INSURANCE LAW
IN A NUTSHELL
THIRD EDITION

By

JOHN F. DOBBYN
Professor of Law, Villanova University

WEST
GROUP

A THOMSON COMPANY

ST. PAUL, MINN.
1996

TEXT IS PRINTED ON 10% POST CONSUMER RECYCLED PAPER

3rd Reprint — 2001

DEDICATION

———————

This dedication is the smallest but most sincere expression of gratitude, love, and admiration for one of the real gentlemen of this world, who devoted the major part of his life to giving to his son the most important things in life—particularly himself.
This one's for you, Dad.

*

PREFACE

The area of Insurance Law is a world unto itself. While theoretically it is merely an enclave of contract law, it is like a mine field, full of hidden traps for those who expect that words in a contract will be applied according to their usual meanings. The reason that cases in Insurance Law frequently read like a chapter out of *Alice in Wonderland* is that the contract (policy of insurance) is only one of three factors that work to swing a decision either to the insured or to the insurer. The second factor is a heavy dose of "public policy," usually on the side of insureds as a class. Courts have long recognized that insurance is one of the major ingredients in the economic planning of most individuals and businesses. To allow the insurance industry to sell and service its product with the same kind of free-wheeling, profit-motivation that is typical of industries dealing in products less close to the core of our economic stability could wreak widespread havoc. This is particularly true where the product, unlike peanut butter or light bulbs, is so complex that the average consumer has very little idea of what he has actually bought (or what he has *not* bought) when he takes out a policy of insurance. For this reason, the courts (and legislatures) tend to apply the public interest factor with a heavy hand to be sure that the product the consumer winds up with is reasonably close to the one he intended to buy. The third factor is one that is little discussed (except by insurers), but that has to be reckoned with in predicting the outcome in many cases. That factor is the fatherly protection of the underdog insured against the powerful insurance company indulged in by both judges and juries in individual cases. Whether it means interpreting an "ambiguity" in the policy language against the drafter of the policy (insurer), when in fact it took a bit of imagination to find the ambiguity in the first place, or simply disregarding the written contract altogether in order to satisfy the "expectations" of the insured, this third factor can, and frequently does, provide a surprising victory for the insured.

It is the purpose of this book to chart the course of Insurance Law as it follows the pulls and tugs of these three factors simultaneously, in order to give the practitioner or law student, not only a comprehensive set of laws and principles, but also a sense of the peculiar directions of Insurance Law to enable him or her to anticipate the areas in which application of the pure principles of contract law would lead to an erroneous prediction as to how a court will deal with a given case.

In any work of this type, acknowledgment must be given to two of the more modern giants whose substantial contributions in this field have gone far toward bringing order out of chaos. Their texts are highly recommended to those who find themselves in need of resources beyond the confines of this book. The first is Professor William R. Vance, whose masterpiece, *Vance on Insurance*, is currently in its third edition, following an able revision by Buist M. Anderson in 1951. The second is the outstanding treatise begun by professor (now Judge) Robert E. Keeton, and brought to a worthy successor edition by Judge Keeton and Alan I. Widiss.

I also want to acknowledge the yeoman services and intellectual contribution of two of the world's finest research assistants—Timothy Levin and Sheila Thompson. They were beyond invaluable.

I appreciate the special recommendations of Neil Reznik.

Finally, by way of a personal note, I must express the gratitude and love that I feel for those most directly responsible for anything that ever has or will come out of my typewriter—my Mother and Father, who have helped and encouraged me in every conceivable way in every project that I have ever considered; and my Bride of twenty-six years, without whose support and love no project would ever be worth undertaking.

JOHN F. DOBBYN

Villanova, Pennsylvania
June, 1995

*

OUTLINE

———

Page

I. GENERALLY

II. WAIVER

Page

Page

TABLE OF CASES

References are to Pages

TABLE OF CASES

TABLE OF CASES

TABLE OF CASES

*

INSURANCE LAW

IN A NUTSHELL

THIRD EDITION

*

CHAPTER ONE

NATURE OF INSURANCE

A. FUNCTIONAL DEFINITION

Just as a horse could be defined as a piece of personalty, a means of transportation, or a slightly larger-than-average pet, depending on the reason for defining it in the first place, the concept of insurance is also subject to a wide variety of definitions, no one of which seems to suit all purposes. In one context, for example, courts and legislatures find it necessary to draw close boundaries around the term to decide whether a particular contract of warranty or indemnity should fall within a regulatory statute. Most of the technical definitions found in cases and statutes are drawn with this rather narrow function in mind, and are, therefore, somewhat off-center for our purposes. As an appropriate jumping-off place, the following functional definition is intended to serve merely to distill from the vast range of contracts that deal in some way with the transference of a risk from one party to another, that distinct core of transactions that are subject to the rather unique body of law, generally termed insurance law.

For our purposes, a contract will be considered insurance when it is characterized by three ele-

1

ments: (1) risk-distribution, (2) among a substantial number of members, (3) through an insurer engaged primarily in the business of insurance.

1. Risk–Distribution

Under the American system of jurisprudence, economic loss incident to any misfortune would fall on one of three individuals absent insurance:

1. Most frequently, the person suffering the misfortune (anything from a broken leg to a burned home) would bear the economic loss;

2. Under the common law, any person who negligently or deliberately causes the misfortune to occur could be compelled to bear the economic loss; and

3. Under certain statutory schemes, the party deemed by the legislature to be the most appropriate from society's point of view is required to bear the loss (such as an employer under Workmen's Compensation Statutes).

While there is no way to transfer the risks of pain, inconvenience, or sorrow that accompany any misfortune, the device of insurance serves to distribute the risk of *economic* loss among as many as possible of those who are subject to the same kind of risk. By paying a pre-determined amount (premium) into a general fund out of which payment will be made for an economic loss of the defined type, each member contributes to a small degree toward compensation for losses suffered by any member of the group. The member has no way of knowing in advance whether he will receive in compensation more than he contributes or whether he will merely be paying for the losses of others in the group; but his primary goal is to exchange the gamble of going it alone, whereby he could either escape all loss whatsoever or suffer a loss that might be devastating, for the opportunity to pay a fixed and certain amount into the fund, knowing that that amount is the maximum he will lose on account of the particular type of risk insured against. This broad sharing of economic risk is the principle of risk-distribution.

In the context of businesses insuring against losses to merchandise and other property, the premium paid into the fund is considered a cost of doing business, and is computed into the prices charged to the public for their products or services. In this way, the distribution of risk is spread even more widely through the entire community.

2. Substantial Membership

The major difference between insurance and a contract whereby one party simply assumes the liability of another for some consideration (as, e.g., a suretyship contract on a note) is the substantial number of members among whom the risk is distributed under a plan of insurance. In fixing premium rates to be paid by each member to cover all losses for the period as well as administrative and other costs, the insurer is required to predict the number and size of losses that are likely to occur during that period. Just as in flipping a coin the number of heads and tails will be more even and predictable as the number of flips is increased, so the probability that the prediction of total losses will not be thrown off by an unanticipated number of losses increases as the number of insurance policies issued increases. This is simply the law of averages at work. It is this predictability that permits an insurer to fix rates that are low enough to make the insurance saleable, and yet high enough to allow the insurer to weather all losses for the period and still cover administrative and other costs. If an insurer does not sell enough of a particular type of policy to reach this comfortable point, the insurer itself can distribute its risk by re-insuring with another insurance company.

3. Insurer Primarily in the Business of Insurance

For purposes of isolating that type of contract to which the body of law that is the subject of this book applies, it is further necessary to distinguish certain contracts that have the common elements of distribution of risk among a sizeable group of participants, but that are generally not treated as insurance *per se.* One example would be broad contracts of warranty on such merchandise as tires, that frequently go beyond defects in workmanship or materials. Another would be pre-paid service contracts for television or appliance repair, or even legal services, that would cover any need for those services that might arise within the designated period. These contracts are generally not subject to the statutory and common law rules that relate peculiarly to insurance, and the distinguishing feature is the third element in this functional definition of insurance. Neither the tire manufacturer, the television repairman, nor the attorney is engaged primarily in the business of insurance. Risk distribution among a large number of individuals is merely incidental to the primary goal of obtaining a fixed and certain income in advance for the services to be rendered.

4. Insurer as Underwriter

Many of the original contracts of insurance took the form of mutual assessment associations, wherein each member paid nothing but administrative costs in advance and merely agreed to be assessed his share of any loss that might occur to any member during the period. This arrangement proved to be inefficient because of the uncertainty that all members would be willing to pay when assessed, and cumbersome because of the repeated necessity for notification and collection. Out of those problems arose the system whereby the insurer assumes the position of underwriter—i.e., the insurer initially fixes and collects a premium for the period, and the insurer assumes *personal* liability to pay the proceeds on any loss. Such functions today are performed almost exclusively by sizeable corporations.

5. Functions of an Insurer

Among the primary functions of an insurer, in addition to the sale of its policies, are the following:

the gathering and interpretation of all data necessary to the fixing of premiums that will cover all costs (including the payment of proceeds on losses); the collection of premiums; the drafting of contracts of insurance in conformity with statutory and case law; the investigation and payment of legitimate claims as well as the defense against illegitimate claims; and the financial management of the funds in its possession. In addition, most insurance companies engage in extensive inspection and educational programs to promote safety and reduce the incidence of loss.

B. TYPES OF INSURANCE

Theoretically, it would be possible, if not practical, for an insurer to evaluate and insure against any risk whatever associated with any lawful activity, as long as there is no violation of that more nebulous restraint—public policy. Historically, however, the specific types of insurance actually written in the United States can be classified according to risks covered in three primary categories: life insurance, fire and casualty insurance, and marine and inland marine insurance. Originally, an insurance company was limited by statute to writing insurance in only one of these three categories. As these restrictions were relaxed, some insurance companies began writing "multiple-line" insurance—e.g., insurance in every line except life insurance. This is occasionally done through an affiliated group of insurance companies, each specializing in a particular line. The expansion ultimately reached the point at which combinations of independent insurance companies (known as "fleets") have added life insurance as well, and write what is now called "all-line" insurance. The separate categories of insurance according to risk are still preserved, however, in the statutory and common law principles that apply uniquely to each category. It, is therefore, important to understand the distinctive characteristics of each.

1. Life Insurance

Life insurance is essentially a contract to make specific payments upon the death of the person whose life is insured. The cast of characters involved in a policy of life insurance other than the insurer includes (a) the *owner* of the policy, who has the power to name or change the beneficiary, the right to assign the policy (under certain conditions), cash it in for its surrender value, or use it as collateral in obtaining a loan, and the obligation to pay the premiums; (b) the person whose life is the subject of the policy (also known as the *cestui que vie*); and (c) the beneficiary to whom the proceeds are paid. One person might occupy all three positions by naming his estate as beneficiary; or each of the three positions may be held by a separate party.

There are various sub-categories of life insurance, the most common of which are the following.

a. *Whole–Life Insurance*

Coverage under whole-life insurance is intended to run for the entire life of the insured, proceeds to be paid upon the death of the insured. Under this plan, ultimate payment of the proceeds is as certain as death itself. An alternative form of payment can come about through the payment of the "cash surrender value" of the policy if it is cancelled by the owner or lapses through non-payment of premiums. The possibility of a cash surrender value is generally available at any time after the policy has been in force for two or three years and prior to the death of the insured. In view of the accumulation of a cash surrender value, as well as the certainty of ultimate payment in some form, whole-life insurance involves a substantial element of investment, as well as insurance.

The category of whole-life insurance is further subdivided according to the various plans for premium payment as follows:

i. *Straight Life Insurance*—premium payments to continue throughout the life of the insured or until he has reached some specific age. This plan is sometimes referred to as "ordinary life insurance."

ii. *Limited Payment Life Insurance*—premiums to be paid for a certain number of years or until a specific pre-planned event such as retirement.

iii. *Single Premium Life Insurance*—The entire premium is prepaid in a lump sum.

b. *Term Life Insurance*

Coverage in this case is to last only for the specified term (one month, ten years, twenty years), and payment of the specified amount of proceeds occurs only if the insured dies within the term.

There is generally no provision for payment of a cash surrender value upon surrender or lapse of the policy. It is, therefore, uncertain that the insurer will be obliged to pay anything in proceeds whatsoever; and consequently this form of life insurance is not considered to carry with it an element of investment. Occasionally, term insurance plans are made more saleable by making them renewable for an additional term or terms, usually without regard to the state of health of the insured at the time of renewal. Because of the necessarily increased age of the insured at the time of renewal as well as the waiver of medical screening by the insurer, rates for subsequent terms are substantially higher than for the initial term. A second option that is frequently added to term insurance is the right of the insured to convert his term insurance policy to one of whole life or endowment life (to be discussed below), again without regard to the state of the health of the insured at the time of exercising the option.

Because of the possibility that the insurer will escape the payment of proceeds entirely if the insured survives the term, rates for term insurance are somewhat lower than those for whole life; but from the point of view of the insured, because the savings aspect inherent in whole life is totally lacking, term insurance serves a function more limited than that of whole life. While whole life insurance is a common element of a broad financial plan of investment as well as protection, term insurance generally fills the more finite need of offering pure protection against a particular economic harm that will occur if the insured dies during a particular period. For example, a homeowner might purchase decreasing term insurance to run for the period of the mortgage on his home to protect his survivors against inability to meet mortgage payments in the event of his death. The amount of proceeds payable under the policy can be made to decrease annually, so that in the event of death, the proceeds will equal, as nearly as possible, the remainder of the mortgage debt due. Similarly, a young married person, realizing that his death within the first fifteen or twenty years of marriage while he is still working his way toward financial security would have a more serious *economic* effect on his family than death subsequent to that period, might be induced to boost his total life insurance coverage during those first fifteen or twenty years without paying the cost of additional whole life insurance by simply adding to his whole life policy a policy of less expensive term insurance to cover that period.

c. *Endowment Life Insurance*

Endowment life insurance differs from the other forms of life insurance in that the insured stands a chance of reaping the benefits while still alive. The usual contract provides for payment of proceeds *either* in the event of death during the specified period, or at the date of "maturity" in the event that the insured has survived the period. Proceeds on maturity can be paid either in a lump sum or as an annuity, making this type of policy useful in retirement planning.

d. *Industrial Life Insurance*

The term "Industrial Life Insurance" derives from the fact that it is tailored to suit the needs of the class that still accounts for the majority of its purchasers—the urban, industrial class of blue-collar workers. Although it is essentially whole life, endowment, or term insurance, it is distinguished by certain common characteristics that make it worthy of special treatment. It is generally written in modest amounts—frequently in the amount necessary to cover burial expenses. There is usually a clause that permits the insurer to make payment immediately upon death to the person equitably appearing to the insurer to be entitled to the proceeds because of having incurred medical or burial expenses in connection with the deceased. This "facility of payment clause" precludes the delay that would result if an administrator or executor's appointment were required to precede payment, or if court action were required to settle disputes between rival claimants.

After years of progress, most industrial life policies today contain non-forfeiture benefits for the insured in the form of cash payments after the policy has been in effect for three to five years, and in the form of insurance after the policy has been in effect as little as six months.

Typically, industrial life insurance is sold through individual solicitation without the requirement of a physical examination. There is, however, usually a general clause included for the protection of the insurer providing, for example, that the policy is invalid if the insured was not in "good health" at the inception date of the policy.

Premiums are collected more frequently than in the case of other types of insurance—usually on a weekly basis. This, together with the high cost of solicitation per policy amount, lack of a medical screening, and the higher-than-average death rate among low-income groups, accounts for the fact that the price of industrial life insurance is higher than that of other types.

e. *Mutual Life Insurance*

A large proportion of the life insurance written in the United States is written by mutual life insurance companies. With mutual (or "participating") life insurance, the insured pays as a fixed premium somewhat more than the estimated cost of his insurance. Depending on the extent of losses, the amount of expenses, and the amount of interest earned on the reserve during the year, the insured receives a dividend from the insurer each year. This dividend is in fact a return of the unused part of the premium previously paid in. Although an insured generally pays a higher premium on a participating policy than on a non-participating policy, if conditions are favorable, he may receive a dividend that will make the net cost less for the participating policy. The decision as to the amount of the annual premium, if any, is in the discretion of the insurer's board of directors.

f. Group Insurance

i. Generally

The term "Group Insurance" refers to a method of marketing standard forms of insurance, such as life insurance, whereby a master policy is issued to the party negotiating the contract with the insurer (frequently an employer), and certificates of participation are issued to the individual insured members of the group (frequently employees). The master policy sets forth all of the terms and conditions of the insurance, while the certificates of participation serve merely to inform the individual members of the major features of the insurance and are not considered to be part of the insurance contract itself.

ii. Types of Insurance

This form of marketing is feasible from the point of view of the insurer because the factors influencing insurability and premiums, particularly on life or health insurance, are fairly homogeneous for a group such as the full-time employees of a particular company. The mere fact that all of the members are employed full-time is a strong positive indication of insurability, and, therefore, the usual physical examination and other methods of screening applicants for life or health insurance can be dispensed with. Membership in the group becomes the necessary and sufficient condition to insurability under the group plan. In this way, the savings to the insurer on costs of administration can be passed along to the group in reduced premiums, compared to the premiums charged for an equivalent individual policy. Further savings in administrative costs arise from the fact that frequently premiums on all of the group policies will come from or be funneled through the one group representative.

The homogeneity of factors relating to insurability that exists in regard to life, health, and accident insurance for any group such as employees, generally does not exist in regard to other forms of insurance such as property insurance. It is not surprising, therefore, that the most common group insurance plans cover only the former types of insurance, with the heaviest portion of the business going to term life insurance, convertible to a more permanent form of individual insurance without medical examination if the employee leaves the company. In fact, the original purpose of group life insurance was to provide funds to take the place of the salary of a deceased insured employee for a period of a year or two after his death. The majority of today's group policies are still in relatively small amounts of face value.

Additional popular forms of group insurance are hospitalization insurance similar to the Blue Cross plan, disability insurance under which an employee receives a percentage of his salary for a limited period during which he is unable to work because of a disability, and group annuities intended to act as a retirement benefit.

While the great majority of group policies are still written for employees, other groups commonly insured include members of unions or professional societies, members of savings or investment associations, and members of fraternal organizations.

iii.　*Contributory v. Non-contributory*

A group insurance plan is considered to be "contributory" if each member pays all or some part of the premiums, and "non-contributory" if the representative (e.g., employer) pays all of the premiums. One reason for the attractiveness of group insurance as a fringe benefit to employees is that the amount of premiums paid by the employer are tax deductible, within limits, while the premiums paid by the employer are not considered taxable income to the employee.

iv.　*Adverse Selection*

The principle of adverse selection (those who are the poorest risks will be those most likely to apply for insurance) is of particular concern to the insurer in the case of group insurance because if the group plan provides for eligibility, for example, for every employee of a particular employer, the insurer does not have the option to screen out the more risky applicants as is possible with individual insurance. The insurer must, therefore, rely on the following methods to counter-balance the inclination of any group toward adverse selection:

　1.　A requirement that a certain minimum percentage (e.g., 100% for non-contributory and 75% for contributory) of the eligible membership be covered;

2. Limitation of the amount of insurance available to any member, generally calculated with reference to some criterion beyond the control of the member, as, e.g., a percentage of his salary, or a function of his position or longevity with the company (upper limits of coverage are frequently fixed by statute);

3. Restriction of the amount of insurance that can be written on any *individual* member to an amount below a certain percentage of the entire amount of insurance written on the group; and

4. Refusal to insure a group that is formed solely for the purpose of taking out insurance.

Any remaining losses due to adverse selection must simply be handled by setting the individual premiums at the level pertinent to the average risk of the participating group. In spite of the fact that this results in the "good risks" carrying the "poor risks" to some extent by paying the same rate of premium, the savings in administrative costs still reduce the premium level, even for the good risks, below those charged for individual policies.

v. Agency of the Representative

The question frequently arises as to whether or not the group representative is acting as agent for the group members or for the insurer. The answer appears to differ depending on the context of the question. For example, it is generally held that in acting as administrator of the group policy (as by adding and subtracting names from the list of insureds and collecting and forwarding premiums), the representative is not acting as agent of the insurer and, therefore, is *not* in a position to waive any of the conditions of the policy or to estop the insurer to rely on any defenses under the policy. Nor is the representative considered the agent of the members for purposes of charging the members with knowledge of information known to the representative. On the other hand, some (though not all) courts hold that if an employee makes payment of the premium to the employer/representative by way of a pre-arranged deduction from his salary, and the employer fails to forward the premium to the insurer, the employer is considered to have received the payment on behalf of the insurer, and the policy will not lapse.

In some instances, the master policy contains such language as, "Unintentional neglect on the part of the employer to furnish the name of any employee eligible hereunder shall not invalidate the insurance on the life of such employee." Here the effect is the same as if the mistake of the employer were attributed to the insurer as principal.

In the case of an employer who gratuitously undertakes to become the representative of his employees in managing a non-contributory plan of group insurance, it is generally held that he is under no liability to the employee/member or any beneficiary for failure to keep the policy in force or to give notice of termination or of the right to convert to a different type of insurance when employment is severed. On the other hand, if the plan is contributory, courts have held that the employer is under a duty to exercise good faith and due care in administering the policy and in notifying the employee of all information needed to keep the policy in effect.

vi. Consent of Members to Amendment or Termination

The parties to the insurance contract are considered to be the representative and the insurer. As a corollary of this, it is generally held that the representative and the insurer together can terminate coverage of an individual member or amend or terminate the entire group policy without the consent of the individual members. Neither an individual nor the entire group of individual members can prevent cancellation or modification by the representative and insurer, absent a provision in the policy to the contrary. On the other hand, a minority of courts hold that in the case of contributory policies, rights in the policies vest in the individual members such that their consent is required for any modification or termination to be effective. Other minority courts extend this rule to all group policies, contributory or non-contributory. It has even rarely been held that rights in the policy vest in the beneficiaries such that their consent to modification or termination is also required.

vii. Notice to Members

While the majority hold that the consent of the individual insureds is not required for amendment or termination of group insurance, it is generally held that the insurer is obligated to give notice to the individual insureds of any such change, as well as notice of any right to convert to individual insurance, so that the insured can take steps to change his entire program of insurance accordingly. Failure to give such notice has led to the holding that the insurance was not terminated or that the conversion period was extended. In some cases, the requirement to give notice is statutory, and on occasion, it is written into the policy.

Absent a change or termination of the policy contrary to its original wording, the general rule is that the individual member is charged with notice of all of the terms of the master policy, particularly where the certificate of membership refers to the fact that the full contract is contained in the master policy. An employee insured under a group policy by his employer is, therefore, held to be on notice that termination of his employment means termination of his coverage under the group policy, and the employer and insurer are under no duty to give notice of that fact.

viii. Assignment and Change of Beneficiary

An individual insured under a group policy usually has the option of changing the beneficiary, but assignment of the policy is frequently rendered legally impossible because of a non-assignment clause in the policy itself.

ix. Standing to Sue on the Policy

There is authority for allowance of an action against the insurer on the policy for proceeds after the death of a member by the representative of the group (acting as trustee for the beneficiary), the legal representative of the deceased member, or the beneficiary, in the case of life insurance, or by the member himself in the case of injury or disability covered by group health or accident insurance. A number of states, recognizing the value of group life insurance to beneficiaries as a temporary relief against the sudden loss of an income, have enacted statutes that insulate the proceeds of such insurance from the claims of creditors.

x.   Conflict of Law

For conflict of laws purposes, the law of the state where the policy was issued and delivered controls in questions of the interpretation or validity of a group policy.

g.   Universal Life Insurance

i.   Generally

Modern variations on the theme of whole life insurance have been created to maximize and combine the benefits of an investment program at competitive rates with the tax and protective advantages of traditional whole life insurance. The most common of these variations is a type of policy known as universal life insurance, which was first marketed in 1979.

The major characteristic of universal life insurance is the continuing flexibility of three figures that are rigidly fixed at the inception of the ordinary whole life policy—the premium, the death benefit, and the interest rate on accumulated cash values. As with whole life insurance, universal life insurance involves an element of investment based on the fact that the cash value of the policy accumulates interest and ultimate payment of the cash value is guaranteed.

ii. Interest Rate

At the inception of the policy, the insured selects the level of death benefit, which is the face value of the policy. Based on that death benefit, the insurer fixes the first premium, from which it deducts mortality and administrative costs. The remaining fund—the cash value of the policy—then begins earning interest. The insurer will each year set the interest rate to reflect current market rates, as opposed to fixing a relatively low permanent interest rate for the duration of the policy. In this way, the universal life insurance policy becomes a competitive means of investment.

iii. Premium

The second flexible feature is that of the premium. After the initial premium is paid, the policy holder is free to pay as little or as much in subsequent premiums as he or she wishes; and the payment can be made, like an investment, at any time. Some universal life policies, however, do set maximum and minimum annual premiums.

The major restriction on the policyholder's ability freely to determine the amount of premium to be paid is the requirement that the cash value of the policy be maintained at a level sufficient to cover the administrative and mortality costs of the insurer. In addition, federal tax law imposes some restrictions on the flexibility of premiums for the universal life contract to continue to qualify as insurance for purposes of exempting accumulated interest from income tax.

Conceivably, if the premiums paid have been sufficiently large, after deduction of costs, the remaining cash value could earn enough interest to pay some or all of the costs of future terms, so that the cash value of the policy could be self-sustaining or even increase with no additional premiums being paid. The application of the cash value to the payment of costs of the policy is generally without interest charge in the case of universal life; while with a whole life policy, such application would be considered borrowing against cash value, and an interest charge would be incurred.

iv. Proceeds

The payment of proceeds on death is guaranteed, just as in the case of whole life insurance. There are generally, however, two options available. The first option is to receive a death benefit that is the greater of a) the policy face value selected by the policyholder, or b) the then-existing cash value plus a "corridor" sum (a predetermined sum—e.g., $10,-000—or a percentage of the cash value). The second option is to receive the face value plus the accumulated cash value.

These options can be changed by the policyholder; but if the change results in added insurance protection, or if the policyholder simply chooses to increase the death benefits, there is usually a requirement of new evidence of insurability. One hedge against this requirement is offered with some policies in the form of a rider enabling the policyholder to increase the face value of the insurance policy to keep pace with the cost of living.

v. Loans and Withdrawals

There are two methods by which a policyholder can take cash out of a universal life policy. One is by borrowing against the cash value of the policy, in which event the insurer will charge interest in one of two ways. Either the insurer will charge a fixed rate, in which case the remaining cash value will accrue interest at a lower guaranteed rate, as opposed to the higher current market rate; or the insurer will charge interest at a variable rate, in which case, the interest paid on the remainder of the cash value will remain at the current market rate.

The second method, unique to universal life policies and their variations, is simply to withdraw funds from the cash value of the policy. There is no interest charge for such withdrawal, but some companies apply a fixed withdrawal fee.

Given this flexibility, the insured can tailor a universal life policy to accommodate investment, protection, and current borrowing needs.

h. Annuities

An annuity contract, unlike the life insurance contracts discussed above, insures against the economic problems resulting from a *long* life, rather than an early death. It provides for payment of a fixed annual (or more frequent) benefit beginning at a specified date and continuing for the life of the insured (annuitant). It is a guaranty against living to an age at which one's income-producing capacity would not be sufficient to meet one's needs. Many such contracts also provide a hedge in the form of a refund of part of the premiums paid in the event of an early death.

A more recent advance on the fixed-benefit annuity is the variable annuity whereby the annuitant buys units of ownership in a portfolio of common stocks. When the period of payment begins, the annuitant receives payment of a certain number of units per year, the number of units being actuarially determined on the basis of the life expectancy of the annuitant. The benefit of this type of annuity is that the value of the units rises as the market value of the common stocks in the portfolio rises, thereby attempting to protect the annuitant against the effects of inflation.

i. Tort Liability of Insurance Companies

Of some relatively recent concern to life insurance companies is the risk of tort liability associated with the issuance of life insurance policies. The question arises when an insurance company issues a policy to a person who has no insurable interest in the life of the person who is the subject of the policy (*cestui que vie*), or neglects to get the signed consent of that person. Liability can arise if the policy holder murders or attempts to murder the (*cestui que vie*) in order to collect the proceeds on the policy.

The cause of action for tort liability is usually brought by the next of kin of the *cestui que vie,* or, in the case of attempted murder, by the *cestui que vie* himself/herself. Plaintiffs typically argue that the insurance company was negligent in issuing a life insurance policy to someone with no insurable interest or without the consent of the *cestui que vie,* and that this negligence was the proximate cause of the *cestui que vie's* death or injury.

On the other side of the argument, the insurance company often asserts first that it was not negligent in ascertaining whether the policy holder had an insurable interest. Secondly, the insurance company frequently argues that even if it were negligent in issuing the policy, that negligence was not the proximate cause of the *cestui que vie's* death or near death, because of the supervening act of the murderer or attempted murderer.

In regard to the defense of absence of negligence, a closer look at the rationale of statutes requiring insurable interests reveals two independent concerns: 1) the avoidance of wagering, and 2) the avoidance of the inducement to murder. Though the former concern has deep historical roots (as outlined in Chapter Two), the latter concern is also expressed from time to time in legislative debate. The legislative history behind a number of current statutes requiring insurable interests indicates that one of the prime objectives of those particular statutes is deterrence of an inducement to murder. In jurisdictions in which this deterrence is at least one of the purposes of the statute, proof of any violation of such a statute may be considered negligence *per se.*

On the other hand, if the state's statutory scheme does not include an insurable interest requirement, or deterrence of gambling is the only apparent purpose of the statute, the negligence *per se* theory will not apply.

If the insurer loses on the negligence issue, a second defense is that of supervening cause. For example, In *Liberty National Life Insurance Company v. Weldon* (Ala.1957), the court dealt with a situation in which an insurance company issued a life insurance policy to an aunt of a minor child. The child was the subject of the policy. Shortly thereafter, the aunt murdered the child. The child's father brought suit against the insurance company, alleging negligence in the issuance of the policy. He claimed that the company knew or should have known that the aunt had no insurable interest in the child.

The company defended by asserting that its action in issuing the policy, whether negligent or not, was not the proximate cause of the child's death. Rather, the murderous act of the aunt was a supervening cause which superseded any negligence of the insurance company.

The court held that the insurer's acts were the proximate cause of the injury despite the supervening criminal act. Because the harm which occurred was the very harm that the statutory duty was intended to prevent, the causal chain connecting the acts of the insurer and the harm was not broken. Moreover, the mere fact that the supervening act was criminal was not enough to negate the foreseeability of the harm. The court held that the insurance company "created a situation of a kind which this court and others have consistently said affords temptation to a recognizable percentage of humanity to commit murder."

Cases subsequent to *Weldon* have addressed the related issue of whether insurance companies can be held liable in tort for issuing life insurance policies without the signed consent of the *cestui que vie*. In *Ramey v. Carolina Life Insurance Company* (S.C.1964), for example, the court held that an insurance company can be held liable in negligence for issuing a life insurance policy insuring an individual's life without that individual's consent.

Other courts have imposed a heavy burden of proof on the plaintiff in a negligence action against an insurer. For example, in *Bacon v. Federal Kemper Life Insurance Company* (1987), the court dealt with a case of a forged signature of the owner of a life insurance policy on a change of beneficiary form. The forger, who became the new beneficiary, murdered the *cestui que vie.* The plurality of the Massachusetts Supreme Judicial Court stated that the plaintiff in a negligence action against the insurer must prove that the insurer *knew or should have known* from the circumstances that the insured did not consent to the change of beneficiary, or that the person who obtained the policy did not have an insurable interest in the *cestui que vie,* depending on the cause of action, and further must prove that the insurer knew or should have known that, in that case, the approval of the change in beneficiary exposed the *cestui que vie* to an "unreasonable risk of harm by criminal conduct."

Nonetheless, it is important to note that the *Bacon* opinion was badly fragmented. Three judges joined in the majority opinion, one judge concurred in the result but wrote a separate opinion, two judges dissented, and one judge abstained. Despite its holding, therefore, the *Bacon* decision is hardly strong precedent in favor of insurance companies.

In addition, there are cases such as *Burton v. John Hancock Mutual Life Insurance Company* (Ga. App.1982), which discuss the issue of an insurer's liability for negligence but do not take a position for or against liability. In these cases, the courts were unwilling to impose liability on the insurer based on the factual elements of the cases, but these courts do not explicitly deny the possibility that such a suit could be viable given the proper factual backdrop. Furthermore, in cases such as *Life Insurance Company of Georgia v. Lopez* (Fla.1983), courts have theoretically accepted the possibility of such liability but have left the question of whether negligence actually occurred to the jury.

On the other hand, although insurance companies have been held subject to tort liability for issuing life insurance policies to someone without an insurable interest, there is the possibility in such a case of the insurer's avoiding payment of policy benefits to anyone under the theory that a life insurance policy issued to one who has the intent to murder the *cestui que vie* is void *ab initio*. It is important to keep in mind, however, that the insurer's success with this argument does not insulate it from potential tort liability. It merely permits the insurer to deny policy benefits, undoubtedly at the expense of having to refund premiums.

2. Fire and Casualty Insurance

Fire and casualty insurance together comprise the second category, and each includes a number of historically related areas of insurance.

a. Fire Insurance

Fire insurance generally covers any loss by fire, other than that deliberately caused by the insured, to property listed specifically (as with real estate) or by location (as with personalty housed within a home, warehouse, or other building). One major exception to the general coverage under a fire insurance policy has been created by the courts with little or no aid from the specific language of the insurance contract. Fire insurance policies are generally held to cover losses caused by "hostile" fires, but not losses caused by "friendly" fires. The dividing line is somewhat indistinct in detail under the cases, but the traditional definition is as follows. A friendly fire is one that is contained in the intended place for a fire, such as a fireplace, furnace, or stove. A hostile fire is one that occurs outside of those usual confines, or one that begins as a friendly fire and subsequently escapes to other areas. Thus the loss of items accidentally dropped into a fire contained within a fireplace would not be covered. There is some dispute as to whether damage through excessive smoke from a fire whose actual flame remained within the fireplace would be covered, since, technically, for purposes of the hostile/friendly distinction, the fire is considered to be the flame (in the chemical sense); and yet, when the fire itself is considered to be hostile, smoke damage is included within the loss.

The origin of the distinction is uncertain, although many courts have rationalized it on the basis of the layman's common understanding of what it means to "have a fire."

Also traditionally included within the coverage of a fire insurance policy are losses through lightning, explosion, earthquake, water, wind, rain, collision, and riot.

b. *Casualty Insurance*

Casualty insurance generally includes coverage for legal liability, burglary and theft, accident and health, property damage, collision, glass, boiler and machinery, workmen's compensation, credit insurance, and fidelity and surety bonds. Fire and casualty insurance together provide comprehensive coverage on realty and such pieces of personal property as cars, boats, and airplanes.

3. Marine and Inland Marine Insurance

a. *Marine Insurance*

Marine insurance is a comprehensive form of all-risk insurance (i.e., all forms of loss are covered except for those specifically excepted), covering ship and cargo against the "perils of the sea." As is implied in that phrase, marine insurance does not extend to floating transportation on inland waterways.

The current pattern of marine insurance is a direct descendant of the custom that developed in the 1600's at the Lloyd's Coffee House in London. A shipper or shipowner interested in insuring a vessel or cargo would pass around a slip of paper among those gathered indicating the relevant facts and the amount of insurance sought. Anyone interested would write on the slip the amount of insurance that he would offer, the rate, and his initials. These latter became known as "underwriters." The major difference today is that most underwriting is done by corporations rather than individuals.

In 1769, the then-existing group of underwriters formed a society which subsequently adopted the standard form of marine insurance that has come down to present day use both in England and the United States with relatively little change. An ex-

cerpt from a modern marine insurance form enu-
merating the "perils" covered serves both to define
those perils and to attest to the survival of the
pristine language:

> "Touching the adventures and perils which we
> the assurers are contented to bear and do take
> upon us in this voyage: they are of the seas, men
> of war, fire, enemies, pirates, rovers, thieves, jetti-
> sons, letters of mart and counter-mart, surprisals,
> takings at sea, arrests, restraints, and detain-
> ments of all kings, princes, and people, of what
> nation, condition, or quality soever, barratry of
> the master and mariners, and of all other perils,
> losses, and misfortunes, that have or shall come
> to the hurt, detriment, or damage of the said
> goods and merchandises, and ship, &c., or any
> part thereof."

b. *Inland Marine Insurance*

i. Origin

Companies engaged in writing marine insurance
have found it a natural extension of their opera-
tions to insure personal property in circumstances
other than on the high seas. The first extension
was to property transported on inland waterways,
such as rivers, lakes, and canals—whence the name,
"inland marine insurance." They subsequently extended coverage to include policies on property subject to the risks of other forms of transportation.
The next extension of inland marine insurance
served to fill a gap in coverage by insuring property
that is neither permanently situated at a fixed

location (and, therefore, not properly the subject of fire or casualty insurance) nor the subject of transportation by a common carrier. Such policies comprise the second major category of inland marine insurance and are referred to as "personal property floater policies."

ii. *Personal Property Floater Policies*

(a) *Definition*

In general, floater policies provide all-risk insurance (subject to specified exceptions) on personal property that is subject to being moved to a different location at any time, and cover the property both while it is at a fixed location and during transit. Floater contracts have become standardized and fall into historically fixed categories. The major division lies between personal and business floater policies.

(b) *Personal Property Floater Policies*

Floater policies on personal property can cover either specific items for stated amounts or all non-business personal property without scheduling each separate item. Coverage usually extends to property belonging to or borrowed or leased by the insured and members of the insured's household. It can also include the property of visitors while on the insured's premises, and the property of a servant, whether on or off of the insured's premises, as long as the servant is engaged in service to the insured and has custody of the property at the time of the loss.

There are generally exclusions of types of property as to which the hazards would be too great for an all-risk policy, such as animals or professional equipment (other than books or instruments kept at home), or which are covered by other forms of insurance such as automobiles, motorcycles, or aircraft.

Certain perils are excluded, such as war, nuclear fission, temperature extremes, insects, and certain types of water damage; and specific limits of liability per loss are placed on certain unscheduled items such as jewelry, watches, furs, stamps, money, and securities.

(c) Business Floater Policies

Business floater policies are all-risk policies on the stock in trade or equipment of a business firm, no matter where the property is located. Standard policies have been tailored to specific businesses and are generally referred to as "block" policies. For example, a jeweler's block policy covers all jewels, precious metals, watches, glassware, etc., belonging to the jeweler, bailed to him by a customer, or consigned to him by another firm, regardless of where in the world the property is located. Similar policies are available to furriers, camera or musical instrument dealers, retail or wholesale dealers in heavy equipment, and others.

A wide variety of movable business property is also insured under *scheduled* property floater policies. For example, a contractor's equipment floater policy covers itemized heavy equipment owned, leased, or borrowed by the contractor, that must be moved from job to job. Standard livestock floater policies cover cattle, horses, hogs, etc., wherever they may be located.

Miscellaneous business floaters have been designed to cover innumerable situations in which the property subject to risk is not kept at a fixed location.

4. Health and Disability Insurance

a. *Health Insurance*

i. Generally

A typical health insurance policy indemnifies the insured for all losses resulting from illness or injury unless those losses emanate from specifically excepted illnesses, such as those arising out of employment, and therefore covered by workers' compensation, or, under some policies, those contracted outside the United States, or those as to which there is a defined limit on coverage for a specific illness or treatment. The insurer will generally indemnify the insured for any loss which is the natural and usual result of a disease, including illnesses associated with cancer and treatments required to control diabetes.

The payment of medical benefits under a health insurance policy is governed by contractual principles. Certain federal and state statutory provisions, however, may dictate the manner in which an insurer can limit its coverage once it has been extended. For example, if a state statute conflicts with insurance policy provisions, and the statute provides broader coverage, an insurer may be obligated to provide the broader degree of coverage set forth in the statute instead of its more restricted coverage.

ii. *Methods of Offering Health Insurance*

Health insurance is offered in a variety of forms, each providing the insured with a unique approach to benefits.

(a) *Service Benefit Plans*

Service benefit plans guarantee the insured specific medical services, such as surgery and immunizations, in exchange for payment of a premium. The insured may choose his or her own health care providers from a group of participating providers. The provider is reimbursed directly by the plan.

Coverage under a service benefit plan may be subject to various exclusions, such as non-coverage for such routine services as eye examinations or dental check-ups, and durational limits. In addition, certain services may require prior authorization by the insurer. Finally, the insured may be liable for significant deductibles or co-payments. The insureds are, however, generally guaranteed that their out of pocket expenses for co-payments will not exceed a specified amount.

The most well-known form of service benefit plan is provided by Blue Cross/Blue Shield. These organizations, established under special state legislative acts, provide for the payment of hospital bills and surgical and medical fees. Further, provided that the plan meets the statutory criteria which characterizes a service benefit plan, it will be exempt from most general state insurance regulatory laws. In addition, Blue Cross and Blue Shield are generally not subject to federal tax on their income and premiums. Nonetheless, Blue Cross and Blue Shield may be subject to special regulation by the state insurance authority in a number of areas including coverage, renewal and termination of subscriber contracts, and appropriate premium levels.

(b) Indemnity Insurance

Indemnity insurance is the most commonly used form of health insurance. Within this framework, the insurer reimburses the insured directly for medical bills in accordance with the terms of an agreement between the parties. This agreement may provide for complete reimbursement of all fees without a limit, or it may provide for reimbursement based on "usual and reasonable" charges for the same services. The policy may require the insured to pay a deductible or co-payment, and the amount reimbursed by the insurer may be limited. With indemnity insurance, the primary relationship is between the insured and the insurer. The health care provider has essentially no part in the agreement between them. The effect of this arrangement may impact upon the provider, however, in that, if the indemnity agreement provides only for reimbursement of charges that are "usual and reasonable" for the same services, and the provider charges more than a fee that is "usual and reasonable", there is, of course, a risk that the provider will not receive full payment for the excess from the insured.

(c) Independent or Self–Insured Plans

This form of insurance exists when an organized group acts as self-insurer and provides health related services to its members. The members make premium payments to the plan and, in exchange, receive services from the group of health care providers who have contracted with the plan. The organization contracts with various health care providers to service its subscribers. This form of health insurance requires few deductibles or co-payments while offering extensive coverage for the subscribers. Self-insured plans generally do not employ fee-for-service billing, but rather, fix a periodic payment to the provider without regard to the actual services provided.

The most common example of an independent plan is a health maintenance organization ("HMO"). It is important to note that HMO's are governed by the Health Maintenance Act, 42 U.S.C.A. §§ 300e–300e–17 (1988), which provides parameters within which each HMO must operate, such as the assumption of full financial risk on a prospective basis for the provision of health services and creation of quality assurance programs.

(d) Hybrid Plans

Individuals may also utilize a number of hybrid health insurance plans which incorporate various characteristics of other types of health insurance.

For example, a preferred provider organization ("PPO") combines characteristics of a service benefit plan with those of the HMO. The PPO includes a) an established set of providers who offer their services at a discounted rate, b) utilization review, and c) financial incentives for participants to use the providers from the established group. Unlike the HMO, however, the PPO does not restrict its subscribers to using specified providers, although the amount of benefits paid decreases if outside providers are used by the insured. Also, the PPO is subject to less regulation than the HMO, and it operates on a fee-for-service basis.

An exclusive provider organization ("EPO") is another hybrid, which is similar to the PPO in that it provides its subscribers with discounted rates by seeking arrangements with certain providers. It also provides for strict utilization review. However, the EPO *requires* the subscribers to receive care from the specified providers as a condition of payment of benefits. The EPO is distinguishable from the HMO in that it operates on a fee-for-service basis.

iii. *Limitations in Health Insurance Coverage*

(a) *Pre-existing Conditions*

Many health insurance policies include provisions which deny coverage for pre-existing conditions. The determination of whether the condition was pre-existing, however, has often been problematic. Some courts have, as a result, developed a *subjective,* two-alternative test for determining whether a condition pre-dated the effective date of the insurance policy. The court may look to the point at which the illness first manifested itself or became active, or the court may look to the point at which the insured first experienced the distinct symptoms or conditions which would lead to a diagnosis of the illness. Other courts have used an *objective* single-prong test, where the inquiry centers upon the point at which a reasonable person should have known of the existence of the illness based on the symptoms.

Disputes arising from the pre-existing condition provision arise frequently, centering on the point at which the illness came into existence. Although courts uphold the pre-existing condition defense where there is convincing evidence that the condition pre-dated the contract, they will generally construe the provisions strictly against the insurer.

(b) Mental Health Exceptions

Many health and disability policies limit or exclude mental illness from coverage. The exclusion is triggered once it is determined that the mental illness at issue arose from behavioral disturbances, i.e., a reaction to environmental conditions, rather than organic or physical sources. Accordingly, it has been held that autism is not subject to the exclusion but manic-depression is.

(c) Requirement of Medical Necessity

A typical health insurance policy limits the extent of coverage to those expenses which are "medically necessary". Conflicts often arise when a doctor determines that a certain treatment or procedure is necessary, but the insurance company disagrees. In response to this problem, many insurance companies have developed their own committees, or contracted with external companies, for the purpose of reviewing the diagnoses and recommendations of health care providers. Ultimately, the decision as to whether a treatment was medically necessary must be made in light of the knowledge which existed at the time the decision was rendered.

iv. Construing Health Insurance Contracts

In resolving disputes that arise with regard to health insurance policies, courts apply general doctrines of insurance policy interpretation. For example, the ambiguity doctrine, which holds that any ambiguity found in the insurance contract is to be strictly construed against the insurer, is frequently employed. The doctrine has been used in the insured's favor, for example, to determine whether an insured had a vested right to continuing coverage under canceled group insurance. The ambiguity doctrine is routinely utilized when the contract can fairly be interpreted in more than one way.

Another doctrine employed by the courts in construing health insurance contracts is the reasonable expectations doctrine. Under this doctrine, the objectively reasonable expectations of the insured regarding the terms of the contract will be honored, even if close scrutiny of the contract provisions would negate these expectations. For example, in *Hemenway v. MFA Life Insurance Company* (Neb.

1982), an insured paid a premium for a health insurance policy and received a conditional receipt which stated that coverage was conditional upon the insured's insurability. Subsequently, the insured incurred medical expenses but was denied coverage because the statements of the insured on the application for insurance did not properly refer to a pre-existing medical condition. When the insured sued for a declaratory judgment as to the insurance company's liability, the court held that even though the insured had not satisfied the conditions required under the receipt, he was under the impression that he had received coverage as a result of the premium payment. As a result, the reasonable expectations of the insured were upheld, despite contrary language in the policy.

b. Disability Insurance

Disability insurance offers coverage for lost wages resulting from illness or injury and generally contains two types of coverage: general and occupational disability. General disability benefits are triggered when the insured is unable to perform the duties of his or her actual occupation and is also unable to engage in any work or occupation for which he or she is reasonably fitted. In contrast, occupational disability benefits are triggered when the insured is unable to perform the usual and customary duties of his or her actual occupation.

Although private insurance companies offer disability benefit plans, these plans are often unattractive to prospective insureds due to the publicly funded disability benefits offered by state and federal government plans such as workers' compensation, social security, or veterans' benefits.

5. Liability Insurance

a. *Generally*

One of the most prevalent types of insurance today is third-party liability insurance. Unlike first-party insurance (life insurance, property insurance, etc.), third-party liability insurance is purchased by an insured to protect against potential tort liability to others. Coverage is not triggered by a loss to insured's property, but by liability of the insured for damage to another's person or property. It further depends on whether the insured's liability to a third party arose out of an "occurrence" or "accident" covered by the policy.

b. *Commercial General Liability Policies*

i. *Generally*

Perhaps the most common type of third-party liability insurance in use today is the Commercial General Liability (CGL) policy. Formerly known as Comprehensive General Liability insurance, these policies are obtained to protect businesses from liability to third parties arising out of a broad spectrum of risks.

The basic CGL insuring agreement provides coverage up to the face amount of the policy for bodily injury and property damage (including damage to intangible property such as good will or trade reputation) which the insured becomes legally obligated to pay as damages. CGL coverage extends broadly to risks ranging from customers' personal injury suits to competitors' libel or slander suits. In the case of liability resulting from bodily injury or property damage, however, CGL policies require that the injury result from an "occurrence." An "occurrence" is defined in the standard policy as an "accident, including continuous or repeated exposure to substantially the same general harmful conditions." This language was recently added to clarify the fact that there is no requirement of temporal suddenness for a loss to result from an occurrence.

ii. Exclusions

(a) Generally

While a CGL policy does provide broad third-party coverage, CGL policies also contain several uniform exclusions from coverage. For example, CGL policies do not cover losses which are, "expected or intended from the standpoint of the insured." In addition, a CGL policy is not a substitute for many other more specialized types of insurance. For example, a CGL policy will not provide coverage for injuries to employees arising in the course of their employment, losses resulting from the, "actual, alleged or threatened discharge, dispersal, release or escape of pollutants, losses arising from the use of an auto, damage to the insured's own property, or damage to the insured's product.

(b) "Work Product" Exclusion

One of the most commonly litigated exclusions in CGL policies is the "work product" exclusion. This exclusion is routinely incorporated into CGL policies that are offered to construction companies, and it generally precludes coverage for property damage to the insured's products and to a third party's property that was worked on by or on behalf of the insured.

Prior to 1973, the work product exclusion, though routinely used, was not effective in precluding coverage for this type of property damage. Courts often found the exclusionary language to be ambiguous in that it did not clearly define what portion of the insured's work was excluded from coverage. In other words, it was unclear whether coverage would be excluded merely for the damage to the defective product or for the entire damage done to the entire project that the insured worked on. For example, if the insured used faulty cement in building the foundation of a house, and the foundation later collapsed and caused damage to other portions of the house, a court was often faced with the decision as to whether the exclusion applied only to the damaged foundation or to the damaged foundation and the damage to the house that resulted from the collapse of the foundation.

In construing the exclusions narrowly against insurers, the courts permitted insureds to recover replacement or repair costs associated with property damage to other parts of a project of the insured caused by a defective product used by the insured. The insured was merely required to prove that some defective product of the insured damaged another identifiable product or work of the insured.

The only coverage that was excluded was the costs associated with repairing or replacing the defective product itself. For example, in the case in which the foundation of the house collapses because it was constructed with faulty cement, and damage results to other parts of the house, the insured would be covered for the damage to the house that was caused by the collapse, but not for the costs of repairing or replacing the foundation itself.

Because the insurance industry was dissatisfied with the trend toward circumventing the full intent behind the work product exclusions, it revised the exclusionary language. In 1973, it modified the work product exclusion to eliminate coverage in any case in which a defective product damages another part of the insured's work, even if the insured's work was performed by a subcontractor or other entity working on behalf of the insured. As a result of the revision of the language in the work product exclusion, many courts upheld the exclusion, finding that it did not contain any ambiguities and, therefore, effectively excluded coverage for all property damage to the insured's products or to work performed by or on behalf of the insured.

For example, the court in *Western Employers Ins. Co. v. Arciero & Sons,* held that the work product exclusion applied to an entire project in which Arciero was the general contractor. The court did not limit the exclusion to the insured's defective work that caused a retaining wall to collapse, but instead, applied it to the cost of repairing the structural damage to various condominiums constructed by the insured that was caused by the collapse of the wall.

One way to expand coverage in spite of the restrictive work product exclusions is by adding endorsements to the policy. One such endorsement is the Broad Form Endorsement to the Commercial General Liability policy. This endorsement modifies the exclusion so that it does not encompass work done *on behalf of* the insured but merely applies to work done directly by the insured. As a result, this endorsement permits coverage for damage to completed work that results from defective work of another entity such as a subcontractor. Additionally, the insured is covered for damage to work of third parties that results from the insured's defective work. The only situations still excluded under the endorsement are those in which the insured's work is damaged by the its own defective work.

It should be noted that not all courts have adopted such a broad reading of the broad form endorsement. Some courts have held, for example, that insureds who, as general contractors, take on full responsibility for an entire project, cannot gain such a broad benefit from the endorsement simply because they use subcontractors. If general contractors were to be given permission to use the endorsement in this way, there would be no incentive for hiring competent and careful subcontractors. Regardless of the manner in which the subcontractor performed the work, the general contractor would be indemnified under the endorsement for any damage that resulted.

The most recent version of the CGL policy contains much of the language used in the broad form endorsement. Most notably, the work product exclusions do not apply to damages resulting from work performed by a subcontractor who is working on behalf of the insured.

(c) Pollution Exclusion

Another common exclusion in CGL policies relates to environmental liability. There are two different pollution exclusion clauses that are important to understand. The first of these is the qualified pollution exclusion which was incorporated into standard CGL's beginning in the early 1970's. It excludes coverage for any damages resulting from the discharge of pollutants or contaminants, except where this discharge is "sudden and accidental".

The sudden and accidental exception to the qualified pollution exclusion has spawned a plethora of litigation. Insureds seek to demonstrate that even a discharge of pollutants that occurs over a lengthy period of time fits within an acceptable definition of "sudden and accidental", and is therefore covered under the policy, while insurers generally argue that the discharge was not what is commonly referred to as "sudden and accidental", and thus, is not covered.

The widespread litigation concerning the correct interpretation of the phrase, "sudden and accidental", was heightened by Congress' enactment of the

Comprehensive Environmental Response, Compensation, and Liability Act (CERCLA). CERCLA essentially imposes strict liability on any party that owns property on which hazardous environmental discharges have occurred or are likely to occur, even if the hazard was not created by the present owner of the property. As a result, insureds have become more eager to seek coverage for environmental claims, and therefore, the ultimate interpretation of the sudden and accidental clause is crucial.

Though a number of courts have faced the problem of defining "sudden" and "accidental", there is no consensus on a single interpretation of the terms. There are, however, several categories into which the interpretations fall.

Most of the controversy centers around the word, "sudden". When dealing with a dumping of pollutants by a corporation over a period of years, it is necessary for the insured to argue that the word, "sudden", does not connote an instantaneous happening in terms of time, but rather relates to the *unexpected* nature of the happening—even if the discharge gradually occurred over a period of years. The counter-argument of the insurer is that the word, "sudden", specifically defines the time span of the occurrence.

The split of opinion among the courts divides generally along the lines of those courts that find the word ambiguous, and are therefore willing to apply the doctrine of *contra proferentum* and adopt the meaning contended for by the insured, and those that find that the word unambiguously conveys a temporal element and therefore excludes a pollutant discharge over a lengthy period of time. In the former case, the insured will recover as long as the damage caused was accidental—i.e., unintended.

Though the qualified pollution exclusion is still litigated today in regard to policies that were in effect when the polluting event occurred, the insurance industry has developed a new pollution exclusion designed to essentially eliminate the insured's liability for coverage of environmental damage. The absolute pollution exclusion was written into standard CGL policies beginning in the mid 1980's and is used in place of the earlier qualified exclusion.

The absolute exclusion eliminates any coverage for damages resulting from environmental discharges, even where those discharges are sudden and accidental. Further, the absolute pollution exclusion typically excludes any "loss, cost or expense arising out of any governmental direction or request that the named insured ... clean up pollutants." In other words, insurers unequivocally exclude coverage for remediation performed pursuant to CERCLA.

In interpreting the absolute pollution exclusion, courts appear to be more accepting of the intent of insurers than they are in interpreting the qualified pollution exclusion. In fact, a number of courts have held that the absolute exclusion is clear and unambiguous and therefore, will effectively bar any recovery under the CGL policy for damage resulting from environmental discharges.

Though it appears that the insured is left without coverage in the event of a discharge, there have been various bases raised by insureds for a finding of coverage in spite of the comprehensive pollution exclusion. These bases were discussed and espoused by the Louisiana Supreme Court in *South Central Bell Telephone Co. v. Ka–Jon Food Stores of Louisiana, Inc.* This court has held that the insured may recover under a CGL policy despite an absolute pollution exclusion where the discharge occurs from routine accidents not generally considered to be "environmental accidents", *e.g.,* where carbon monoxide gas leaks from a heater and causes bodily injury. Alternatively, the insured might recover if it was not properly advised by the insurer that without additional endorsements, the policy absolutely excluded environmentally related damages. Finally, the insured might argue that it reasonably believed that the qualified pollution exclusion was still in effect. In a case where there had been no reduction in premiums after the insertion of the absolute exclusion, the insured could argue that it was not adequately forewarned of a reduction in the risk assumed by the insurer, and therefore, the absolute exclusion should not apply.

6. Title Insurance

a. *General*

Title insurance is a promise on the part of the insurer to indemnify the insured for a loss suffered as a result of a variance in the actual title to realty from that stated on the face of the policy. Policies of title insurance are issued to both property owners and mortgagees, and many mortgagees now require that a policy of title insurance be purchased to protect their security. Title insurance is generally considered a unique type of insurance, because, unlike other forms of insurance, it protects the insured from losses which result from the legal rights of others which already exist. Title insurance policies provide coverage only for defects in title which exist at the time of issuance of the policy. There is no coverage for impairments which are created by the insured after the inception of the policy. It is only the subsequent assertion of those pre-existing rights which may be seen as the fortuitous, loss-causing event.

Title insurance does not insure that the quantity of land conveyed is correct; and further, where a mortgagee is the insured, it does not insure that the property is worth the amount of the debt or that the debt will be paid.

b. *Exclusions*

The most significant of the common exclusions from coverage under title insurance is that title insurance policies do not cover defects which are known to the insured at the inception of the policy. Thus, the insurance company ordinarily will perform a search of the title records and append a list of defects to the policy. Neither these recorded defects, nor any other defects known to the insured will be covered. Courts are split as to whether a title insurance company has a duty to conduct a title search and report the results of the search to the insured. Where insurers are so required, they are generally held to the standards of care of a reasonable title abstractor.

In addition, title policies generally exclude defects which result from the exercise of the state's zoning or police power, rights of eminent domain, rights of parties in possession, and unrecorded mechanic's liens. Defects which a survey of the land would disclose are also generally excluded, because they are defects which would be made apparent only by investigations outside of the recorded deeds.

Even granting these exclusions, however, title insurance is preferable to a simple title search. For example, title insurance will cover losses due to a forged deed, undisclosed spouses, or undelivered instruments, all of which would impair title, but go undetected by a title search. Also, some courts have held that title insurance will protect the insured when the insured is sued on a warranty deed given by the insured if the defect existed as of the policy date.

c. Damages

Disputes over the determination of damages under a title policy may arise because of the uncertainty of determining the value of land. This problem can be compounded by the fact that damages under a title policy may accrue even if the encumbrance on the title is not permanent.

Two general rules have developed. First, in cases where the owner is the insured, the owner will recover to the extent that the property value is less than it would be without the defect of title. Second, in cases where a mortgagee is the insured, the mortgagee will recover to the extent that the value of the security has been impaired.

d. Duty to Defend

In addition to indemnifying the insured for losses which result from the defect, the insurance company also has the duty to defend the insured in suits that arise because of a covered defect of title. This duty is separate from the duty to indemnify, and the cost of defense is neither a part of, nor constrained by, the policy limits. The insurance company does, however, reserve the right to attempt to cure defects as they arise.

e. Successors in Interest

A general rule of title insurance is that the policy does not run with the land to the insured's grantees. There are, however, certain exceptions to this rule. An individual's policy will protect subsequent owners who take as heirs or devisees. Corporate successors will also benefit from the policy in cases such as those involving merger or consolidation. Also, in the case of a mortgagee, the lender's policy will run with the land to an assignee of the mortgage.

C. NO–FAULT COMPENSATION

The primary flaws of the existing tort (fault) system for compensation of people injured in automobile accidents that are addressed by a system of no-fault compensation include the following:

1. *Gross over-compensation of minor injuries.* The rampant settlement by liability insurers of inflated and fraudulent minor claims and legal actions places a serious burden on the cost of automobile insurance under the fault system that is in turn passed on to the insureds in the form of raised premiums.

2. *Gross under-compensation for legitimate, serious injuries.* Recovery, even to the extent of actual damages, excluding pain and suffering, is frequently eliminated completely by inability of the injured victim to locate a hit-and-run driver, by inability to obtain and present actual proof of the negligence of a tortfeasor, or by a possible jury finding of contributory negligence. Recovery of the full loss is frequently seriously reduced by contingent fees to counsel, other expenses of trial, and the possible finding of comparative negligence.

3. *Delay in recovery of losses.* If the case goes through the full process of trial, or serious settlement negotiations do not occur until the eve of trial, payment for losses by the tortfeasor can lag years behind the incurring of expenses by the victim, sometimes forcing the acceptance of an unreasonably low settlement by the victim because of the pressure of expenses caused by the injuries. If an

appellate procedure follows, the delay can be extended by years.

The most promising approach to the curing of these defects in the fault system of compensation has been the introduction of the no-fault system—*if done properly*. The keynote of the system is a radical change in the philosophy of compensation for injury. It begins with recognition first, that the automobile is an essential element of our lives, and second, that the automobile is an inherently dangerous instrumentality that will predictably cause extensive personal injury. Based on that principle, the no-fault system in its purest form would base recovery for the expenses of an automobile injury on first-party insurance required to be carried by every driver in the state. The twin goals of the system would be 1) to provide rapid compensation, truly measured by the expenses incurred, including lost wages and loss of ability to perform household functions; and 2) in exchange for certain and adequate compensation, to eliminate the costly burden of litigation for any injuries compensated by first-party insurance and for pain and suffering, in order to be able to provide this full compensation, while at the same time, actually reducing automobile insurance premiums.

The first state to deviate from the system of compensating victims of automobile accidents through the liability of tort-feasors was Massachusetts. In 1970, the legislature of Massachusetts enacted a provision for compensation for bodily injury arising out of automobile accidents that generally required the physically injured party to look to his own insurer for compensation for damages up to $2000 and granted immunity from tort liability to that extent to the tort-feasor. While the systems enacted in the states that have followed the lead of Massachusetts vary somewhat, the Massachusetts system provides an adequate prototype for understanding the basic functioning of no-fault compensation in an area traditionally characterized by liability compensation.

Under the Massachusetts statute (M.G.L.A. c. 90 §§ 34A, D, M, and N) personal injury protection included in an automobile policy is required to provide, in addition to liability coverage in the amount of $10,000 for injuries to any one person with a limit of $20,000 per accident, coverage to the extent of $2000 for personal injury expenses incurred in a motor vehicle accident that takes place in Massachusetts by a named insured, members of his household, any authorized operator or passenger, or any pedestrian struck by the insured's vehicle. Coverage is to include medical, surgical, X-ray, and dental expenses as well as funeral expenses and any net loss of wages if the injured party is employed or lost earning power if the injured party is unemployed. Also included are expenses for necessary services performed for the injured party that he would otherwise be able to perform for himself. Any owner, registrant, operator, or occupant of a motor vehicle to which personal injury benefits apply, who would otherwise be liable to the injured party for damages in tort, is made exempt from tort liability to the extent that the injured party is entitled to recover under a policy providing personal injury protection, or would be entitled to recover if the party taking out the policy under which he is covered had not elected one of the deductibles to be discussed below. The tort-feasor is similarly exempt from liability in any subrogated action by an insurer.

Under M.G.L.A. c. 231 § 6D, the injured party is entitled to bring an action against the tort-feasor for pain and suffering (including mental suffering) but only if the reasonable and necessary expenses for medical, surgical, X-ray, and dental services exceed $500, or the accident resulted in death, loss of a bodily member, serious and permanent disfigurement, or loss of sight or hearing.

The Massachusetts plan enables the insured to select an endorsement to his policy which would provide that his $2000 coverage is subject to a deductible in the amount of $100, $250, $500, $1000, or $2000. If he selects the $2000 deductible, he has effectively eliminated no-fault coverage for himself and those covered by his policy, but the exemption from liability for the tort-feasor nevertheless remains in effect. This possibility benefits those who have adequate coverage under other policies.

So far, there has not been a strong movement toward extending the no-fault principle to property damage arising out of automobile accidents. A no-fault statute covering property damage was enacted in Massachusetts in 1972, but it was repealed in 1976.

Though Massachusetts was the first state to adopt some form of no-fault insurance, it has not been the only jurisdiction to do so. Approximately half of the states in the country have some form of no-fault statute in effect. These systems are divided generally into two groups. The first group, of which the Massachusetts statute was the pro-genitor, has been generally labeled "modified", or occasionally "true no-fault", since this type of statute makes a fundamental change in the existing fault system by restricting the ability of the insured to bring a tort action.

The most comprehensive statute of the modified type to be adopted was that of Michigan. It has also been the most successful in terms of meeting the twin goals of reduced automobile insurance premiums and full, accurate, and timely compensation of victims for automobile injuries. The sole secret to success in the no-fault approach is to provide adequate compensation for injury and to eliminate as far as practicable the ability of the injured person to resort to an action at law against the tortfeasor. The statute originally passed in Michigan provided for the elimination of the right to sue a tortfeasor for any losses covered by the first-party no-fault insurance or for pain and suffering except in the case of deliberate conduct or injuries resulting in death, loss of a limb, or permanent and serious disfigurement (the so-called "verbal restriction"). On the other hand, Michigan no-fault insurance provided for medical coverage, compensation for up to three years for lost wages, and replacement of services such as housekeeping and child care of which the victim was rendered incapable for up to three years—and that coverage was without upper limit. Under the Michigan system, three types of insurance coverage were made mandatory: personal protection insurance, property protection insurance, and residual liability insurance.

While it would seem that medical and other coverage without upper limit would send automobile insurance premium rates soaring, the net effect of the savings on the costs of litigation was to greatly reduce the premium for automobile coverage.

The Michigan experience with no-fault insurance in its purest form was a courageous experiment in the face of serious opposition. It was also highly successful, as compared to the no-fault program of Massachusetts and other states that passed a no-fault bill with the seeds of its own downfall sown within it. In Massachusetts, for example, the relatively low level of coverage ($2000) fairly insured that a significant number of accidents would slip over the top and wind up in litigation. More significantly, the low threshold for elimination of tort suits for pain and suffering ($500 for medical, surgical, X-ray, and dental costs—the so-called "monetary limitation") was both an easy limit to exceed legitimately with the increase in medical costs, and an invitation to artificially inflate medical bills to boost the injured person over the threshold and into a lawsuit for lucrative recovery for pain and suffering. Since the three controlling parties concerned—the injured party, the injured party's doctors, and the injured party's lawyer—all stood to profit from elevating medical costs over the $500 limit and into the litigation range, it was predictable that "no-fault" would result in increased automobile premiums, and in some cases, a resulting rejection of the no-fault system without its ever having a fair test.

The second form of no-fault system that was adopted in a number of states is purely cosmetic and clearly doomed to failure in terms of reducing premiums. It is generally referred to as "add-on" no-fault. In this instance, all of the ills of the fault system are retained, and the expense—without the benefit—of no-fault insurance is added to it. In some states, insurers are required to offer, and insureds are required to purchase, first-party no-fault insurance. In others, insurers must offer, but the insured can reject, first-party no-fault insurance. In a third group of states, both the offering and acceptance of no-fault insurance is optional. The theory of add-on no-fault is that if the injured party is compensated for medical losses through first-party no-fault insurance, he/she will voluntarily forego bringing a lawsuit for pain and suffering. Such a consummation is devoutly to be wished—but nonetheless naive to a fault (no pun intended).

D.　UNINSURED AND UNDERINSURED MOTORIST COVERAGE

1.　Generally

The recurring problem of inadequate automobile liability insurance coverage, and the resultant concern over the inability of insureds to receive full indemnification for personal injury in automobile accidents, led to the creation of uninsured and underinsured motorist coverage.　These types of coverage indemnify insureds when they are injured by another driver who either has no insurance or who does not have enough insurance to cover the cost of the injuries.

2.　Uninsured Motorist (UM) Coverage

Uninsured motorist ("UM") coverage offers first-party accident insurance, paying benefits directly to the insured for personal injury (though usually not property damage), covering insureds when they are *legally entitled* to recover from another driver who is not insured, or when that other driver cannot be identified, *i.e.,* a hit-and-run situation.　This coverage extends to three classes of insureds: the named insureds and members of the insureds' household, persons injured while in an insured vehicle, and people who suffer consequential damages as a result of personal injuries suffered by the previously noted classes of insureds.

Uninsured motorist coverage is provided for by statute in most of the fifty states.　In some states, automobile insurers are required to include UM coverage in all automobile liability policies. In others, the insurer is merely required to offer UM coverage to its insured, who has the option of refusing it, thereby saving the additional premiums and generally relying on his/her own health insurance to cover such accidents.

To be entitled to UM proceeds, the insured is required to establish that he/she is "legally entitled" to recover for personal injuries from the uninsured tortfeasor because of the tortfeasor's legal liability. The tortfeasor is considered to be "uninsured" if the tortfeasor does not carry required liability insurance, the tortfeasor's insurer denies coverage, or the tortfeasor's insurer is insolvent.

Insurers who pay proceeds under uninsured motorist coverage are generally subrogated to the cause of action of the insured against the tortfeasor—for whatever that may be worth.

3. Underinsured Motorist Coverage (UIM)

Underinsured motorist coverage is designed to provide first-party indemnification in situations where the automobile liability insurance of the responsible party has policy limits that are not as high as the level of either the liability insurance or the underinsured motorist coverage carried by the injured insured. Underinsured motorist coverage, though commonly not required by statute, is increasingly included in automobile insurance policies for an added premium.

4. "Stacking" of Uninsured or Underinsured Coverage

The practice of making claims under multiple insurance policies or multiple coverages within one insurance policy in order to obtain total indemnification for the expenses resulting from an injury where no one policy or coverage compensates for the total loss is commonly referred to as "stacking". The practice of stacking occurs frequently with uninsured and underinsured motorist coverage.

There are two main methods that insureds use to stack uninsured coverage: 1) combining uninsured coverages from more than one policy, or 2) combining uninsured coverage for one vehicle with the uninsured coverage for another vehicle on the same policy. Whether the insured uses the former or the latter method, stacking does not involve double recovery, but rather is an attempt to provide the injured party with full indemnification for his or her injuries.

Stacking of underinsured coverage is often approached in a similar manner. In cases where underinsured coverage is mandated by a statute which defines the term "underinsured" in terms of the relationship between the injured party's underinsured motorist coverage and the tortfeasor's liability coverage, there are unique ways of stacking which can be used to determine whether the underinsured motorist coverage is triggered. For example, some courts determine whether the tortfeasor is underinsured by aggregating, or stacking, all of the insured's uninsured motorist coverages and then comparing that amount to the amount of liability coverage carried by the tortfeasor. If the tortfeasor's coverage is less than the insured's aggregated uninsured motorist coverage, the underinsured motorist coverage will be activated.

Frequently courts will prohibit a tortfeasor from stacking his/her liability benefits in a way that is detrimental to the injured party. In other words, the underinsured policy will be activated in any case where the tortfeasor's liability coverage is insufficient to fully compensate the injured party for his/her loss.

For example, if the tortfeasor has a combined liability policy limit of $120,000, but the tortfeasor must answer in damages to five injured parties— *i.e.,* each injured party will receive only $24,000— the courts will not permit the insurer to deny underinsured motorist coverage to the injured party on the basis that the injured party's underinsured motorist coverage, *e.g.,* $50,000, is less than the total policy limits of the tortfeasor, *i.e.,* $120,000. Instead, the court compares the total liability limits of the tortfeasor as to a *particular injured party, i.e.,* $24,000, with the underinsured motorist coverage of the injured party, *i.e.,* $50,000. If the liability coverage is less than the underinsured motorist coverage, the underinsured motorist coverage is triggered.

Finally, a court may activate the insured's underinsured motorist coverage whenever the tortfeasor's liability coverage is insufficient to fully compensate him or her for the loss.

In order to combat efforts by insureds to stack coverage, insurers often include language in automobile insurance policies which expressly or impliedly prohibits stacking benefits. For example, a policy may provide that "This is the most we will pay regardless of the number of vehicles or premiums shown on the Declaration", thus preventing the stacking of more than one uninsured motorist coverage under the same policy. Challenges have frequently arisen with regard to the validity of these anti-stacking provisions. In ruling on these challenges, courts have focused on several factors, including the public policy considerations behind uninsured and underinsured motorist coverage, the specific language of the policy, and the reasonable expectations of the insured.

Whether stacking of benefits is permitted depends on the proclivities of the specific jurisdiction. Some jurisdictions explicitly prohibit the practice of stacking by statute. Other jurisdictions permit the practice, but only if there is no clear and unambiguous policy language to the contrary. Still other jurisdictions consistently permit stacking despite contrary policy language.

E.   ORAL CONTRACTS

Although a number of states require that contracts of life, accident, and health insurance be in writing, the general rule is that oral contracts of insurance are enforceable as long as they can be performed within one year. Oral contracts are frequently used to provide immediate temporary insurance until a written binder can be issued, primarily in cases of fire, casualty, and marine insurance. Although the time period during which the oral binder is in effect is kept to a minimum, there is always the danger of fraud on the part of the insured or even the agent of the insurer in collusion with the insured, in claiming an oral contract of insurance after a loss occurs.

Of necessity, when an oral contract of insurance is entered into, the parties discuss only the essential terms of the contract. Proof of other terms of the contract generally consists of evidence of an understanding that the standard form of policy was intended to fill in the missing terms.

If an agent represents more than one insurer that writes the type of insurance that the agent has agreed to issue effective immediately, it is required that there be some objective evidence other than the mere mental decision of the agent as to which insurer the agent has selected to write the policy. Even a mere mention of the insurer to the insured or written memorandum by the agent to himself has been held to be sufficient for this purpose.

F. WRITTEN BINDERS

In cases in which a formal policy of insurance cannot issue immediately because of administrative delays or the necessity for normal investigation, in order to satisfy the need of the insured for immediate coverage, and to prevent losing a customer in the interval, the practice has developed of issuing cursory written binders, incorporating by reference the terms of the full policy form, to be effective until the actual policy is issued or rejected by the home office. In the case of life insurance, documents accomplishing this purpose are issued upon payment of the first premium and are referred to as "binding receipts."

In an attempt to limit or control the effectiveness of binders, insurers frequently worded the binder form so that it was made subject to a later acceptance on the part of the home office of the insurer. Theoretically, the insurer retained the power under the binder to reject the contract, and thereby render the binder ineffective in the case of an individual who died prior to the issuance of a formal policy. Numerous court decisions have avoided this attempt at reserving discretion by "strict interpretation" of the language against the insurer, or by resolving "ambiguities" in favor of the insured, frequently in ways that suggest that the court is simply rewording the binder to provide coverage for the insured.

G. PREMIUMS

Since the basic purpose of insurance is to provide the mechanism whereby the covered losses suffered by any member of the insured group will be spread equally among the entire group, the most fundamental problem is to predict at the beginning of the period the total amount of losses that will occur during the period. This figure, combined with the total costs of administering the program (including any profit to be anticipated) form the basis for arriving at the premium to be charged per unit of insurance. Each of these elements should be considered separately.

1. Net Premium

The net premium is the amount that must be collected by the insurer (in advance, or annually, or on some scheduled basis) in order to cover all of the losses that will occur during the period of insurance. In the case of life insurance, mortality tables, reflecting the carefully accumulated data of actual experience, give a reasonable prediction of what the percentage of a class of men or class of women of a particular age will die in successive years. From this, the insurer can predict the total amount that will have to be paid out of the collected fund in any given year by way of proceeds. By dividing that figure by the total number of $1000 units of insurance to be issued, the insurer can determine the amount to be collected from an insured for each one thousand dollars worth of insurance purchased. This figure is referred to as the net single premium. It is somewhat complicated by other factors such as the fact that premiums are generally collected in advance, at least on an annual basis; and, therefore, the insurer can collect a slightly smaller figure since it will be able to add to it the interest that it can earn through having the use of the premium from the beginning of the period.

Because mortality tables are a practical application of the law of averages, their reliability has improved through the years since the first table was constructed on the basis of baptismal and death records in London by John Gaunt in 1662. They require periodic revision, not only on the basis of more extensive data, but also on the basis of an increasing life expectancy.

Net single premiums for fire insurance on residential buildings are arrived at in a similar way. Tables based on experience have been constructed to predict the dollar amount of losses that will occur per $100 of building value. Separate tables apply to various classes of residential buildings depending on the type of construction. This "manual rating method" of predicting losses, and thereby fixing the rate per unit of insurance on the basis of past experience, is also used in the cases of workmen's compensation, liability, automobile, health, and surety insurance.

A system of "schedule rating" is used in the case of commercial property both to provide an incentive to owners to prevent losses, and to provide fairly for the difference in likelihood of fire loss among the large variety of commercial buildings (farm, factory, retail store, etc.). Under the system of schedule rating, a basic figure is arrived at for a particular type of commercial building, not on the basis of experience, but on the basis of an engineering judgment as to the likely danger of fire damage. Debits and credits, either in dollar amounts or percentages, are then applied to that basic figure according to a fixed schedule for particular fire prevention features (such as a sprinkler system) or hazards on the premises.

2. Loading

The "gross" or total premium is arrived at by adding to the net premium a certain amount of "loading" to cover all costs to the insurer in administering the program over and above the payment of losses. Loading includes such fixed costs as office expenses, executive salaries, and rent. It also includes such variable costs as agent's commissions, loss of interest through installment rather than initial collection of premiums or through early occurrences of losses, or high mortality costs because of an element of adverse selection (e.g., of the total class of those who are eligible to convert their term policies to permanent policies, it is preponderantly those who are in poor health who will exercise the option rather than an average cross-section). Also included in the loading charge is a contingency surplus to cover the eventuality of losses in excess of those predicted by the mortality or other tables.

H. RESERVE FUND

The liability of an insurance company on all of its outstanding policies at any one point in time is not measured by the total face value of those policies because its liability is contingent on the happening of the event insured against, and it is, therefore, predictable that the company will not be called upon to pay the full face value of every outstanding policy at once. Rather, its anticipated liability for any given year is based on a prediction of the number of payments it will be compelled to make on the basis of experience tables. If, for example, an insurance company issued ten life insurance policies in the face amount of $20,000 each to ten identical males, and the mortality tables indicated that among the group one would die in each of the next ten years, it would be predictable that the company's liability on those policies would be $20,-000 for each of the next ten years. It is also predictable that it will be collecting premiums from each of the ten in the first year, and from the nine remaining in the second year, and from the eight remaining in the third year, etc. The total number of premiums is, therefore, known in advance. On this basis, it is possible to establish the amount that must be *reserved* out of each premium to enable the insurer to meet the proceeds that it must pay in any given year. The fund so reserved is called the "reserve fund." It is generally fixed conservatively on the high side to hedge against losses in excess of those predicted by the mortality tables.

If at any time the assets of an insurer fall below the amount necessary to maintain the reserve fund plus any other liabilities, the laws of most states empower the commissioner of insurance to take control of the company for purposes of rehabilitation, or if necessary, to liquidate it for the benefit of creditors.

I. SURPLUS

As a precaution against allowing its assets to fall below the amount necessary to maintain its reserve in the event of losses far in excess of those predicted, all insurers set aside, out of income, a fund in addition to the reserve fund called the "surplus fund", "contingency fund", or "special reserve". In this way, an insurer can weather a massive disaster without risking insolvency.

J. SURRENDER VALUE

It is a common feature of whole life and endowment life insurance policies that once the policy has been in effect for a specified period (generally two or three years), upon surrendering the policy for cancellation the insured will receive from the insurer its "cash surrender value." While the amount of the surrender value is based on the reserve value of the policy, it is generally set considerably below the reserve value for the purpose of discouraging cancellation.

The cash surrender value is usually collectible at the option of the insured in cash, or in paid-up insurance in a lesser amount than the face value of the policy, or in term insurance in the full face amount.

K. CANCELLATION OF AN INSURANCE POLICY

An insurance company will often deny coverage or defend its decision to deny coverage based on the cancellation of the policy. There are several ways to achieve cancellation, and it can be accomplished either by the insured or the insurer.

The most straightforward method of canceling a policy is by mutual agreement between the parties to the insurance contract. However, it is more probable that the termination will be unilateral, either due to action taken solely by the insured or the insurer.

If the insured wishes to cancel the policy, it may be done in a number of ways. First, the insured could choose not to renew a policy at the time of its termination. Alternatively, because most insurance policies contain a provision that the policy may be canceled upon non-payment of premiums, the insured could cause the policy to be canceled simply by failing to make payment of any additional premiums. In addition, the insured is generally permitted under the policy provisions to cancel the policy upon written notice to the insurer.

The insurer also enjoys the right to cancel the policy in a number of instances. For example, the insurer may cancel the policy if the insured has concealed or misrepresented a material fact at the time the insurance contract was entered into. The insurer may also cancel the policy where the insured has breached a warranty in the policy. Additionally, the insurer may take action to cancel the policy if the insured does not pay the premiums.

Despite the insurer's ability to cancel an insurance policy, however, there are significant restrictions on how it may do so. State statutes, for instance, may impose procedural requirements which the insurer must follow if it is to effectively cancel the policy, and these statutes are generally applied strictly against the insurer.

Statutory requirements may include timely and sufficient notice to the insured regarding cancellation and provision for a grace period which forestalls cancellation for some period after the premium has become due. Moreover, in cases involving, for example, compulsory automobile insurance, a statute may also require that notice of cancellation be given to a state agency such as the division of motor vehicles. This reporting requirement is intended to encourage the state to take steps to prevent individuals from operating vehicles without adequate coverage and thus protect innocent third parties.

Public policy may also have an impact upon the validity of an insurer's cancellation of a policy. For example, it has been held that where a dentist's malpractice insurance was canceled after he testified against another dentist being accused of malpractice, the witness could bring a claim against the insurer for breach of contract. This holding was based on the public policy against intimidating witnesses to give testimony. This public policy was deemed by the court sufficient to override an insurer's ability to cancel a malpractice insurance policy.

Related to the cancellation issue is the question of whether premiums must be refunded upon cancellation of the policy. The answer to this question may depend on the type of policy involved and the particular refund provisions in the policy. If a life insurance policy is involved, for example, provisions in the policy generally permit refund of a portion of the premiums not applied to the purchase of coverage up to the time at which the insured cancels the policy. A property insurance policy generally permits a refund of a portion of the policy in an amount determined by specific tables established by the insurer. Finally, an automobile insurance policy will generally permit a refund in an amount determined by the insurer's manual.

CHAPTER TWO

INSURABLE INTEREST

A. GENERAL

Consistent with the concept of insurance as a means of indemnifying an insured against a loss is the corollary that insurance should not provide an insured with the means of showing a net profit from the event insured against. One rather rough-hewn method of enforcing that corollary is the doctrine of insurable interest.

B. HISTORICAL DEVELOPMENT

Prior to 1746, insurers had developed the practice of writing insurance on ships and cargoes with the stipulation that they would not demand proof of any interest of the insured in the subject matter of the insurance. The results of this practice were well stated in the preamble to an Act of Parliament in 1746:

"[I]t hath been found by experience that the making insurances, interest or no interest, or without further proof of interest than the policy, hath been productive of many pernicious practices, whereby great numbers of ships with their cargoes, hath either been fraudulently lost or destroyed, or taken by the enemy in time of war: * * * and by introducing a mischievous kind of gaming or wagering, under the pretense of assuring the risque on shipping, and fair trade, the institution and laudable design of making assurances, hath been perverted * * *."

Consequently, Parliament gave birth to the principle of insurable interest as a rule of law:

"[B]e it enacted * * * That * * * no assurance or assurances shall be made by any person or persons, bodies corporate or politick, on any ship, or ships belonging to his Majesty, or any of his subjects, or on any goods, merchandizes, or effects, laden or to be laden on board of any such ship or ships, interest or no interest, or without further proof of interest than the policy, or by way of gaming or wagering, or without benefit of salvage to the assurer; and that every such assurance shall be null and void to all intents and purposes." Act of 1746, St. 19 Geo. 2, c. 37 § 1.

That statute was followed in 1774 by a second act of Parliament that made it unlawful to issue insurance on "the life or lives of any person or persons, or on any other event or events whatsoever, wherein the person or persons for whose use, benefit, or on whose account such policy or policies shall be made, shall have no interest, or by way of gaming or wagering. * * *" Act of 1774, St. 14 Geo. 3, c. 48.

These statutes precluded court enforcement of policies issued without some form of insurable interest, but they missed the mark of eliminating the practice of issuing such policies. Not only has it proven nearly impossible to quench gambling instincts entirely by legislation, but there were also any number of legitimate commercial situations in which the interest of the insured would be difficult to prove by legal standards. An example of the latter would be the issuance of insurance on "anticipated freight," whereby the insurance policy is issued prior to sailing, but the contract for the cargo is not entered into until it is taken on board at some distant port. Policies issued under these circumstances, therefore, simply moved, in terms of enforcement, from forums of law to forums of "honour", in that they depended for the payment of proceeds upon the honour of the insurer who could have pleaded the defense of lack of insurable interest in an action at law. Phrases commonly found in these policies include "policy proof of interest" or "P.P.I." (i.e., no further proof of insurable interest required than the existence of the policy), "interest or no interest", and "without benefit of salvage to the insurer" (because the insured had no benefit of salvage to give).

The English courts enforced the insurable interest statutes with a vengeance, holding a policy that contained any of the offending phrases listed above to be unenforceable even though the insured actually had an insurable interest. In fact, the very making of such a policy became a criminal act under the Act of 1909. American courts have taken a somewhat more lenient view, holding that while such phrases are themselves unenforceable, they do not affect the enforceability of the rest of the policy.

The American version of the insurable interest doctrine originated in court decisions following English precedent based on the Statutes of George II and George III referred to above. Subsequently, a number of states codified the general rules into statute.

C. PURPOSES

Throughout the development of the insurable interest doctrine in case and statutory law, two primary purposes have captured the attention of lawmakers, both rooted in public policy. The first is the elimination of insurance as a vehicle for gambling, an activity to which has been attributed idleness, vice, a socially parasitic way of life, increase in impoverishment and crime, and the discouragement of useful business and industry. Patterson, Insurable Interest in Life, 18 Colum.L.Rev. 381, 386 (1918). The second is the removal of the temptation provided by a prospect of a net profit through insurance proceeds to deliberately bring about the event insured against, whether it be the destruction of property or human life. A third purpose, the elimination of an inducement to defraud the insurer by destroying the thing insured, has been all but totally overlooked in the genesis of the doctrine, perhaps because it is overshadowed by the first two, and perhaps because of a sense that in this regard the insurer can and should protect itself by investigation prior to issuance of the policy.

D. DISTINCTION BETWEEN PROPERTY
AND LIFE INSURANCE

Since the time of the early English statutes referred to above, the single doctrine of insurable interest has been stretched to accommodate two widely disparate forms of insurance—property and life insurance. While the purposes to be served by the doctrine in regard to the two types of insurance are basically the same—i.e., prevention of wagering and protection of the entity insured—there are major distinctions between life and property insurance that call for the application of different rules in order to achieve those purposes. For example, property insurance is purely a form of indemnity (restoration, dollar for dollar, as nearly as possible within policy limits, usually to the insured, of the value of the thing lost). Life insurance, on the other hand, is more accurately characterized as a form of investment, whereby the insured makes periodic contributions to a fund that is ultimately to be paid for the support of a beneficiary other than the insured after the death of the insured. Secondly, the "loss" to the beneficiary caused by the death of the insured can seldom be measured accurately in terms of cash value, while the reverse is generally true of the loss of property. Thirdly, the degree of public interest in protecting human life from deliberate destruction far exceeds that in protecting property. In order to understand the radical differences in rules encompassed within the insurable interest doctrine as it pertains to these two forms of insurance, it seems appropriate to treat each form separately.

E.   INSURABLE INTEREST IN RELATION TO PROPERTY INSURANCE

1.   Definition

As a functional definition, it might be said that "insurable interest" is that interest that the law requires a beneficiary of an insurance policy to have in the thing or person insured in order that the contract of insurance will not be held to be void as a wager or an inducement to bring about the event insured against. Focusing more directly on the nature of that interest, section 281 of the California Insurance Code defines it as "Every interest in property, or any relation thereto, or liability in respect thereof, of such a nature that a contemplated peril might directly damnify the insured." That will suffice for the moment until the following discussion can highlight areas of contention that require further particularity for a working definition.

2.   Legal Interest v. Factual Expectancy
a.   *Origin*

One of the most ancient yet continuing controversies in defining the law of insurable interest involves the question of whether the insured is required to hold some *legally* recognized interest in the property or whether a simple *factual* expectancy of loss in the event of its destruction is sufficient. Modern cases determining current policy continue to draw for their roots upon one or the other of two early English cases interpreting the Statute of George II. Those opting for the "factual expectancy" test harken back to the case of *Le Cras v. Hughes* (1782). During the war with Spain, British naval forces captured the Spanish ship, Santo Domingo, in the harbor of St. Fernando de Omoa, together with its cargo. By virtue of custom, the British captain and crew had every expectation of being granted rights of Prize in the captured ship and cargo since "wherever a capture has been made, since the Revolution, by sea or land, the Crown has made a grant: there is no instance to the contrary." Ibid. The captain and crew insured the vessel and cargo for the voyage back to England, during which it was lost due to the perils of the sea. In an action on the policy, Lord Mansfield held as one alternative ground that although "Master Holford's insurance was not a legal interest," the mere factual expectancy of a profit to be made by way of Prize if the ship had survived the voyage was sufficient. "An interest is necessary [under the Statute of George II], but no particular kind of interest is required."

The second case, *Lucena v. Craufurd* (1806), provided the cornerstone for the "legal interest" school. The subject was again a captured vessel, insured by the Royal Commissioners during a voyage from the point of capture to a British port. The issue of insurable interest in the Commissioners was tried and resulted in a verdict for the Commissioners. On appeal, the House of Lords remanded the case for a new trial because of erroneous directions to the jury. The opinion of Lord Eldon in that case continues to be cited by adherents to the legal interest doctrine. He imposed upon the definition of insurable interest the requirement that it be a "right in the property, or a right derivable out of some contract about the property, which in either case may be lost upon some contingency affecting the possession or enjoyment of the party." If any doubt of the additional requirement remained, he further stated that "if the [*Le Cras v. Hughes*] case was decided upon the expectation of a grant from the Crown, I never can give my assent to such a doctrine. That expectation, though founded upon the highest probability, was not interest, and it was equally not interest, whatever might have been the chances in favour of the expectation." He reasoned that "hundreds, perhaps thousands" anticipated some advantage from the safe passage of the ship, from the dock company down to the porter, and concluded, without stating a further rationale, that without a legal interest in the ship these latter should not be permitted to insure their expectancy. It is conjecturable that the true basis for the "legal interest" distinction lay in the traditional English predilection for defined property rights. In the same opinion, Lord Eldon quoted the words, "Courts of justice sit here to decide upon rights and interests in property; rights in property, or interest derived out of contracts about property. They do not sit here to decide upon things in speculation. Speculative profits are nothing."

Once Lord Eldon made the technicality of a legally recognized right the touchstone of insurable interest, he went on to carry it to extremes by allowing it to suffice "even if the factual expectation was that the right would be economically worthless." His famous example ran as follows:

"Suppose A. to be possessed of a ship limited to B. in case A. dies without issue; that A. has 20 children, the eldest of whom is 20 years of age; and B., 90 years of age; it is a moral certainty that B. will never come into possession, yet this is a clear interest."

b. Early Case Law

If the end to be served is the prevention of gambling or inducement to destruction, it seems clear that the factual expectancy theory is the more appropriate. It is the lack of prospective gain from the practical point of view of the insured that produces the desired effect, rather than some technical legal right, regardless of value. Nevertheless, until recent years, the majority of American jurisdictions had opted for Lord Eldon's legal interest theory.

This choice produced results at odds with the indemnification theory in a number of instances. For example, in *Hartford Fire Ins. Co. v. Cagle* (10th Cir.1957), the insured contracted to purchase a farm for $3500. He was to live on the farm, paying $35 per month until title could be perfected in the seller, at which time he would be obligated to pay the full remaining purchase price. The contract gave the insured the option of calling off the agreement if the seller could not acquire title, whereupon the $35 installments would be considered rent. It became obvious before the destruction of the property by fire that the seller would be unable to perfect title. After the property was destroyed, the insurer challenged the insured's insurable interest because of the total worthlessness of the legal right. Following Lord Eldon's view, the court affirmed an award for the insured. In the same vein, in *Insurance Co. v. Stinson* (1880), a mechanic's lien that was factually worthless because of a prior security interest that exceeded the value of the property was considered adequate to support an insurable interest to the full extent of the debt. In both cases, the technicality was served, but the insured stood to profit substantially from the fire.

The rationale for this counterproductive approach to insurable interest has occasionally been stated to be that it would be an excessive burden on the insured to require him to prove the dollar value, as well as the existence, of his legal interest, especially in instances in which the value is not subject to accurate proof. Where cases are to be won or lost, not on the facts, but on the insured's inability to prove the facts one way or the other, it is not extraordinary for the courts to favor the insured, placing the burden on the insurance company to protect itself by being more circumspect in limiting the amount of prospective liability it assumes under its contracts.

In applying the legal interest approach, courts have generally fixed upon three categories of interest in property that will suffice as an insurable interest. They are property rights, contract rights, and legal liability.

i. *Legal Title*

Legal title of practically any nature and quality will apparently suffice as an insurable interest. It could be as remote from a fee simple as that of Lord Eldon's hypothetical remainderman in *Lucena v. Craufurd,* supra (ship limited to remainderman in case A dies without issue, A having twenty children, the eldest of which is twenty years of age). Insurable interest exists in the lessor, lessee, and sublessee in the same property, as well as in the holder of any form of life estate. Similarly, one who holds mere legal title after executing a contract to sell realty has an insurable interest. Legal title may be voidable, or even void and yet suffice as long as the insured is under an honest and reasonable belief that he holds valid title. This was the case in *Home Ins. Co. of New York v. Gilman* (Ind.1887) wherein the insured was in bona fide possession, unaware of the invalidity of an executor's conveyance. (In fact, it has been held to be immaterial as between insurer and insured that the insured obtained title by fraud.) A number of courts have taken the position that possession under claim of ownership is prima facie evidence of title.

The actual value of the particular title would seem to be immaterial in qualifying as an insurable interest.   In the case of *Insurance Co. v. Stinson* (1880), the holder of a mechanic's lien had an insurable interest although a prior mortgage far exceeded the value of the property, making the lien of no practical value.

ii.   Equitable Title

Just as any form of legal title will provide an insurable interest, so any form of equitable title will also suffice.   For example, the holder of equitable title under a contract for the sale of realty has an insurable interest, as is appropriate in view of the fact that the risk of loss is generally placed on the vendee.   Similarly, a beneficiary of a trust has an insurable interest in the trust res, as does the holder of any beneficial interest recognized by a court of equity.

iii.   Possessory Interest

Anyone having a mere possessory interest in property, has an insurable interest to the full extent of its value.   This applies to one who hires or borrows property, even when he is not legally liable for its loss.   Ordinarily, he is required to hold the proceeds, over and above the value of his interest in the property, for the benefit of the owner.

iv.   Creditor's Interests

While an unsecured creditor may have an insurable interest in the *life* of his debtor (as discussed below), he does not ordinarily have an insurable interest in the property of his debtor.   On the other hand, a secured creditor does have an insurable interest in the property that is subject to the security interest. This applies whether the security interest arises by way of a mortgage, mechanic's lien or otherwise, and whether it is recognized by a court of law or equity. As was held in the case of *Insurance Co. v. Stinson* (1880), the fact that a prior security interest exceeds the actual value of the property and renders the lien predictably worthless does not destroy the lien-holder's insurable interest. Nor is the insurable interest affected by the fact that destruction of the particular insured property would still leave ample security to cover the debt.

v.   *Future Interests in Property*

Courts have upheld an insurable interest in property which the insured has not yet acquired, or which is not in existence at the time of contracting for insurance as long as it is understood that the insurance attaches only in the future at such time as the insured shall acquire an actual interest in the property. Shippers are thereby able to contract in advance for insurance on cargo that they will take on board in the future, perhaps at some distant port. Similarly, retailers are able to insure in advance their revolving stock of inventory.

vi.   *Representative's Interest*

In situations in which legal title is held in a representative capacity, as by an executor, administrator, receiver, or trustee, the representative is considered to have an insurable interest for the purpose of taking out insurance on the property under his control, and any proceeds from such insurance are considered to be held for the benefit of those for whose benefit the representative is acting.

vii. Stockholder's Interest in Corporate Property

Under the American rule, a stockholder, whose ability to receive dividends depends on the continued existence of corporate property, is considered to have an insurable interest in corporate property to the extent of his pro rata share in the value of the property in the event of liquidation.

viii. Liability Interest

As was even noted by Lord Eldon in *Le Cras v. Hughes,* supra, if a person is so situated that loss or damage to the property will render that person legally liable for damages, as in the case of a bailee, that person is considered to have an insurable interest in the property. In the same vein, one who is contractually bound to obtain insurance on property for another has sufficient interest, because of potential liability, to insure the property, even in his own name.

c. Current Case Law

In recent years, a surge of case law adopting the factual expectancy test has made it the current majority rule. In a number of decisions during the 1980s, courts have gone out of their way to adopt the factual expectancy test even though the choice was unnecessary since an actual legal interest existed in the insured.

One of the earliest and most conspicuous jurisdictions to opt for the factual expectancy test for insurable interest is New York. In the case of *National Filtering Oil Co. v. Citizens' Ins. Co. of Missouri* (N.Y.1887), National Filtering had licensed Ellis & Co. to use its patent in oil filtering and reduction. The license granted was to remain exclusive even if royalties were reduced by destruction of Ellis' plant. The plaintiff, therefore, insured against such loss by taking out a fire insurance policy on the plant. When the building burned, the insurance company claimed lack of insurable interest in National since it had no property rights whatever in the building. The court held for National, stating that an "interest legal or equitable in the property burned is not necessary to support an insurance upon it; that it is enough if the assured is so situated as to be liable to loss if it be destroyed by the peril insured against. * * *"

A subsequent New York statute (N.Y.Ins.Law § 148 McKinney 1966) stated that an insurable interest "shall include any lawful and substantial economic interest in the safety or preservation of property from loss, destruction or pecuniary damage." In view of the apparent purpose of the New York legislature to codify rather than reverse the *National Filtering* approach to insurable interest, the words, "lawful and substantial interest" are generally understood to mean a *lawful* as opposed to an *unlawful* interest (as, e.g., an expectancy of profit from a shipment of illicit drugs), and not to introduce a requirement of a legal or equitable interest in the property.

A common fact pattern in which courts have faced the issue in recent years involves persons who purchase and insure a stolen car without knowledge that the car is stolen. The great majority of courts passing on the issue have held that the insured does have an insurable interest in the car, and the trend is to base that determination on the factual expectancy of loss to the insured if the car is damaged or stolen. The test is generally stated to be whether the insured will gain a benefit by the continued existence of the insured property or suffer a loss by its destruction.

It is interesting that even in current case law, courts adopting the factual expectancy doctrine do so specifically in terms of the "Lawrence" view, as opposed to the "Lord Eldon" view, harkening back to their debate in the 1805 case of *Lucena v. Craufurd,* supra.

In determining whether a factual expectancy exists in, for example, a house or automobile, the courts have frequently considered whether or not the insured had a possessory right in the thing insured and whether or not the insured had invested money or labor in improving or maintaining it.

3. When Insurable Interest Must Exist

The rule in this area took an unfortunate turn in 1743 when Lord Chancellor Hardwicke stated by way of *dicta,* "I am of opinion, it is necessary the party insured should have an interest or property at the time of the insuring, and at the time the fire happens." In numerous American cases, judges have echoed the rule without considering the fact that as long as the insured has an insurable interest at the *time of the loss,* the purposes of the indemnity principle will be totally accomplished. The requirement of an insurable interest at the time of insuring as well would preclude insurance on after-acquired property. It would require a contractor to take out a new builder's risk insurance policy every day, to add coverage on the previous day's construction, and would preclude a marine policy on cargo to be taken on at a later point in the voyage. It would also deny recovery to one who sells insured property and subsequently reacquires it prior to the loss.

Fortunately, the rule apparently applied in cases in which it would actually affect the outcome is substantially different from the rule generally quoted in case law. The reason for this is that courts have been in the habit of restating Lord Hardwicke's rule as *dicta* in cases in which an insurable interest existed at *both* times or at *neither* time— i.e., cases in which the requirement of an insurable interest at the time of insuring as well as at time of loss would not affect the outcome of the case. In cases in which it matters, the predominant rule is that an insurable interest is only required at the time of the loss. Adding to the demise of Lord

Hardwicke's rule is the fact that insurers generally will not raise the defense of lack of insurable interest at the time of insuring even when it is available because of the prospect of losing the profitable business of writing policies on such things as after-acquired property.

In terms of legislation, the statutes of fourteen states require an insurable interest only at the time of the loss, while only three state statutes require an insurable interest both at the time of insuring and at the time of the loss. The New York statute requiring an insurable interest in property is non-specific as to the time, but the New York courts have applied the requirement only at the time of the loss.

According to Professor Vance, there is one small aspect of Lord Hardwicke's rule that remains in force. If an insured takes out a policy that is a pure wager, such as a policy on someone else's home, the policy will not generally be allowed to become valid even if the insured subsequently acquires an interest in the property before the loss.

F. INSURABLE INTEREST IN RELATION TO LIFE INSURANCE

For purposes of the insurable interest doctrine, life insurance is divided into two distinct groups— insurance taken out on one's own life, and insurance taken out on the life of another.

1.　Insurance on One's Own Life

The traditional statement that "Every person has an insurable interest in his own life" is a cryptic way of saying that when one takes out a life insurance policy on himself, there are sufficient inherent safeguards in the situation to preclude the need for the usual rules concerning insurable interest. The insured has it within his power to name himself (more accurately, his estate) or any other person of his choice as beneficiary; and this is considered a sufficient guaranty of good faith and confidence to protect the insured against an early and deliberate demise and also to preclude wagering. Except in the state of Texas, it is not necessary that the named beneficiary, if it is other than the insured, have any insurable interest in the life of the insured.

An exception to that general rule exists in cases in which the court finds that a wagering policy has been taken out by the insured on his own life at the behest of a third person who is named as beneficiary. Evidence of a wagering policy is usually found in such facts as (1) that the original proposal to take out the insurance was that of the beneficiary, (2) that premiums are paid by the beneficiary, and (3) that the beneficiary has no interest, economic or emotional, in the continued life of the insured. On finding that such a policy is primarily a wager, the court will generally void the policy entirely.

2. Insurance on the Life of Another

It has been argued that life insurance frequently involves relationships of consanguinity or affection that afford extra protection against deliberate destruction or wagering not present with property insurance, and, therefore, less stringent rules should apply in the case of life insurance. The counter-argument is that life is so much more precious than property that *any* danger of deliberate destruction or wagering should call for more rigorous protection than in the case of property insurance. The resultant rules of insurable interest in regard to policies on the life of one other than the owner of the policy reflect this bi-polarization.

In discussing the rules, it will be convenient to use the term *cestui qui vie* (CQV) to refer to the person whose life is the subject of the policy.

a. Family Relationships

It is universally held that one has an insurable interest in the life of his or her spouse, without more. Generally, one who is living with another in the mistaken but good faith belief that they are lawfully married has the same insurable interest. (This does not apply to parties deliberately living in unlawful cohabitation.) At the outer reaches of this rule, courts have held that a person has an insurable interest in a fiance.

The only other relationship to which courts universally accord insurable interest without more is that of parent and minor child. Each is considered to have an insurable interest in the other. Beyond that degree of consanguinity, the courts split as follows.

Some courts extend an automatic insurable interest to the relationships of parent-adult child, brother-sister, brother-brother, sister-sister, and grandparent-grandchild, while others require some additional pecuniary interest. In this area, pecuniary interest is tested by the factual expectancy rather than legal interest test. As long as the benefit to be obtained from the continued life of the CQV is pecuniary rather than merely sentimental, a mere reasonable expectation that it will be forthcoming from the CQV will be sufficient, regardless of the absence of legal enforceability. In addition, the dollar value of the expected benefit is not considered a limit on the amount of insurance that can be obtained.

The relationship between aunts and uncles and nephews and nieces and between cousins have generally been held to be too remote to support an insurable interest. Again, a factual expectancy of economic benefit is required. Although clear lines are difficult to draw from the cases, the clarity of proof of a financial interest required seems to vary inversely with the closeness of the actual family ties. The closer the family relationship, the less stringent the requirement of proof of economic interest. For example, in a case involving an aunt and niece who lived together for many years, the mere expectation that the niece would feel disposed to help the aunt financially if the need arose was sufficient to give the aunt an insurable interest in the niece. *Cronin v. Vermont Life Ins. Co.* (R.I. 1898).

It is universally held that such legal relationship as those between a mother-in-law, father-in-law, son-in-law, daughter-in-law, brother-in-law, sister-in-law, stepfather, stepmother, and stepchild do not alone support an insurable interest. Again, an economic expectancy must be proven.

b. *Contractual Relationship*

It is generally held that if one person is in a position to suffer an economic loss by the death of another because of a business or contractual connection with that person, the former has an insurable interest in the life of the latter, at least to the extent of that economic interest. This means that a partner has an insurable interest in his partners, and a partnership has an insurable interest in each of the partners. Because of this, insurance is a common way of funding an agreement between partners for the continuation of the partnership business after the death of any of the partners and the removal of the deceased partner's share of the assets of the business. It also means that an employer and employee each has an insurable interest in the life of the other. A typical example of this is "key person" insurance. Also, a creditor can insure the life of his debtor (although an unsecured creditor cannot insure the *property* of his debtor).

While the amount of insurance obtainable on a spouse or relative is not limited by the dollar value of the insurable interest, even if some pecuniary interest is required, in the case of an insurable interest based on commercial or contractual rights, the dollar value of the interest usually does fix a *general* limit on the amount of life insurance that will be permitted. For example, the aunt who insured her niece on the basis of anticipated financial assistance in her old age in *Cronin v. Insurance Co.,* supra, could take out insurance in any amount; while life insurance taken out by a creditor on his debtor will be stricken as a wager if the amount of insurance greatly exceeds the amount of debt plus costs, interest, and insurance premiums payable during the life of the debtor.

3. When Insurable Interest Must Exist

The insurable interest requirement for life insurance, as well as other forms of personal insurance such as accident and health insurance, is almost exclusively controlled by statute. Thirty-three states have statutes requiring an insurable interest in order to take out a policy of personal insurance on someone other than the owner of the policy. Of these, twenty-seven state statutes require only that the interest exist at the time of inception of the policy, as opposed to the time of the loss. Another five state statutes do not specify a point in time; and the North Dakota statute requires an insurable interest for both personal and property insurance both at the inception of the policy and at the time of loss.

The result of the majority rule requiring an insurable interest for personal insurance only at the inception of the policy is that the owner of the policy can lose the insurable interest during the life of the policy (as, for example, by a divorce) without affecting the validity of the insurance or the ability of the beneficiary to collect proceeds at the time of loss.

4. Assignment of a Life Insurance Policy

Assignment of a policy of life insurance differs from merely naming a beneficiary in that the entire bundle of rights of ownership of the policy is transferred permanently. Of particular concern is the fact that the insured no longer retains the power to change the beneficiary in case of a deterioration of their relationship. This becomes pertinent in deciding whether the rule permitting the naming of one without an insurable interest as beneficiary should be carried over to permit assignment of a life insurance policy to one without an insurable interest. Two arguments favoring free assignability are the following. (1) While property insurance is viewed exclusively as a means of indemnification against loss, life insurance is primarily considered investment property. In order to maximize the usefulness of life insurance as an investment, it should be freely marketable. (Note additionally: in the event that an insured is unable to keep up premium payments on a life insurance policy of which the market value exceeds the cash surrender value because the insured has become uninsurable since the beginning of the policy, the only possibility of the insured's realizing the additional market value frequently lies in his ability to sell it to any buyer free of the constraints of the insurable interest rule.) (2) Several cumbersome methods permit an insured to accomplish the same end result as an assignment (such as the method suggested by Keeton of naming his estate as beneficiary and binding himself contractually to leave the proceeds to the "assignee" in his will).

The primary argument against permitting assignability to persons without an insurable interest is that the net effect is the same as permitting that person to take out the insurance policy in the first place, giving rise to concerns about wagering and the deliberate hastening of the death of the *cestui que vie.*

Courts are widely split on this issue, but the majority favor free alienability for the reasons mentioned above, while the minority invalidate assignment to anyone without an insurable interest. The often-cited wording of the Massachusetts court in adopting the majority view clearly flags the limitation on this freedom:

"We see nothing in the contract of life insurance which will prevent the assured from selling his right under the contract for his own advantage, and we are of opinion that an assignment of a policy made by the assured in *good faith* for the purpose of obtaining its present value, and *not as a gaming risk* between him and the assignee, or a cover for a contract of insurance between the insurer and the assignee, will pass the equitable interest of the assignor; and that the fact that the assignee has no insurable interest in the life insured is neither conclusive nor *prima facie* evidence that the transaction is illegal." *Mutual Life Ins. Co. v. Allen* (1884) (Emphasis added.)

Even under the majority view, if it is found that the assignment was part of a scheme from the beginning on the part of the assignee to obtain a wagering policy, the assignment will be held invalid. The usual evidence in cases of this sort is the fact the assignment occurred almost immediately after the policy was initiated.

5. Consent of the Insured

To provide an extra measure of control and protection to the *cestui que vie,* the general rule is that before a policy may be taken out by anyone other than the *cestui que vie,* his consent is required. Absent that consent, the policy is invalid. The only exceptions to this rule are that in some jurisdictions, insurance on a spouse may be initiated without his or her consent, and in nearly all jurisdictions, insurance on the life of a child does not require his or her consent.

6. Industrial Life Insurance

The usual rules regarding insurable interest have frequently been held not to apply to industrial life insurance for several reasons. First, since the proceeds of industrial life policies are typically small, they present little danger as an inducement to murder. Secondly, the investigation and processing of the potential defense in each case would be time consuming and nullify the advantage of speedy payment of proceeds for funeral and burial expenses under the "facility-of-payment" clause. Thirdly, in view of the diminutive size of the proceeds, the addition of pointless administrative costs for either the insurer or the beneficiary could destroy the current usefulness of this type of insurance. While there exists the possibility of wagering by buying up the industrial life policies of those unable to meet the premiums, the evil has not been considered sufficiently serious to impose the insurable interest rule on all such policies.

G.　STANDING TO RAISE DEFENSE OF INSURABLE INTEREST

In spite of the fact that the insurable interest doctrine was devised out of a *public* concern rather than concern for the interests of insurers, the majority view is that only the insurer has standing to raise the defense. This standing limitation is invoked most frequently to prevent an alternate claimant to the proceeds from arguing that they should not go to the named beneficiary for lack of insurable interest. This limitation in standing seems particularly in conflict with the purpose of the insurable interest doctrine in view of the fact that frequently the insurer will find it more to its interest to overlook the defense in order to preserve a good client (particularly in dealing with large commercial organizations), and even more frequently will be indifferent as to which of two claimants recovers the proceeds as long as it is not required to pay more than once.

The basis for the standing limitation is that only a party to the insurance contract has a legitimate interest in raising the defense. Numerous courts have, however, overlooked this technicality and permitted an outsider to raise the issue, particularly in cases involving challenged assignments of policies or proceeds. It should also be noted that the apparent "majority" view may be deceptive in that the rule is frequently found stated as mere *dicta* or as a secondary ground for the holding. If the outcome of many of these cases were to depend solely on this standing question, it is far from certain that the result would be the same.

H. COUNTER–DEFENSES TO THE INSURABLE INTEREST DOCTRINE

1. Waiver and Estoppel

The typical situation in which the counter-defenses of waiver and estoppel arise is that in which the beneficiary makes claim to the proceeds of a policy from the insurer, the insurer defends on the grounds of lack of an insurable interest, and the beneficiary counters by proof of some statement or action on the part of the insurer that amounts to a waiver of the insurable interest defense or should be held to estop the insurer to rely upon it. The court is then faced with the question of whether or not the public interest in enforcing the insurable interest doctrine outweighs the desire to reach an equitable result between the parties before it. A substantial number of decisions have held that the insurable interest doctrine is not subject to the counter–defenses of waiver or estoppel. Other decisions appear to take a more moderate position, holding that waiver and estoppel will not prevail against a defense of no insurable interest whatever, but will be permitted to defeat a claim that the existent insurable interest is not as valuable as the proceeds claimed under the policy.

CHAPTER THREE
DEFINITION OF RISKS

In a number of specific areas, courts have applied public policy to enlarge or diminish coverage in ways that ignore the express wording of the contract. In this chapter, we shall examine the primary areas of this kind of judicial amendment of insurance policies.

A. UNLAWFUL CONTRACTS

As a general principle, courts will render unenforceable any insurance policy that violates a statute, violates public policy, or is an integral part of some prohibited activity. While it might be argued that in such a case the risk never attached since the policy was unenforceable from inception, and therefore premiums should be refundable, courts will frequently take the position that the insurer and insured are *in pari delicto,* and decline relief in any respect.

1. Policies in Violation of Statute

As discussed above in chapter two, any policy of insurance that is issued to one without such insurable interest in the subject of the insurance as is required by the pertinent statute is unenforceable.

Similarly, contracts of insurance that violate statutes rendering gambling illegal are also unenforceable. For example, a life insurance policy is generally assignable to one without an insurable interest in the life of the cestui que vie *except* when the assignment is obtained for purely wagering purposes. Businesses that evolved for the purpose of buying up industrial life insurance policies from their impoverished holders were found to be "vocational wagering," generally rendering the assignment invalid so that the policy could not be enforced by the assignee. Another such example is the classic tontine and its multiple variations, whereby a number of individuals take out insurance on themselves under an agreement that the proceeds of all of the policies shall go to the last survivor of the group.

2. Policies in Violation of Public Policy

In theory, any insurance policy, "the tendency of which is to endanger the public interests or injuriously affect the public good, or which is subversive of sound morality, ought never to receive the sanction of a court of justice or be made the foundation of its judgment." *Ritter v. Mutual Life Ins. Co.* (S.Ct.1898). The difficulty in drawing clear lines or predicting the outcome of cases involving novel fact situations in this area stems from the fact that any area of law that is so dependent on the individual court's concepts of "the public good" and "sound morality" is bound to look like a patchwork quilt, particularly when these varying views are being counterbalanced against equally varying views of the respect to be accorded freedom of contract. For example, it has generally been held that any insurance contract that might act to discourage marriage is unenforceable. This rule has been applied primarily to so-called "marriage benefit insurance," whereby the insurer is bound to pay a fixed sum to the beneficiary or his wife at the time of the beneficiary's marriage on condition that he remain single for a specified period of time. Another variation obligates the insurer to pay, at the time of marriage, a sum which increases the longer the insured remains single. On the other hand, the same courts will enforce a contract of insurance wherein the insured names as beneficiary his or her unmarried partner.

3. Policies Related to Unlawful Activity

Courts have drawn an equally uneven line between enforceability and unenforceability with ad hoc decisions on policies relating in some way to unlawful activity.

a. Insurance on Property Relating to Unlawful Activity

Courts have drawn a distinction in terms of enforceability between insurance on property which it is unlawful to possess and insurance on property which it is lawful to possess but which is used in the perpetration of unlawful activity. For example, insurance policies on gambling equipment, burglary tools, and inventory of a business carried on without a required license have been held to be unenforceable, while insurance policies on buildings and their furnishings used as brothels have been enforced. The rather vague rationale for enforcing the latter contracts is that the insurance is not illegal per se, and any support that it lends to the business of prostitution is purely incidental. The inconsistency that one finds from case to case can be seen in comparing the brothel cases with a holding by the Minnesota court that insurance on a barn that housed an illegal still was unenforceable. *Vos v. Albany Mut. Fire Ins. Co.* (Minn.1934).

Insurance on intoxicating liquors tends to straddle the line of enforceability. Such insurance has been upheld in some states in which the sale and even use under certain conditions is illegal on the rationale that the liquor *could possibly* be used lawfully. In areas in which liquor or particular drugs are considered contraband per se, the majority view is that insurance on these items is an integral part of the unlawful possession, and therefore void.

One generally adopted distinction is that if the insured is not himself involved in the unlawful activity, he can legitimately insure the unlawfully used property. For example, a mortgagee or lienholder can insure the debtor's automobile against confiscation for the unlawful transportation of liquor, provided the insured himself is not involved in the operation.

b. Life Insurance on Individuals Involved in Unlawful Activity

i. Death as a Result of Unlawful Activity

Courts are more reluctant to find public policy exceptions to the enforcement of life insurance than to the enforcement of property insurance due to criminal activity on the part of the insured because (1) the beneficiary is of necessity someone other than the person who is the subject of the insurance and is involved in the unlawful activity, (2) the all risk nature of life insurance precludes the expectation of implied exceptions on the part of laymen, and (3) insurance proceeds are frequently all that stand between the beneficiary and pauperism.

The public policy issue is squarely presented when the insured is killed in the course of committing a crime. A minority of courts have taken the highly technical position that it would contravene public policy if the insured had expressly insured himself against being killed by a policeman's bullet in the course of an armed hold-up, and therefore the same effect cannot be permitted by implying coverage of that eventuality under a general policy of life insurance. Underlying this rationale is the sense that the insurance acted, if not to induce, at least to remove an impediment to the commission of the crime. The majority view favors allowance of the recovery of proceeds under these circumstances, particularly if the beneficiary is other than the estate of the criminal cestui que vie, as long as the policy was not taken out in contemplation of committing the crime. As stated in *Home State Life Ins. Co. v. Russell* (Okl.1936), the distinction between *express* coverage for death while involved in criminal activity and the mere inclusion of that loss within coverage by *implication* is that in the former case, the policy was clearly obtained in contemplation of committing the criminal act, while in the latter, the opposite is probably the case. Furthermore, it is not the wrongdoer who reaps the proceeds, nor one whose rights should be measured by those of the wrongdoer, but rather one whose rights arise under the insurance contract and who was not responsible for the loss. In the majority view, whatever deterrence to crime would inhere in the denial of recovery of insurance proceeds would be more than outweighed by the benefit of permitting insurance proceeds for the payment of creditors and the support of dependents.

Occasionally, policies contain an express exception to coverage for losses caused by "criminal acts" of the insured. Courts have interpreted such exceptions restrictively against the insurer, limiting their application to such major crimes as murder. Their rationale is that if the exception applied to every technical assault, battery, false imprisonment, etc., coverage under the policy would be reduced well below the expectations of the insured.

ii. *Death by Execution*

Courts are fairly evenly split on the question of permitting recovery when death is caused by execution for crime. One of the key factors that can swing the balance is whether the proceeds are to go to the estate of the insured or to another. In the latter case, courts are more prone to allow recovery of proceeds.

iii. Suicide

It is the view of a number of courts that as a matter of public policy, recovery of proceeds under a policy of life insurance, naming as beneficiary the estate of the insured, is to be disallowed in the event of death by suicide while the insured is sane. Most courts will allow recovery, however, if the beneficiary is other than the estate of the insured, as long as the policy was not obtained with the intent of committing suicide.

In the event of a specific provision in the policy excepting coverage in the event of suicide, and *a fortiori,* in the event of no express exception for suicide, recovery is *not* prevented when suicide is committed by an insured while insane. A reasonable definition of the distinction between sanity and insanity in this context is to be found in *Mutual Life Ins. v. Terry* (S.Ct.1872):

> "If the assured, being in the possession of his ordinary reasoning faculties, from anger, pride, jealousy, or a desire to escape from the ills of life, intentionally takes his own life, the proviso attaches, and there can be no recovery. If the death is caused by the voluntary act of the assured, he knowing and intending that his death shall be the result of his act, but when his reasoning faculties are so far impaired that he is not able to understand the moral character, the general nature, consequence and effect of the act he is about to commit, or when he is impelled thereto by an insane impulse, which he has not the

power to resist, such death is not within the contemplation of the parties to the contract, and the insurer is liable."

Frequently, a policy will contain a broad exception for "suicide, sane or insane." In interpreting that clause, a majority of courts have held that an act which would be considered suicide if committed by a sane insured will be so considered if committed by an insane insured. A minority view, however, restricts the word, "insane," as used in the exception, to a person who cannot comprehend the moral or legal consequences of his act, but will not extend it to a person who cannot comprehend the *physical* consequences of his act on the grounds that an act by such an individual does not fit the definition of suicide as the intentional taking of one's own life.

Policy clauses excepting coverage in case of suicide frequently limit the exception to a period of one or two years from the commencement of the policy period. The contract generally provides for a minimal return (e.g., the return of the premiums paid) in the event of a suicide during that initial period on the theory that an insured who takes out a policy in contemplation of suicide will not wait longer than a year or two to consummate his plan. In some instances, the limitation of the exception to coverage for suicide to a one or two-year period, with full coverage of death through suicide after that period, is mandated by state statute.

A majority of courts have held that when a policy lapses through forfeiture and is subsequently revived by a reinstatement, it is the original policy that is continued in force, so that the period of contestability for suicide runs merely from the date of the original policy, and not from the date of reinstatement.

When the insurer raises the suicide exception as a defense under a life insurance policy, the burden is upon the insurer to overcome the presumption against suicide and to establish such facts as would exclude any reasonable theory of accidental death.

c. *Punitive Damages*

i. *Class of Cases*

The issue of whether or not an insurer is to be permitted or obligated to pay punitive damages on behalf of an insured under a liability policy arises in a limited class of cases. One limitation is the fact that punitive damages are practically never assessed for conduct that is merely negligent. On the other end of the scale, if the tortious conduct of the insured defendant is deliberate, the general policy against the insurability of liability arising from deliberate conduct prevents coverage for either compensatory or punitive damages. This means that insurability of punitive damages arises as an issue only in cases involving gross negligence or wanton or reckless conduct on the part of the insured.

A second limitation is a function of the definition of coverage in liability policies. Except where overcome by such doctrines as *contra proferentem* and reasonable expectations of the insured, an express exclusion of coverage for punitive damages prevents the issue from arising. Where the policy language is general, however, covering all "damages" or "sums the insured is legally obligated to pay", courts have generally held punitive damages to fall within coverage of the liability policy.

ii. Public Policy

In those cases, then, in which punitive damages are assessed against the insured tortfeasor for wanton or reckless conduct or gross negligence, and there is no express exclusion for punitive damages in the policy, the courts generally go on to apply competing elements of public policy to determine whether or not the punitive damages *ought* to be permitted to be covered by insurance.

Public policy arguments disfavoring the allowance of insurability are the following:

a. The purpose of punitive damages, as implied in the name, is to exact a civil form of punishment on the tortfeasor guilty of culpable conduct. To allow the punishment to fall on the tortfeasor's insurer would miss the mark. The only apparent counter-argument is that, despite the name, punishment per se, as opposed to deterrence of future misconduct and compensation of the victim, is not a major purpose of punitive damages.

b. The intended effect of punitive damages is to deter the tortfeasor and others from future wanton, reckless, or grossly negligent conduct. If the insurer bears the sting, the message to the tortfeasor and the public is neutralized. The counter-argument is that, while this argument might be applicable to various forms of deliberate conduct, there is no clear indication that punitive damages actually have the effect of deterring wanton, reckless, or grossly negligent conduct. Furthermore, permitting insurance coverage of punitive damages does not mean that no ill effects will result to the tortfeasor from the imposition of punitive damages. In addition to the effect on the tortfeasor's reputation (not an inconsiderable effect if the tortfeasor depends economically on its good will in the community), there is the likelihood of radically increased insurance premiums, if not cancellation of the policy, as well as the possibility that punitive damages will exceed policy limits.

c. Since the insurer must offset the expense of the payment of proceeds for punitive damages, it is required to raise premiums for the entire class of liability insureds. This results in ultimate payment of the punitive damages by the public that is endangered by the wanton, reckless, and grossly negligent conduct of this tortfeasor.

Public policy arguments favoring the insurability of punitive damages are as follows:

a. The line between negligence and gross negligence is, in many cases, indistinguishable, and the allowance of insurance for punitive damages in cases of the latter will no more increase the incidence of that type of conduct than the allowance of insurance for compensatory damages increases the incidence of negligence. Therefore, they should be treated alike, and insurability should be allowed in both cases.

b. Jurors are aware that any punitive damages awarded will be paid to the plaintiff. As often as not, therefore, the jury's purpose in awarding punitive damages is to provide further compensation to the plaintiff for any damages beyond those that could be proven. Insurability would therefore aid the plaintiff in collecting those punitive damages that exceed the tortfeasor's means to pay. The counter-argument is that the plaintiff is not entitled to be compensated beyond proven damages, and therefore collectability by the plaintiff is not an appropriate concern.

c. The final consideration, when it is not overcome by any more compelling public concern, is the court's respect for the insurer's and insured's freedom to contract.

The great majority of courts that have faced the issue of insurability of punitive damages have weighed the public policy considerations and come down on the side of insurability.

iii. Vicarious Liability

A special situation is presented when punitive damages are awarded against a defendant that is held vicariously liable for the tortious acts of another. In the case, for example, of an employer that is held, under the doctrine of *respondeat superior,* liable in punitive damages for the acts of its employee, the predominant rule, even among courts that generally disallow insurability of punitive damages, is that insurability is permitted.

iv. Uninsured Motorist Coverage

Another special circumstance arises in the case of an insured under an automobile policy who recovers a judgment for punitive damages against an uninsured or underinsured motorist. The issue presented is whether or not the uninsured motorist coverage of the injured insured's policy should be permitted to cover the punitive damages.

The first question is whether the standard language of the coverage clause, obligating it to pay "damages which a covered person is legally entitled to recover from the owner or operator of an uninsured motor vehicle because of bodily injury", encompasses punitive damages. The majority view appears to be that the language is broad enough to encompass punitive damages, at least under the *contra proferentem* theory of interpretation. One court took the view that the insurer places itself squarely in the shoes of the uninsured tortfeasor, being liable for *any* damages found against the tortfeasor—punitive or compensatory—within policy limits. This coverage is, in fact, generally more broad than that of the usual liability insurer, since even the deliberate acts of the tortfeasor are within coverage.

The second question is whether or not public policy should permit such coverage. Even in states strongly adhering to the punishment theory of punitive damages, coverage of punitive damages under uninsured motorist insurance is generally permitted. The justification is that the ultimate penalty will be paid by the tortfeasor, since, unlike the situation with normal liability insurance, the insurer under uninsured motorist coverage is able to bring an action in subrogation against the tortfeasor. A minority of jurisdictions, however, stress the compensatory connotation of the words, "damages * * * because of bodily injury", found in both insurance policy and statute, and deny coverage.

B. IMPLIED EXCEPTION FOR INTENTIONAL CONDUCT

1. Generally

Courts will universally recognize an implied exception to coverage under any form of insurance policy for a loss deliberately caused by the insured. This exception is implicit in the nature of insurance which is intended to indemnify against losses which are fortuitous—i.e., beyond control, from the point of view of the party intended to be protected by the insurance.

A loss which is deliberately caused by one person may nevertheless be fortuitous as to another. For example, an employer may be held vicariously liable for a deliberate assault on a third party by one of his employees. If the employer is insured, there will be no implied exception to coverage because of the deliberate nature of the act since as to the insured employer, the act was fortuitous.

The court will generally make a determination first as to whom the policy of insurance is intended to protect economically, and then determine whether or not the loss is fortuitous as to that person. For instance, in some cases involving liability insurance in areas governed by financial liability statutes (e.g., compulsory automobile liability statutes), courts have made the determination as to fortuity from the point of view of the injured third party. In such a case, if the injury was deliberately caused by the insured, the insurer should have a cause of action for reimbursement of proceeds against the insured.

Under a policy of life insurance, where the beneficiary is someone other than the estate of the insured, death by the deliberate act of the cestui que vie (suicide) would be fortuitous as to the beneficiary, and therefore recovery is permitted in most jurisdictions. *A fortiori,* death of the cestui que vie caused by deliberate homicide by some third person is fortuitous as to the beneficiary (absent implication in the crime), and there is no implied exception to coverage.

Courts will further distinguish between insureds, so that deliberateness in causing a loss on the part of one insured will not preclude recovery on the same insurance policy by other insureds as to whom the loss is fortuitous. For example, where a single liability policy covers two partners, and one partner deliberately causes an injury for which, under partnership law, the other partner is equally liable, it has been held that coverage is not excepted as to the innocent partner.

Responsibility for deliberately causing loss in the context of excepting coverage under an insurance policy does not exactly parallel responsibility for tort law purposes. For instance, where an insured intends to inflict a relatively minor impact, and the resultant harm is far out of proportion to that intended, the loss might be considered fortuitous for purposes of insurance coverage, although tort law will hold that the defendant takes the frail plaintiff as he finds him for purposes of liability.

In some instances, a mistake will save the insured from loss of coverage for a deliberate loss. For example, if an insured deliberately cuts down trees or shrubs mistakenly believing them to be on his own property, in most jurisdictions he will not lose coverage under a liability policy. Similarly, where an insured causes personal injury or property damage in an attempt to avoid injury to himself, there is precedent for allowing coverage, even where the insured is mistaken as to the danger, and in some instances, even if his mistake is the result of his own negligence.

When the issue is raised, courts will consider the *capacity* of the insured to form the necessary intent. For example, in certain cases, the youth or lack of mental capacity of the insured has led the court to disallow an exception to coverage for an act which, if committed by a sane or older person, would have induced the court to negate coverage.

2. Fortuitous Element

Occasionally, an incident is composed of both an intentional act of the insured and fortuitous element. In such a case the court will isolate the fortuitous element to see if it is a fortuity against which the policy was intended to insure. For example, in *Argonaut Southwest Ins. Co. v. Maupin* (Tex. 1973), the court held that there was no coverage under a *contractor's* liability policy when he purchased and removed 5000 cubic yards of material from a piece of property, later discovering that the vendor was not the true owner of the property. Compare the case of *Big Town Nursing Homes, Inc. v. Reserve Ins. Co.* (5th Cir.1974), in which liability for false imprisonment sustained by a nursing home whose employees restrained an alcoholic patient from leaving was held to be covered by a malpractice policy. In each case, the court focused on the fortuitous element. In *Maupin,* the fortuity lay in a mistake as to the true owner of property—a fortuity against which the contractor's liability policy was *not* intended to insure. In *Big Town,* the fortuity was an error in professional judgment—a fortuity against which a malpractice policy *is* intended to insure.

3. Express Exclusion for Intentional Conduct

In interpreting exclusions for "injury * * * caused intentionally by or at the direction of the insured," particularly in the case of liability policies, courts generally require a specific intent to cause harm as the threshold requisite for application of the exclusion. Negligence, and even gross negligence, do not satisfy this requirement.

4. Intentional Conduct Leading to an Unintended Result

In addition to having to determine coverage on the basis of whether conduct was accidental or intentional, it is also occasionally necessary to consider the issue of coverage from the aspect of the intended result. The insured may argue that while the particular conduct was intentional, the specific consequence of that conduct was accidental. Courts have taken several views when determining coverage based on non-intended consequences. The reasoning employed by courts varies widely, and the tests range from those which greatly restrict coverage to those which will allow coverage in most circumstances.

At the restrictive end of the spectrum, some courts will simply consider whether there was a purpose to do some harm. It is irrelevant that the particular harm which resulted was unintended, if, in fact, any type of harm was intended. Similarly, knowledge that the particular harm would result is unimportant. This test can lead to a very broad limitation of coverage.

Other courts will consider whether or not the injury was the natural and probable result of the conduct. This test removes the focus from the intent of the insured and puts it on the judgment of the ordinarily reasonable person as to the foreseeability of the harmful result. While this test also creates broad exemptions from coverage, it is justified by the court's applying it on the theory that it is more in keeping with the language in newer policies which excludes coverage unless injuries are "neither expected nor intended." This test is driven more by principles of contract interpretation than a public policy favoring compensation of injured parties.

Other courts consider whether there was an intent to cause the specific type of injury which resulted. This test has also been restricted further by some courts by requiring evidence that there was an intent to cause injury to the particular individual who was injured. Thus, there would be coverage where the insured either caused an unintended type of injury or intended to injure someone other than the person who was actually injured. This test results in a much greater likelihood of coverage. It has been justified on the basis that it is more protective of injured third parties.

Lastly, there are situations in which courts are persuaded that the insurer should not be allowed to deny coverage on the basis of intentional conduct. This reasoning has been most persuasive in cases in which the liability insurance policy is required by statute for the protection of third parties. The most typical example is that of mandatory automobile liability insurance. Recently, however, the principle has gained acceptance in employment discrimination coverage. The rationale underlying this approach is that limitations of coverage for intentional conduct should not prevail over the public policy enunciated in a statute that injured parties should not be left uncompensated for their injuries. This principle could potentially apply in situations in which the public policy favoring compensation of injured victims arises from sources other than statutes.

5. Highly Expectable Losses

In certain instances, the losses which are claimed do not result from conduct intended to cause harm, but are simply too easily foreseen to be treated as other than a calculated risk or cost of doing business. As a result, they are treated similarly to those caused by intentional conduct, since it is deemed inappropriate to allow the insured to shift the losses to insurers. Thus, determining whether a loss was highly expectable is a frequently occurring issue in coverage disputes, particularly under business liability insurance.

The rule can be stated generally that insurance will not cover losses that are so expectable as to be considered a calculated risk by the insured. For example, where a petroleum company discovers that a pipeline valve is nearly worn out, but elects not to replace the valve for economic reasons, any loss which then results from the breaking of the valve may be said to have resulted from the company taking a calculated risk in not replacing the valve.

Coverage can also be denied on the basis of highly expectable losses arising from an insured's creation of a nuisance. It is a catch-all theory and has been used to deny coverage where, for example, a contractor burned logs, tires, and fuel, and the fires resulted in soot and smoke damage to nearby residents. The conduct was simply considered too reckless to warrant coverage.

C. IMPLIED EXCEPTION FOR NORMAL WEAR AND TEAR OR INHERENT DEFECT

Since property insurance is intended to cover fortuitous, as opposed to predictable, losses, courts have created an implied exception for any loss through normal wear and tear of the property as well as through any inherent defect. Even in the case of all risk insurance, as to which the burden of proof is generally held to be favorable to the insured, the burden is upon the insured to establish that the loss was the result of some casualty rather than the result of normal wear and tear or of an inherent defect. The burden then shifts to the insurer to prove that the loss fell within some excepted cause, express or implied.

D. IMPLIED EXCEPTION FOR FRIENDLY FIRE

In interpreting policies that insure against loss by fire, courts have generally followed the practice of implying a distinction between "hostile" and "friendly" fires, holding the insurer liable for loss caused by the former, but not the latter. A friendly fire is defined as one that remains in control within an area within which fire is intended to exist, such as a fireplace, incinerator, or boiler. All others are considered hostile. In this unique instance, courts have ignored the apparently clear, all-encompassing language of the policies (e.g., "all direct loss or damage by fire") and created a limiting interpretation favorable to the *insurer*. Early cases refer to the implied intention of the parties to cover losses only in those instances in which, in layman's terms, the insured would be said to have "had a fire." Some of the more modern courts take the position that even if they would disagree as to the intent of parties at the time the friendly/hostile distinction was being forged by the courts, continued application of the distinction by the courts has resulted in common understanding and acceptance of the distinction by insureds. See, e.g., *Youse v. Employers Fire Ins. Co.* (Kan.1951).

A fire that is originally friendly can become hostile by escaping beyond its intended confines, and the damage is then within coverage, even if the escape is caused by the negligence of the insured. Some modern courts have even considered a friendly fire to have become hostile when it has grown beyond the intended intensity and caused damage, though remaining within the original confines.

Courts generally do not permit recovery for damage caused by soot, smoke, or heat escaping from a fire that remains within "friendly" confines as to the chemical flame. If, however, the flame is in such an area as to be considered hostile, the accompanying damage from smoke, soot, and heat are generally held to be within coverage.

It is possible to insure *expressly* against loss through friendly fire, as under a floater policy, since the distinction between hostile and friendly fire is based upon an interpretation of the intent of the parties rather than a public policy against recovery for damage caused by friendly fire. The only limitation in this respect is that the loss must be fortuitous as to the insured, since recovery of proceeds is never permitted in the case of deliberate destruction by the insured.

E. DEFINITION OF "ACCIDENT"

Policies of liability insurance as well as property and personal injury insurance frequently limit coverage to losses that are caused by "accident." In attempting to accommodate the layman's understanding of the term, courts have broadly defined the word to mean an occurrence which is unforeseen, unexpected, extraordinary, either by virtue of the fact that it occurred at all, or because of the extent of the damage. An accident can be either a sudden happening or a slowly evolving process like the percolation of harmful substances through the ground. Qualification of a particular incident as an accident seems to depend on two criteria: 1. the degree of foreseeability, and 2. the state of mind of the actor in intending or not intending the result. As discussed above in regard to the implied exception to coverage for intentional conduct, a loss which is intended by the person causing it may still be within coverage if it was accidental from the point of view of the insured.

In cases involving policies covering product liability, foreseeability of the harm is often evaluated in terms of the frequency of the occurrence. When foreseeability reaches an excessive level, the loss through liability is considered a cost of doing business rather than an accident.

It is not uncommon for policies to define coverage in terms of loss by "accidental means," as opposed to the more sweeping "accidental result." If the courts were to give this term literal interpretation, the extent of coverage would be minimal, and probably far short of that anticipated by the insured. It would be limited to incidents of loss caused by some bizarre means, and would exclude unanticipated harmful results of conduct that is not ordinarily considered extraordinary. For example, in the case of the sunbather who falls asleep and suffers sunstroke, the harm would be considered the *accidental result* of normal (rather than accidental) *means*. The same would be true of the insured who unintentionally takes an overdose of a normal medication. Insurers have frequently attempted to place that limitation beyond doubt by clearly limiting coverage to those losses "caused solely and exclusively by external, violent, and accidental means," or words to that effect.

Prior to 1946, courts interpreted the language of policies in this respect according to the clear purport of the words. In that year, however, in the landmark case of *Burr v. Commercial Travelers Mut. Acc. Ass'n* (N.Y.1946), the New York court set the new trend among courts of disregarding any distinction between "accidental means" and "accidental result," thereby including within coverage for loss by "accidental means" any loss that would be considered an "accidental result," regardless of the clarity of the limitation within the policy. The court held in that case that death caused by exertion in walking through a snowstorm and attempting to shovel an automobile out of the snow was within coverage limited to losses caused solely and exclusively by external, violent, and accidental means. The rationale behind the court's expansion of the clear policy language was as follows. "Our guide must be the reasonable expectation and purpose of the ordinary businessman when making an insurance contract such as we have here." Id.

The court in *Burr* did distinguish between cases of overexertion in the course of the natural and customary acts of a workman or householder and overexertion in situations unanticipated by the insured, such as accidentally falling into the water and having to swim ashore. Only the latter cases would be considered "accidental" losses within coverage.

Policies covering loss through accident will generally exclude injuries or disabilities caused wholly or partly by disease or infirmity. Courts will generally allow this exception to operate, however, only in cases in which the disease or infirmity is so serious and abnormal that in its natural course of development, it can be expected to cause a loss. For example, an insured who slipped while carrying a milk can which struck him and caused the perforation of an existing ulcer the size of a pea, resulting in death, was held to be covered. *Silverstein v. Metropolitan Life Ins. Co.* (N.Y.1930). Mere conditions of frailty, such as bones that have become brittle with age, or an abnormally thin skull, which would not of themselves cause a problem, but which are a source of more extensive damage than would be caused to the normal individual by the same accidental blow, will not preclude coverage.

F.   ALL RISK v. SPECIFIED RISK

There are two basic approaches to defining the risk insured against in a policy. The distinction between them is significant because of the radically different treatment accorded the two approaches by the courts.

1. *All Risk* insurance frequently referred to as "open perils" insurance is that which covers damage to the specified subject matter of the policy from any cause whatever other than those specific causes expressly excepted by way of exclusion, condition, or exception. Occasionally the risk is limited to all risks incurred in a particular type of undertaking, e.g., "all risks involved in conveyance by land, air, or water." One other common type of express limitation on all risk coverage is a limitation as to the interest in the property covered as, e.g., in a policy covering only the leasehold or remainder interest of the insured in the property covered.

2.   *Specified Risk* insurance, now called "specified perils" insurance covers damage to the subject matter of the policy only if it results from one of the specific causes listed in the policy.   Typical examples are fire insurance and collision insurance.

Courts do not look to any particular key words in a policy to classify it as all risk or specified risk, but rather make the determination on the basis of the conclusion that would be reached by a reasonable insured as to whether he was buying all risk or specified risk insurance.   In some instances, the historical development of the policy is pertinent. For example, jewelers' block insurance developed as a new and distinct type of insurance to fill the peculiar needs of jewelers for coverage against loss whether caused by theft, fire, or *any* unforeseeable cause.   This type of insurance was deliberately created as all risk insurance.   By way of comparison, the standard form of homeowners' insurance and automobile insurance are examples of policies that were historically created by merely joining in one policy a variety of specific coverages, such as fire, theft, and liability insurance.

There are two major distinctions in the courts' treatment of these two types of policies.   First, the courts appear to be much more liberal in interpreting the coverage of an all risk policy expansively to cover even losses that, in some instances, seem to be expressly excepted from the policy, in order to accommodate the expectation of the insured that his all risk policy in fact covers all risks.   In the case of *Northwest Airlines, Inc. v. Globe Indem. Co.*

(Minn.1975), the insurer argued that the theft of money by a hijacker did not technically fall within the express provision for "loss inside the premises coverage" or that for "loss outside the premises coverage." The court took the position that the policy, when read as a whole, would be interpreted by a reasonable insured to be an all risk policy, and therefore the loss would be covered unless *this specific risk* were expressly excluded. The benefit to the insured is that with all risk insurance, he is far less likely to be caught in the gaps between specific, technically defined coverages.

The second distinction has to do with burden of proof. Under the ordinary specified risk policy, the burden is on the insured to prove that the loss falls within the policy's definition of coverage. Under an all risk policy, once the insured establishes that the loss occurred through some casualty, rather than through an inherent defect or normal wear and tear, the burden is generally upon the insurer to prove that the loss fell within some clear exception to coverage as to which the insured can fairly be held to have been on notice. This shifting of burden of proof is of considerable benefit to the insured, particularly in cases in which it is impossible to prove exactly how the loss was caused.

G.   REASONABLE EXPECTATIONS RULE

Perhaps the most extreme examples of the courts' remaking of contracts of insurance between the parties are those that involve application of the reasonable expectations rule. It is a matter of carrying the rule of interpreting a contract *contra proferentem* beyond the extreme, so that the policy is held to cover whatever a reasonable insured would believe it to cover, frequently in spite of clear language to the contrary. As was stated by the court in *Storms v. United States Fidelity & Guar. Co.* (N.H.1978), "If a policy is so constructed that a reasonable man in the position of the insured would not attempt to read it, the insured's reasonable expectations will not be delimited by the policy language, regardless of the clarity of one particular phrase, among the Augean stable of print."

Professor Llewellyn has justified this approach on the grounds that there is not true "assent" to all of the boiler plate clauses by the two parties in the first place. There is at most, in the generality of cases, an agreement on the broad outlines of coverage and an implied agreement to any reasonable boiler plate, contained in the policy delivered after the agreement, that will not change or reduce the coverage expressly agreed to. See Llewellyn, "The Common Law Tradition—Deciding Appeals."

In *C & J Fertilizer, Inc. v. Allied Mut. Ins. Co.* (Iowa 1975), the court permitted recovery of proceeds for a burglary loss in spite of absence of "visible marks [of forced entry] made by tools, explosives, electricity or chemicals upon, or physical damage to, the exterior of the premises at the place of such entry," as required by the definition of burglary in the policy. The court based its decision on what is coming to be an effective three-sided attack on any and all of the painstakingly drafted definitions, exclusions, conditions, and warranties which are contained in standard form policies but which are not actually called to the attention of the insured by the agent or bold print on the policy, or are not "common knowledge" among insureds generally. Side one is the "reasonable expectations rule" discussed above.

Side two is a particular adaptation of the implied warranty concept, recognizing that as it affects the public generally, the insurance business should realistically be characterized as the sale of a product, rather than as the negotiation of a commercial contract. In this context, the insurer should be held to warrant to the insured that the actual policy delivered is reasonably fit for the purpose intended, i.e., that it states the obligations of the parties without altering or reducing the protection bargained for between the parties.

Side three is the doctrine of unconscionability, which can be called into play whenever the court is convinced that the "fine print" of the policy diminishes the protection which the insured (who is presumed not to have read or understood the contract) reasonably expects as a result of the insurer's advertising, discussions with the agent, or broad statements of coverage in bold type on the face of the policy.   Under the unconscionability doctrine, courts have stricken defenses for the insurer in the policy even if the insured had read and was aware of the limitations as long as the defense would, in the opinion of the court, upset the reasonable expectations of the majority of insureds.

This process of "equalizing" the positions of the insured and insurer began with the courts' liberal use of the tool of interpreting any discoverable ambiguity in the policy language strictly against the insurer who drafted the policy form and sold it on a take-it-or-leave-it basis. This doctrine of *contra proferentem* has been pushed to the brink, and in some cases, over the brink of intellectual honesty by courts that were intent on reaching a just verdict for the insured, but that were not quite ready to openly espouse the radical (in terms of traditional contract law) and direct approach of the reasonable expectations rule. Courts have frequently strained to find ambiguities where none logically existed. In the case of *Northwest Airlines, Inc. v. Globe Indem. Co.* (Minn.1975), the court used an interesting test for the determination of ambiguity: "the very fact that [the parties'] respective positions as to what this policy says are so contrary compels one to conclude that the agreement is indeed ambiguous." Id. at 837. The necessary conclusion was then that "[t]he rule is well settled that ambiguous language will be strictly construed in favor of the insured." Ibid. It would appear under that test that in any case in which the fertile imagination of counsel for the insured could find an interpretation of policy language that would differ from the interpretation of counsel for the insurer, there would be an ambiguity to which the court could apply the doctrine of *contra proferentem*.

Even stretched to that point, however, a growing number of courts have recognized that the doctrine of *contra proferentem* is too limited an ally for the insured in the face of the insurers' ability to continue to rework the language of conditions, exclusions, and definitions in the policy until they "get it right." It is these courts that have shown an increasing willingness to face directly the fact that insurance policies are a breed of contract set apart from all others, partly because of the institutionalized inequality of positions between the parties, and partly because of the public interest in fulfilling the expectations of insureds in being economically compensated for losses. It is these courts that have made the break with traditional contract precepts in adopting the reasonable expectations rule.

An interesting corollary to this protective attitude of the courts toward insureds can be found in the court's opinion in *C & J Fertilizer, Inc. v. Allied Mut. Ins. Co.,* supra:

> "Nor can it be asserted the above doctrine [reasonable expectations rule] does not apply here because plaintiff knew the policy contained the provision now complained of and [the plaintiff] cannot be heard to say it reasonably expected what it knew was not there. A search of the record discloses no such knowledge." Id. at 176.

It would seem that the evolving system rewards those insureds who follow the perceived pattern of the crowd—i.e., those who buy, but under no circumstances *read,* the policy.

CHAPTER FOUR

PERSONS INSURED

A. DEFINITION OF INSURED

The "insured" can generally be defined as the person whose *loss* is the occasion for the payment of proceeds by the insurer. He is not always, however, the person to whom the proceeds are paid. In the case of life insurance, for example, of necessity the person whose life is the subject of the policy is not the person who receives the proceeds in the event of death. In the case of property or casualty insurance, the person whose insurable interest is the subject of the insurance may assign the proceeds to another, as in the case of a mortgagor who assigns the benefits of his insurance on the mortgaged property to the mortgagee. And in the case of liability insurance, the injured third party is frequently permitted to bring a direct action against the insurer for the proceeds of the policy, even, on occasion, when the insured himself would be precluded from recovering the proceeds because of a defense available to the insurer. (See infra.)

B.   IDENTIFICATION OF THE INSURED

There is a variety of standard methods of identifying the insured in the insurance contract.   The following are the most frequently used methods.

1.   "Does Insure" Clause

The most common method of identification is to insert the name of the insured in a clause stating that the insurer "does insure _____."   Where there is more than one insured, they can simply be listed, with the result that they share the proceeds equally, or their names can be followed by the phrase, "as their interests may appear," in which case they will share the proceeds in proportion to the economic loss to their peculiar interest in the property.   A third approach is to specify in the same clause the interest of each insured, as, e.g. "[the insurer] does insure A, as mortgagor, and B, as mortgagee."   The same can be done for lessors and lessees, life tenants and remaindermen, bailors and bailees, etc.

It is common practice, particularly in the case of fire insurance, to specify as insured not only the named insured, but also his legal representative, so that in the event of his death, the property will continue to be covered during the administration of the estate.   If a loss occurs during the term of the policy but after the death of the insured, because the contract of insurance is personal in nature between the parties, the cause of action for the proceeds lies in the personal representative of the insured rather than in the heir or devisee of the property insured. The proceeds are, however, held in trust by the personal representative for such heir or devisee. On the other hand, if the policy designates as insured "John Jones, his heirs and assigns," the cause of action for the proceeds lies in the heir or assign having title to the property at the time of loss.

2. Endorsement

Additional insureds can be added to a policy, once it is in effect by appending an endorsement. This frequently happens, for example, when an insured vendor wants to extend the policy to protect the interests of a vendee pending the actual transfer of title to the property. This device is also occasionally used to add as party insured a lessee, mortgagee, or bailee. The effect of such an endorsement is that the added party acquires full status as an insured, rather than that of a mere assignee of the proceeds of the policy, and, therefore, the requirements of the doctrine of insurable interest apply to the added party. Such an endorsement can only be accomplished by written agreement with the insurer.

3. Omnibus Clause

In order to meet the needs of insureds who wished to expand the coverage of their automobile policies to cover the changing class of persons who might use the insured's automobile with his permission, and also under compulsion from legislatures to provide insurance coverage in cases of accidents caused by otherwise uninsured and financially irresponsible drivers, insurers responded with the omnibus clause. Such clauses generally define a class of insureds in terms of a relationship to the named insured, e.g., members of the insured's household, or persons driving the automobile with the permission of the insured.

Originally, such clauses were limited in application to automobile *liability* coverage, but they have since been extended to include collision and even medical payments coverage. As applied to medical payments coverage, omnibus clauses generally expand coverage to include persons injured while "occupying" the automobile, or while "in or upon or entering into or alighting from" the automobile. Since their inception in the automobile liability field, omnibus clauses have found their way into other forms of insurance such as health and accident policies (extending coverage to members of the insured's family), and comprehensive personal liability policies, as well as homeowners policies.

Each person encompassed within the omnibus clause has full standing as an insured, and, therefore, has a right to bring action against the insurer for losses. As insureds, they are also immune from any action by the insurer in subrogation, as e.g., in the case of a member of the insured's household who negligently causes damage to the insured automobile.

Omnibus clauses have given rise to extensive litigation, particularly in determining whether or not an individual using the insured automobile was doing so with the "permission, express or implied," of the insured. Case law seems to divide the jurisdictions into three primary groups. First, those that opt for a *liberal* construction to obtain maximum coverage will disregard any express restrictions imposed by the owner on permission to use the automobile as long as permission was granted for *some* purpose. This includes the situation in which an employee who is permitted to use the company car for business actually uses it for social purposes. Secondly, jurisdictions that hesitate to warp the contractual intent of the parties to serve a social purpose give conservative interpretation to the word, "permission", and require proof that the actual use was within the permission granted by the insured. Thirdly, the majority of jurisdictions steers a middle course between the two and are, therefore, more difficult to predict in any given fact situation. These jurisdictions permit some deviation from the scope of actual permission but will deny coverage in the event of a major deviation. For example, in one jurisdiction, use of an employer's truck on Christmas day for a personal trip to a town fifteen miles distant was held to be within coverage, but a trip out of state to a point one hundred miles distant was held to be beyond coverage. As a generality, this third group of jurisdictions tend to imply extended permission more readily if the original permission were granted for social purposes than if it were granted for business purposes. It is also historically true that the word "use" is frequently extended to others than drivers or passengers. For example, in *Lukaszewicz v. Concrete Research, Inc.* (Wis.1969) those participating in the loading of the insured truck by operation of a hoist loader were considered "users."

One point of agreement among the three types of jurisdictions is that legal inability to give permission will void any implied permission under the omnibus clause. If, for example, an owner has transferred title to an automobile but not the insurance on it at the time of an accident, the driver will not be held to be a permittee of the insured since the insured could no longer grant such permission legally.

Another area of litigation has centered on the so-called second string permittee, or the permittee's permittee. An example of this would be the case in which a father permits his son to drive the car, and the son in turn permits one of his friends to drive it. The issue is whether or not the son's friend was within the scope of permission granted by the father within the meaning of the omnibus clause in the father's policy. The minority rule is that the original permission is effective as to the second string permittee as well, regardless of attempts to expressly limit the scope of the permission. The majority of courts look to the particular facts of the case to answer three distinct questions: (1) Did the owner's permission in fact extend to the second string permittee; (2) Did the first string permittee in fact grant permission to the alleged second string permittee; and (3) Was the actual *type* of use by the second string permittee within the scope of the owner's permission. In the usual case in which the owner has expressed neither permission nor prohibition, the majority of courts hold that the second string permittee does fall within the implied permission, especially if the second string permittee is using the automobile for the benefit of the first string permittee.

4. Beneficiaries Under Life Insurance Policies

a. *Designation of Beneficiaries*

Originally, when life insurance policies were initiated, the beneficiary was named irrevocably. It is now common for the owner of the policy to expressly reserve the right to change the beneficiary at any time up to the death of the cestui que vie. Another option frequently employed to designate contingent or secondary beneficiaries so that if the primary beneficiary predeceases the cestui que vie, the proceeds will automatically go to the secondary beneficiary without the necessity of amending the policy. The estate of the owner is generally designated as the final contingent beneficiary in the event that all named beneficiaries predecease the cestui que vie.

Modern policies also provide a broad selection of methods of payment of the proceeds to accommodate the tax and other interests of the beneficiary. Through these options, the life insurance policy has become a major functioning part of the owner's estate plan. In addition to the option of spelling out the disposition of the proceeds in the policy, the beneficiary clause can simply designate an individual or trustee as recipient with the ultimate disposition of the funds to be spelled out in a contract, trust document, or will. These documents have the advantage of being amendable without the insurer's consent.

b. Interest of the Beneficiary

i. Irrevocable Beneficiary

When a beneficiary is named irrevocably—i.e., the owner has not retained the power to change beneficiaries—the right to receive the proceeds on the death of the cestui que vie is considered to be vested in the beneficiary regardless of lack of delivery of the policy to the beneficiary or even knowledge of the policy by the beneficiary. This right, however, being one of contract under the policy, is subject to any defenses available under the policy. If, for example, the cestui que vie commits suicide within an exclusion of the policy, or engages in military service which voids the policy by its terms, there is a valid defense against the beneficiary. Default in payment of premiums by the owner will also provide a defense, with the exception that in this case the beneficiary can generally prevent the default by paying the premiums himself.

The rights of the beneficiary prior to the death of the cestui que vie are protected by statute in all states against attachment by creditors of the owner of the policy, and a number of states have added protection against attachment by creditors of the beneficiary. Absent this protection, since the only right of ownership retained by the owner who has named the beneficiary irrevocably is the right to pay the premiums (even the right to cancel the policy is illusory because the beneficiary can take up payment of the premiums), the policy is subject to attachment by the creditors of the beneficiary if it has matured or has a cash surrender value.

When a life insurance policy names several irrevocable beneficiaries in common, it is generally held that if one beneficiary dies, his rights pass to the surviving beneficiaries, and not to his estate, unless otherwise specified in the policy.

ii. Revocable Beneficiary

Under a policy in which the owner has retained the right to change the beneficiary, the named beneficiary has a very minor interest during the lifetime of the cestui que vie. It is generally referred to as a mere expectancy. It is, however, somewhat protected by statute in that the creditors of the owner cannot cut off the rights of the beneficiary by attaching the cash surrender value of the policy unless the owner enters bankruptcy, in which case the trustee in bankruptcy has the power to extinguish the interest of the beneficiary by taking the cash surrender value of the policy.

Whatever power the owner has retained to change the beneficiary terminates at his death and does not pass to his executor or assigns. The expectancy of the beneficiary becomes a vested right at that time and continues to be protected against the claims of the creditors of the owner unless it is found that the premiums were paid by the owner in fraud of his creditors, or unless otherwise provided in the policy or by statute.

c. *Common Disaster Clause*

In the situation in which a husband takes out a life insurance policy on himself, naming his wife as primary beneficiary and his children as secondary beneficiaries, if both husband and wife should die in a "common disaster," such as an automobile or airplane accident, the rules of distribution of the proceeds are as follows. If the insured is shown to have survived the wife, even by a matter of seconds, the secondary beneficiaries will receive the proceeds; but if the wife is shown to have survived the insured, again even by a matter of seconds, the proceeds go to the wife's (primary beneficiary's) estate, to be distributed through her estate to persons who may not have been of the insured's choosing. Two provisions are available to approximate more closely the intent of the insured. The first is statutory. The Uniform Simultaneous Death Act, adopted now by the majority of states, provides that "Where the insured and the beneficiary in a policy of life or accident insurance have died and there is no sufficient evidence that they have died otherwise than simultaneously, the proceeds of the policy shall be distributed as if the insured had survived the beneficiary."

To provide for the situation in which it can be proven that the primary beneficiary survived the insured, but only for a short period of time, policies frequently contain a "common disaster clause", which provides that the primary beneficiary is to receive the proceeds only if he or she survives the insured for at least a specified period of time, such as two months, and that otherwise, the proceeds are to be paid to the secondary beneficiaries.

d. Beneficiary Who Predeceases the Insured

Situations in which the beneficiary predeceases the insured fall into two categories. The first is the situation in which the beneficiary has given value to the insured in exchange for the designation as beneficiary. An example of this would be the case of a debtor taking out a policy of life insurance on himself and naming his creditor as beneficiary to secure the debt. Another would be the case of a beneficiary who, in good faith (not as a wager), pays all of the premiums on the policy. In each of these cases, the estate of the beneficiary would take the proceeds.

The second category involves the situation of the pure donee-beneficiary. If the condition of surviving the cestui que vie is expressly stipulated in the policy, even if the owner has not retained the power to change the beneficiary, the vested interest of the beneficiary, is subject to divestment if the condition is not met. On the other hand, if the beneficiary is named in the policy as "X, her executors, administrators and assigns," or words to that effect, the proceeds go to the beneficiary's estate. In the typical case of simply designating the beneficiary by name and relationship, most courts find an implied condition of survivorship in the intent of the insured to provide support for the beneficiary after the insured is no longer able to provide it. In this case, if the beneficiary predeceases the insured, the proceeds go to the estate of the insured. Although most policies today expressly contain the condition of survivorship, the last rule of interpretation has been widely adopted statutorily. In fact, these same statutes generally permit the surviving insured to name a new beneficiary after the death of the designated beneficiary, even if that right has not been expressly reserved.

e. Effect of Divorce

Absent a statute to the contrary, divorce between the insured and beneficiary does not automatically terminate the right of the beneficiary, even if the right to change beneficiaries has been reserved. The same rule applies even though the beneficiary may have been described as "wife" of insured. Courts generally hold the designation of "wife" to be merely descriptive and not limiting.

Statutes in some jurisdictions provide that an insured can change the beneficiary in the event of divorce, even if he has not retained the power to do so. This is particularly true in situations in which the insured is not found to be the party at fault in the divorce proceeding.

f. Creditors as Beneficiaries and Assignees

When a creditor of the insured is named as beneficiary or assignee, the question frequently arises as to whether the beneficiary was to take any proceeds in excess of the outstanding debt (plus interest and charges) at the time of death of the debtor. The deciding criterion is the intent of the insured, and absent any express statement in the policy, that intent must be divined by the court on the basis of circumstantial evidence. The indemnity principle has little apparent bearing because of the refusal of courts in other contexts to limit the collection of proceeds by the dollar value of insurable interest or to restrict assignment to those with insurable interests. The court will frequently look to such indicia as whether or not the creditor had any relation to the insured other than as creditor. If the creditor is named as assignee of the policy rather than beneficiary, the case is stronger for limiting his share of the proceeds because it is more customary to assign a policy as security for a debt than to change the beneficiary.

When the policy is taken out by the creditor and premiums are paid by him, it is generally considered proper that he be allowed to retain the entire proceeds because he has the full interest in the policy. This conclusion can be challenged, however, if it can be shown that the creditor obtained the policy himself purely for ease and certainty of administration of the debt, and that the debtor in fact bore the premium payments in the form of increased interest or administration charges.

g. Community Property

In jurisdictions applying concepts of community property, if a husband during the marriage takes out a life insurance policy on himself, naming as beneficiary his estate or personal representative, and he pays the premiums with community property, when he dies, the proceeds belong to the community. If the husband has named the wife as beneficiary, the proceeds belong to her separately.

h. Disqualification for Murder

Any beneficiary who intentionally and unlawfully, as opposed to negligently or even recklessly, causes the death of the cestui que vie is held by the courts to be disqualified from receiving the proceeds. The word, "intentional", in this context is limited to the actual specific intent to bring about the death of the cestui que vie, and is not coextensive with the more expansive tort or criminal definition of the word. As two clear exceptions to this rule, however, the beneficiary is not disqualified if he caused the death as an act of self-defense or while insane.

When a beneficiary is thus disqualified, the proceeds go either to the remaining beneficiaries or, if none, to the estate of the cestui que vie, just as if the disqualified beneficiary had predeceased the cestui que vie. The only case in which the insurer is totally relieved of liability is when the murderous beneficiary was also the sole heir of the cestui que vie and had himself taken out the policy and paid all of the premiums so that the cestui que vie had no interest in the policy whatsoever.

Some courts have felt constrained by statutes of descent and distribution that do not disqualify a murdering heir from inheritance, to distinguish between murderers who are named beneficiaries under a policy and those who are to inherit the proceeds through the estate of the deceased, disqualifying the former and allowing the latter to receive the proceeds. In other jurisdictions, statutes prevent such inheritance.

i. Facility of Payments Clause

Industrial life insurance policies generally contain a "facility of payments" clause which provides that on the death of the cestui que vie, the insurer may pay the proceeds of the policy to the administrator or executor, husband or wife, or any close relative of the cestui que vie, or to any person who appears to the insurer to be reasonably entitled to the proceeds by having paid the funeral or last hospital expenses of the cestui que vie. This comports with the purpose of most industrial life policies, which is to provide funds for the payment of last hospital and burial expenses, in that it enables the insurer to make quick payment without fear of suit by another claimant requiring a second payment. This clause provides a valid defense even against a named beneficiary as long as the insurer has acted in good faith. The defense is void if the insurer failed to exercise due care in selecting the recipient of proceeds or has paid the proceeds to one who is not in the class specified in the clause. The option of employing the facility of payments clause or not lies with the insurer, except that it cannot be employed to make payment after suit has been begun against the insurer by a named beneficiary or the personal representative of the cestui que vie.

j. *Change of Beneficiary*

The procedure specified in the "change of beneficiary" clause generally requires a written request by the owner of the policy to the insurer to change the beneficiary to a designated new beneficiary, and return of the policy (or proof that it has been lost) for the insurer's endorsement of the new beneficiary. The policy is then returned to the owner, or, in the event of a lost policy, one is reissued. In other policies, a written request submitted for the insurer's consent is all that is required.

If the power to change the beneficiary has been reserved to the owner in the policy, the change can be made without the consent or knowledge of the original beneficiary. If, however, there is a contract between the owner and the original beneficiary binding the owner not to change the beneficiary, courts of equity will enforce the contract by holding that an equitable interest in the proceeds was vested in the original beneficiary that is superior to the rights of the subsequent beneficiary. For example, when a husband agreed with his wife after divorce that he would not change the designation of their daughter as beneficiary in exchange for the wife's agreement not to levy on arrears in support payments, the daughter was held to have a superior claim to the proceeds over the husband's second wife whom he had named as new beneficiary. *Kelly v. Layton* (1962).

As opposed to the general allowance of *assignments* without compliance with formalities specified in the policy (see infra), courts generally disallow changes of beneficiary that do not substantially comply with the required formalities. The conflict between honoring the apparent intent of the owner based on informal evidence and preserving a more certain foundation in divining the intent of the owner inherent in requiring compliance with the formalities is, in this case, generally resolved on the side of the formalities. There are inconsistencies among the decisions in defining fact situations that will amount to "substantial compliance". Generally, however, when the insured has done everything reasonably in his power to effect the change, courts will consider compliance to be substantial. Such a situation arises when a beneficiary has possession of the policy and will not surrender it for endorsement of the change.

One of the more common errors is for an owner of a policy to attempt to change the beneficiary in his will rather than through the formalities. Such an attempt will generally not be considered substantial compliance. A simple way of enabling the owner to successfully accomplish that result would be to formally change the beneficiary to the owner's estate, and then dispose of the proceeds through his will.

In some cases, courts have required *strict,* rather than substantial compliance with formalities, and have disallowed the attempted change in beneficiary. This has occurred in instances in which the insurer has paid the proceeds in good faith in accordance with the formal provisions to the original beneficiary, and also in cases in which the equities were particularly strong in favor of the original beneficiary.

In the event that the insured executes a request for change of beneficiary and sends in the policy for endorsement, but dies before the insurer completes the endorsement, some courts will accept the change as valid, particularly if the insurer was at fault in delaying the endorsement. Other courts give rigid effect to the clause which states that the effective date of the change of beneficiary is the date of the insurer's endorsement. This will be the result particularly if the insured is in some way responsible for the delay.

k. *Standing to Contest Change of Beneficiary*

There are two points of view expressed in the cases on whether or not the insurer should be the sole party to have standing to contest the validity of a change of beneficiary. From one point of view, the specified formalities for making the change are required primarily, if not solely, for the benefit of the insurer to enable it to decide with certainty who is entitled to the proceeds. Limiting standing to the insurer has the effect of protecting the insurer against having to pay the claim twice, once to the apparent beneficiary and again to the claimant who successfully challenges the naming of the beneficiary. The position has also been taken as a corollary of the above that the insurer, for whose benefit the formalities are specified in the contract, should also have the power to waive the formalities in accepting a change of beneficiary. This does not imply, however, that the insurer should have the power to arbitrarily choose between beneficiaries after the death of the cestui que vie.

The second point of view is that the formalities also protect the insured against an ill-considered or rash change of beneficiary, and, therefore, a prior beneficiary should have standing to contest the change. Of necessity, this implies the danger to the insurer of having to pay the claim twice and can hinder the rapid payment of proceeds. The most effective protection for the insurer in this situation is interpleader if the insurer becomes aware of the multiple claims in time.

C. ASSIGNMENTS

1. Chose in Action

In addition to naming additional insureds under the "does insure" clause of the policy, a third person, *with or without* an insurable or other interest in the subject matter of the insurance, can be named as payee of the proceeds by designation in the clause usually worded "loss, if any, payable to _____." This arrangement is used, for example, when a debtor wishes to assign any payments made by an insurer in the event of destruction of his property to a creditor who is otherwise unsecured. Since without a lien or mortgage the creditor could have no insurable interest in the property of a solvent debtor, this form of assignment of proceeds is the closest alternative to being named an additional insured. The phrase, "as his interest may appear," is occasionally appended to the "loss payable" clause to signify, in the example above, that the loss payee is to receive proceeds only to the extent of his debt outstanding at the time of payment, the remainder of the proceeds to be paid to the named insured.

Such an assignment of a chose in action against the insurer can occur in the policy with the consent of the insurer or in a separate agreement between the insured-assignor and the assignee without the consent of the insurer. It can occur before or after the loss, as long as it occurs before the payment of proceeds by the insurer.

For purposes of a subrogated cause of action against the assignee, assignment of the mere chose in action does *not* render the assignee an "insured" under the policy.

2. Entire Policy

An alternative to assigning merely the chose in action (right to proceeds), is the assignment of the entire policy, including the obligation to pay premiums. With the exception of the case of life insurance (discussed below), it is generally held to be necessary that the assignee of the policy have an insurable interest in the subject matter since the assignee becomes the substituted insured. Unlike the case of addition of a party insured, after assignment of the policy, the assignor is no longer an insured. He, therefore, becomes subject to being sued by the insurer in subrogation for any cause of action the assignee may have against the assignor for causing a loss within the coverage of the policy. It also follows that the assignee, being now an insured, is no longer subject to a subrogated action by the insurer. At this point, because of radical differences in legal consequences, it is necessary to treat assignment of property insurance separately from assignment of life insurance.

a. *Property Insurance*

Because an insurer bases its decision to enter into a contract of insurance on property to some extent on trust and confidence in the individual insured not to cause a loss deliberately or negligently, a policy of insurance on property cannot be assigned without the insurer's consent. In the event that such an assignment is attempted without the insurer's consent, most courts hold that the assignment is void as to the insurer, but valid as a contract of assignment of proceeds as between the assignor and assignee. In such a case, the assignor remains the insured under the policy which continues in effect, absent a provision to the contrary in the policy.

Assignment with the consent of the insurer creates, in effect, a novation, and the assignee takes what amounts to a newly formed contract, free of defenses available to the insurer against the insured under the old contract between the insurer and the assignor.

Assignment of a policy of property insurance does not automatically occur when the property that is the subject of the insurance is sold or otherwise transferred. The insurance does not run with the property, so to speak. The assignment must be specifically contracted for between the parties and the insurer. It is, in fact, important to remember to take this formal step when full ownership of the property is transferred, since without the consent of the insurer, the insurance would not pass to the new owner, and since the original owner no longer has an insurable interest, the insurance would become void.

In the event that property insurance is assigned to a mortgagee or lien-holder as a protection of collateral security, the assignor retains an interest in the insurance; and if a loss should occur, any excess proceeds, after payment of the amount of the secured debt to the assignee, will be paid to the original insured. Since this assignment does not work a complete novation (the original insured retaining an interest in the policy as an insured) the assignee's interest in the policy has been held to be subject to any defense available to the insurer against the original insured that was not known to the insurer at the time that it consented to the assignment. The insurer is, however, estopped to assert any defense as to which it was on notice at the time of consent to assignment against an assignee who took assignment without notice of the defense.

b. *Life Insurance*

In an effort to maximize the investment value of life insurance to the owner, the majority of courts have held that a life insurance policy can be freely assigned to one without an insurable interest in the cestui que vie. This is but one step removed from allowing the owner to name any beneficiary in a life insurance policy, regardless of insurable interest. The justifying rationale is that the owner of the policy having an insurable interest, will naturally protect the life of the cestui que vie by the discreet selection of an assignee.

Full assignment of the policy includes transfer of the right to change the beneficiary (if, indeed, the assignor had retained that power), the right to any cash surrender value, the right to obtain loans on the policy, and the rights of conversion and assignment, as well as the obligation to pay premiums.

In view of the fact that, unlike property insurance, life insurance involves a large element of investment and a relatively small element of personal trust and confidence in the *owner* of the policy (as distinguished from the cestui que vie who remains the same regardless of assignment), absent an express clause to the contrary in the policy, courts have generally held that the consent of the insurer is not required for a fully effective assignment. On the other hand, if the owner of the policy has irrevocably named the beneficiary—i.e., has not retained the power to change the beneficiary, the owner cannot assign the policy without the consent of the beneficiary.

As in the case of property insurance, where an assignee obtains assignment of a life insurance policy expressly or impliedly for the purpose of securing a debt, although the assignment is in form absolute, proceeds will be paid to the assignee only to the extent of the debt secured, the remainder going to the assignee.

Occasionally an assignment of a life insurance policy will occur without formal action being taken to exercise the right to change the beneficiary. The question then arises as to who has the prior right to the proceeds. In their attempt to further favor assignments, courts have resolved that question by granting priority to the assignee—at least to the extent of the assignment. (Occasionally less than the entire interest in the policy is assigned, as in the case of assignment of a policy to secure a debt.)

The question is further complicated at times by the fact that the assignor has not observed all of the formalities specified in the assignment clause of the policy. The issue then is whether the formalities were included in the policy solely for the protection of the insurer, in which case the assignment is good against the beneficiary if the insurer consents, or whether failure to follow the formalities gives the beneficiary grounds to challenge the assignment. Courts have generally decided this issue in favor of assignees, especially if there has been substantial, though not strict, compliance with the formalities. This not only comports more closely with the wishes of the original owner of the policy, but again favors assignability.

By way of protection of assignors and beneficiaries against the dangers inherent in allowing assignment without full formalities, however, courts have strictly enforced statutes of frauds which require that any assignment of a life insurance policy be in writing. They will only permit exceptions in cases analogous to the "part performance" exception to the usual statutes of frauds. These usually involve such factual indications as the take-over of premium payments by the assignee and delivery of the policy to the assignee.

One exception to the rule that the assignee of a life insurance policy need have no insurable interest in the cestui que vie, is the case in which the court finds that the assignee procured the assignment to effect an unlawful wager on the life of the cestui que vie. Strong evidence of such a scheme would be assignment immediately after the policy is initiated and payment of all of the premiums by the assignee. While a majority of courts will hold the policy void *ab initio,* the minority will hold the *policy* valid and only the *assignment* void, allowing the assignee to recover out of the proceeds the amount of premiums paid, the remainder going to the assignor's estate. This outcome is particularly common where the litigation is between the assignor's representative or the beneficiary and the assignee for the proceeds. When the *insurer* chooses to set up the illegality as a defense, however, if the defense is established, the court will generally find that the insurer is not liable for the proceeds.

One universal rule is that an assignment by an insane person or one found to be mentally incompetent is invalid. The same rule applies to a change of beneficiary. The burden of proof is on the party asserting mental incompetency, and the test is basically the same as that for determining mental capacity to execute a will or deed—does the person understand the nature of the transaction? An insurer is protected in that it is not required to check into the mental competency of an insured who makes an assignment, and if the insurer pays the full proceeds to the assignee without notice of the mental incompetence of the assignor, it is subject to no further liability.

D. REINSTATEMENT OF LAPSED POLICY

1. Generally

Nearly all life insurance policies, and frequently other types of policies such as those of health and accident insurance, include a provision permitting the insured to reinstate his policy on certain specified conditions after it has lapsed for non-payment of premiums. In many states, this clause is required by statute. This right of reinstatement can have significant value if premium rates have risen, or, in the case of life insurance, if the settlement or annuity options in the lapsed policy are more favorable than those currently being offered. Also, one of the primary benefits to the insured is that the process of reinstatement is less complicated than that of taking out a new policy.

If the policy does not expressly grant to the insured the right of reinstatement, the insurer can nevertheless effect reinstatement, as by accepting a late premium, on such conditions as it may prescribe. For example, the insurer can specify as a condition that the reinstated policy will not cover losses that occurred during the period of the lapse. The insurer can also condition reinstatement on the acceptance by the insured of changes in the terms of the policy. In the case of life insurance, a standard condition to reinstatement is that the insured furnish evidence of "good" or "sound" health, or "insurability" (which has been held to be a broader requirement than good or sound health). Another common condition to reinstatement is the payment of any premiums in default.

If the insured has a contractual or statutory right to reinstate his policy upon complying with specified conditions, the reinstated policy is considered to be merely a continuation of the original policy, and any attempt by the insurer to add conditions, exclusions, or restriction, or to amend the policy in any way other than as specified in the conditions to reinstatement without consideration would be ineffective. If, on the other hand, the insured does not have the right to reinstatement, the reinstated policy is considered to be a new contract.

2. Incontestability Clause

The majority of courts hold that if a policy lapses after the contestability period fixed by an incontestability clause has passed, and the reinstatement was procured by means of fraud or a misrepresentation in the application, the reinstated policy is contestable by the insurer on those grounds for a period equal to the original contestability period, running from the date of reinstatement.

3. Time of Reinstatement

The cases divide on the question of the effective date of a reinstatement, which may be critical in the event of death or other loss during the period of lapse if the insurer has conditioned reinstatement on the non-coverage of losses occurring during that interim. Many courts take the position that if the insured has a statutory or contractual right to reinstatement, it becomes effective as soon as the insured has complied with all of the specified conditions. Other courts hold that reinstatement is not effective until the insurer has approved the application or at least had a reasonable time within which to process the application. If the insured does not have a right to reinstate the policy or the policy provides that reinstatement requires the approval of the insurer, the general holding is that reinstatement is not effected prior to actual approval by the insurer, absent a statute to the contrary.

E. SPECIAL PROBLEMS OF VENDOR/VENDEE OF REALTY

Courts have differed widely in their treatment of the situation in which a vendor and vendee of realty have signed a contract of sale, with transfer of title to take place at a later date, and the property has been damaged by fire in the interim. The majority rule in such a situation is that the vendee bears the risk of loss during that interval and is, therefore, subject to a bill for specific performance for the full purchase price, even if the property is totally destroyed. The question with which we are concerned is which of the parties is to be allowed to receive the benefit of insurance proceeds. In a case in which the vendee has taken out a policy of his own to cover the risk of loss, he simply collects the proceeds and is indemnified. A more complex question is presented when the vendor continues his policy of insurance on the property in effect through that interval prior to transfer of title (with the vendee frequently being unaware that he bears the risk). The issue is whether or not the vendor should be permitted to receive full payment from the vendee for the damaged property *and* collect and retain the proceeds of his insurance as well. On this issue there is a wide split of authority.

One faction of courts stresses the indemnity principle and seeks to prevent the vendor from *profiting* from his insurance. There are three basic approaches to this end. One is to allow the vendor to collect the insurance proceeds, but then to subrogate the insurer to the vendor's claim against the vendee on the contract of sale to the extent of proceeds paid. In this way, the vendor is precluded from receiving a double recovery. A second approach is to simply deny the vendor recovery against the insurer to the extent that the contract right against the vendee will cover the value of the property destroyed, on the grounds that to that extent there is no loss.

The third approach is a bit more complex. A number of courts take the position that since the vendor is merely the holder of legal title while the vendee is the true beneficial owner of the property, the vendor should be permitted to recover the proceeds from his insurer, but he should be considered to hold them in constructive trust for the benefit of the vendee. In the case of *Paramount Fire Ins. Co. v. Aetna Cas. & Sur. Co.* (Tex.1962), the Texas court found, however, that the equities behind that rule are changed when the vendee has also taken out his own insurance policy on the property, and is, therefore, indemnified for his loss. The court refused to follow a line of Pennsylvania cases which permitted a vendee to receive the benefit of both his own and the vendor's insurance, even to the extent of making a net profit. The underlying premise of this result in Pennsylvania is that the loss to the insured is determined at the time of the destruction of the property, regardless of subsequent events.

A second faction of courts places heavy emphasis on the personal nature of the contract of insurance, and refuses to look beyond the provisions of the contract itself to accommodate the indemnity principle or create equitable rights in nonparties to the contract (such as the vendee). As was stated in the New York case of *Brownell v. Board of Education* (N.Y.1925), while we speak of insurance as being "on the property," it is actually a personal contract to indemnify the owner from financial loss in the event of its destruction and does not in any sense "run with the land." Courts that follow this approach permit a vendor to collect and retain proceeds on his insurance regardless of his ability to collect the purchase price for the property. The two contracts are considered separate and distinct, and have no effect on each other.

The one exception to this general rule is that if the vendee assumes the payment of premiums when the contract of sale is signed, proceeds of the insurance are applied to the purchase price of the property for his benefit, even if the insurance policy remains in the name of the vendor.

F. SPECIAL PROBLEMS OF MORTGAGOR/MORTGAGEE

In the common situation in which real property is mortgaged to secure a debt, there are several methods of insuring the interest of the mortgagee in the property. Since the mortgage has an insurable interest in the property, he can be added as a party insured to the policy of the mortgagor, or he can take out a separate policy. The most common method, however, has been to provide in the policy of the mortgagor that the proceeds of the insurance were to be paid to the mortgagee to the extent of his interest. Several important consequences turn on a determination of whether the mortgagee is a party insured or merely an assignee of the chose in action under the mortgagor's policy. For example, if the mortgagee is merely an assignee rather than a separate insured under the policy, all defenses of the insurer against the mortgagor are good against any claim of the mortgagee. This includes the situation in which the mortgagor has no insurable interest in the property because, for example, he has conveyed it to another prior to the loss. With no insurable interest in the sole insured, the company is not liable on the policy.

It also follows that if the mortgagor has a cause of action against the mortgagee for causing the loss, the insurer will not be subrogated to that cause of action if the mortgagee is a party insured (under the rule that an insurer cannot be subrogated to a cause of action against its own insured under the policy), but it can be so subrogated if the mortgagee is a mere assignee of the chose in action.

It is generally held that where the mortgagee is an assignee under the loss payable clause of the mortgagor's policy, payment of proceeds to the mortgagee extinguishes the underlying debt *pro tanto*.

The more modern method of affording protection to the interests of the mortgagee is through inclusion in the mortgagor's policy of the "standard" or "union" mortgage clause. This differs from a simple assignment of the chose in action under a "loss payable" clause in the following ways. Following the standard provision that loss shall be payable to the mortgagee "as interest may appear," it is provided that the policy shall not be invalidated as to the *interest of the mortgagee* by any act or neglect of the mortgagor, by foreclosure, by change in ownership of the property, or by occupation of the premises for purposes more hazardous than are permitted by the policy, provided that the mortgagee will pay on demand any premium that is left unpaid by the mortgagor, as well as any increase in premium assessed by the insurer because of an increase of hazard.

In view of the fact that the mortgagee can collect under the policy even in the situation in which the mortgagor is barred from collection by a full defense against his claim (as, e.g., by his sale of the property and loss of an insurable interest, or by breach of a condition of the policy), it is generally considered that the standard or "union" mortgage clause gives the mortgagee the status of an insured. This means that the insurer is not subrogated to any cause of action against the mortgagee for causing the loss. On the other hand, the standard mortgage clause generally provides that in the event that the insurer pays the proceeds to the mortgagee when it has a good defense against a claim on the policy by the mortgagor, the insurer will be subrogated to the claim of the mortgagee against the mortgagor on the underlying debt to the extent of the proceeds paid. This does not violate the rule against subrogation of an insurer to a cause of action against its own insured since in view of the defense available to the insurer against the mortgagor's claim to proceeds, the mortgagor is no longer considered an "insured" for these purposes.

One question raised by the fact that under the standard mortgage clause the mortgagee is considered an insured is whether or not an assignment by the mortgagee of his rights under the policy, incident to an assignment of the debt and security, is valid without the consent of the insurer. Ordinarily a chose in action can be assigned without such consent, but not an insured's interest in the policy. In this case, however, it has been held that the assignment without consent is valid. Professor Keeton has strongly favored this decision because of the desirability of facilitating assignments of secured debts, and because the identity of the mortgagee is of far less concern to the insurer than the identity of the mortgagor in terms of the moral hazard of loss. (Keeton, Insurance Law, Basic Text, pp. 192–3.)

In the situation in which the mortgagee takes out his own separate policy on the mortgaged property, in the event of loss and payment of the proceeds to the mortgagee, the insurer is subrogated to the claim of the mortgagee on the debt to prevent a windfall to the mortgagor by way of cancellation of the debt on the basis of insurance paid for by the mortgagee.

G. SPECIAL PROBLEMS OF LIFE TENANT/REMAINDERMAN

Courts have split on the question of whether a party having a simple life estate is to be permitted to insure the property to the full extent of its value and personally recover and retain the entire amount of the proceeds in the event of loss. A substantial number of jurisdictions do so permit, and the issue in such situations is frequently whether it was the *intent* of the life tenant in insuring the property to cover his own interests solely or those of himself and the remainderman. In the interests of the indemnity principle, these courts will frequently presume, unless otherwise specified, that if the life tenant insured the entire fee, his intent was to protect the interest of the remainderman as well. In such a case, the life tenant would receive the entire proceeds but hold the excess over the value of the damage to his life estate in trust for the remainderman. In cases in which the original owner insured the property before death, and that insurance remained in force after the property passed under a will naming a life tenant and remainderman, the presumption is that the insurance was for the benefit of both life tenant and remainderman. This can be of serious consequence to a life tenant whose major concern is the restoration of his destroyed dwelling, but who does not have control of the entire proceeds from the insurance.

In some jurisdictions, enforcement of the indemnity principle precludes a life tenant from insuring the full fee and recovering the entire proceeds. It has been held in some jurisdictions of this persuasion that the life tenant can recover the proceeds, but that he holds the entire fund in trust for the remainderman, being entitled only to the interest on the fund for life.

In cases limiting the recovery of the life tenant to the value of the life estate, that value is generally determined by multiplying the value of the fee by a fraction, the numerator of which is the life expectancy in years of the life tenant according to actuarial tables, and the denominator of which is the expected useful life of the property.

H. THIRD PARTY INTERESTS IN LIABILITY INSURANCE

Liability insurance originated solely as a protection for the interests of the insured against loss suffered through liability to third-parties. It began in the area of employers' insurance against loss through liability to employees for work-connected injuries. Since indemnification of the employer/insured was the sole function of the insurance, the injured third-party could not bring a direct action against the insurer even after obtaining a judgment against the insured. Even the insured could not bring action on the policy until he had sustained an actual loss by payment of the judgment debt to the third-party. If the insured happened to be insolvent and judgment proof, no claim could arise under the policy.

In subsequent years, legislation has radically transformed the function of liability insurance in many areas to make the injured third-party with a cause of action against the insured a quasi third-party beneficiary of the liability policy. One of the first areas under legislative attack was the inequity of allowing an insured to pay premiums to an insurer to keep liability insurance current and then to allow the insurer to hide behind the shield of the insolvency of the tortious insured to prevent payment of the judgment debt owed to the third-party victim. Under these circumstances neither the injured victim nor the insured received any benefit from the insurance. Eventually, legislation in several states required the inclusion in liability policies of a clause to the effect that insolvency or bankruptcy of the insured would not prevent liability on the part of the insurer. When it became evident that legislatures across the country would adopt this approach, insurers decided to face the inevitable and voluntarily include as a standard term in liability policies the provision that "Bankruptcy or insolvency of the insured or of the insured's estate shall not relieve the company of any of its obligations hereunder."

One major distinction to be drawn among the various types of policies that protect an insured from loss due to his causing harm to another's person or property is that between a liability policy and a pure indemnity policy. Some policies provide that "no action shall lie against the company" until the insured has actually suffered an economic loss by the actual payment to the third party of an amount fixed by a final judgment or an agreement between the insured, the third-party, and the insurer. Such a policy is considered a pure indemnity policy and generally gives rise to no cause of action by the third-party directly against the insurer. Courts have split over the question of whether an insurer that takes advantage of its contractual right to come in and defend the claim against the insured thereby waives its rights under the "no action" clause to the extent that it becomes liable to satisfy the judgment against the insured. The majority rule is that no such waiver is to be inferred from defense of the action.

A second form of "no action" clause provides that "No action shall lie against the company * * * until the amount of the insured's obligation to pay shall have been finally determined either by judgment against the insured after actual trial or by written agreement of the insured, the claimant and the company." A policy containing this type of clause is considered a policy of liability insurance, meaning that the insured has a cause of action on the policy as soon as his liability to the third-party is fixed as to amount. The next step was to recognize a right in the third-party, following a judgment or agreement fixing liability, to bring a direct action against the insurer on the policy under a theory of garnishment of the debt owed by the insurer to its insured, or occasionally a theory of subrogation of the third-party "creditor" of the insured to the insured's cause of action against the insurer. Under either theory, the third-party is afforded the position of a quasi third-party beneficiary of the insurance contract.

A third aspect in which legislation has created rights for the third-party victim in the insured's liability policy involves defenses against recovery on the policy. In the area of automobile liability insurance particularly, legislatures have generally provided in financial responsibility statutes for the protection of tort victims that defenses that would bar collection of the proceeds by the insured, such as fraud in the application, non-cooperation in defense of a tort action, or failure to notify the insurer of an accident, will be of no effect in a direct action by the third party tort victim against the insurer. This is particularly true of insurance intended to satisfy a statutory requirement such as compulsory automobile liability coverage. Automobile liability policies generally provide that in the event that the insurer is statutorily required to pay proceeds to a third-party which it would not ordinarily be obligated to pay because of a defense available against the insured, it shall have a cause of action for reimbursement against the insured. In this way, the risk of non-payment because of insolvency of the insured is placed on the insurer instead of the third-party tort victim; and in this way also, the third-party becomes a quasi third party beneficiary with rights under the insurance contract.

I. TORT IMMUNITY

In the past, the issue of tort immunity has occupied a more important place in the determination of insurance issues. With the trend in the law toward limiting tort immunity for charitable institutions and other parties, the issue of tort immunity in insurance law has become less of a factor. However, where the tortfeasor is immune from suit, the issue as it relates to liability insurance is generally addressed in one of three ways.

First, a policy may be silent on the issue of tort immunity. In this case, it is generally left to the insurance company to decide whether to attempt to exercise this immunity. Courts generally reason that the insurer is only required to pay when an obligation is imposed by law on the insured. Invocation of tort immunity by the insurer acts as a bar to the imposition of liability on the insured. Courts have also held that the mere purchase of liability insurance is insufficient to waive immunity on the part of the insured.

Second, the policy might reserve to the insured the right to determine whether tort immunity will be exercised. This type of clause has been criticized on the ground that it gives the insured unpoliced license to favor certain parties and invites fraud. The practical value of such a provision is also questionable, because it provides little premium savings over an absolute refusal to allow the insurance company to invoke tort immunity.

Third, the policy may totally forbid the insurance company from exercising a right to tort immunity. This type of provision has generally been held valid by courts.

CHAPTER FIVE

PROCEDURE FOR FILING CLAIMS

A. GENERALLY

Policies commonly contain specific provisions requiring the insured to comply with certain requirements as conditions to the payment of proceeds. Non-fulfillment of any such requirement may provide the insurer with a defense against payment. As with other attempts to limit liability on the part of the insurer, however, such provisions are frequently limited in their effect by statutory or decisional restrictions to preclude an inequitable loss of rights to the insured.

B. NOTICE OF LOSS

Insurance policies generally require that the insured give notice of any loss to the insurer immediately upon its occurrence. The purpose is to enable the insurer to gather information while the condition is still fresh, and, in the case of property insurance, to take whatever steps are necessary to prevent further loss to the property.

Regardless of the words chosen by the insurer to express the idea of immediacy of notice, the courts have consistently interpreted them to mean within a *reasonable time* considering all of the circumstances. Delays in excess of fifty days have been excused where the assignee of an insurance policy did not have possession of the actual policy and was, therefore, unaware of the condition.

Courts will frequently also restrict the effectiveness of the requirement as a defense to payment of proceeds by requiring that the insurer establish that it was substantially prejudiced by the failure of the insured to give notice of the loss. If, for example, the insurer had obtained knowledge of the loss from another source, it would be precluded from denying recovery on the basis of the failure of the insured to give notice.

C. PROOF OF LOSS

Insurance policies generally also require as a condition to recovery of proceeds that within a certain period after the loss (e.g., sixty days), the insured file with the insurer a "proof of loss." This is a written statement providing specific details concerning the type and extent of the loss, sworn to and signed by the insured.

In some jurisdictions, statutes regulate any possible defense of the insurer based on misstatements in the proof of loss by providing that no such misstatement shall be the basis for a defense unless it is *material* to the risk. In other jurisdictions it has been held that statutes regulating the use of misrepresentations in applications for insurance as an insurer's defense also apply to misstatements in any proof of loss. In other jurisdictions where no statute of either type exists, courts have fashioned their own requirement of materiality. The purpose in each case is to prevent the upsetting of reasonable expectations on the part of the insured on the basis of immaterial misstatements.

In the event that the proof of loss does not provide all of the information called for by the policy and which is within the ability of the insured to provide, the insurer has the right to reject the proof of loss. The insurer must, however, give notice to the insured of any objections with sufficient detail to enable the insured to correct the deficiency. If the insurer accepts the proof of loss and fails to make objections within a reasonable time, it is generally held to have waived any defense based thereon.

If it is impossible for the insured to provide any of the information called for in the proof of loss clause (as, e.g., when the source of the information has been destroyed in the fire), the insured is excused from that part of the requirement.

The time period within which the proof of loss is to be submitted generally runs from the time of the occurrence of the loss, unless the insured neither knew of the loss, nor, as a reasonable insured, ought to have known of the loss, in which case the period runs from the time the insured can reasonably be held to be on notice of the loss. Notice is considered to exist when the insured is aware of facts which would lead a reasonable insured to conclude that a loss within coverage has occurred.

The primary purpose of such time limitations is to allow the insurer to investigate the claim while the evidence is still fresh, thereby helping the insurer to root out fraudulent claims before the evidence has grown stale or disappeared. A second purpose is to provide the insurer with a current picture of its liability to facilitate the more accurate fixing of reserves.

Because of the severity of such time limitations on unwary insureds, their effectiveness is generally limited by an assortment of judicial doctrines. For example, some courts require as a condition to the insurer's defense that the insurer prove that it was *prejudiced* by the failure of the insured to file a timely notice or proof of loss. Other courts take a middle position by merely permitting the insured to overcome the insurer's defense by proving that the insurer suffered no prejudice from the delay. Still others hold that prejudice is immaterial to the defense since the condition is a clear term of the contract.

In a number of cases, courts have held that they will not enforce the timeliness provision as a defense if the insured can prove that he had a *reasonable excuse* for not filing the notice or proof of loss within the required period. For example, an insured under a liability policy being sued for negligence has been excused from timely reporting the incident to the insurer or filing a proof of loss on the grounds that he reasonably believed that the incident was too insignificant to result in a law suit against him. In other cases, insureds have been excused because of their belief on reasonable grounds that they were not liable for the loss.

In their effort to satisfy the reasonable expectations of the insured or to protect him from what some consider an unconscionable term, courts have also seriously limited the effectiveness of timeliness terms in regard to notice and proof of loss by the artistic use of such judicial concepts as waiver, estoppel, and election, usually finding the grounds for their application in some action or lack of action on the part of the insurer after notice of the loss. These courts will also interpret the policy provisions as strictly as reason will allow against the insurer and will generally require that a breach be *substantial* before it will provide a defense for the insurer.

D.   TIMELINESS FOR FILING ACTIONS

Insurance policies frequently contain a provision to the effect that no action shall be brought on the policy after a specific period (e.g., one year) following the date of the loss. These periods of limitation are, in some cases, prescribed by statute. In dealing with such provisions, courts will, on occasion, permit the filing of an action beyond the specified period if the insured can establish that it would have been impossible for him to file the action within the period, as in the case of incapacity or insanity. Courts will also apply the doctrines of waiver and estoppel against the insurer where, for example, the insurer has been instrumental in inducing the insured to postpone filing his action by holding out the promise of a settlement.

E.   COOPERATION OF THE INSURED

Liability insurance policies consistently require as a condition to payment of proceeds that the insured cooperate and assist in the investigation and defense of any action against the insured as to which there is coverage under the policy.   Cooperation and assistance encompass not only the passive aspects of not admitting liability or making payments or engaging in settlements with the third party or assisting the third party in the prosecution of his action, but also the affirmative aspects of attending hearings and depositions, furnishing information for drafting and answering interrogatories, supplying evidence, and generally assisting the insurer's defense counsel as reasonably required.

Here again, courts will frequently deny the insurer a defense based on non-cooperation of the insured unless the insurer can prove prejudice. While various tests for prejudice are found in different jurisdictions, the most common is a determination of whether non-cooperation made the trial or settlement of the third party's action substantially more difficult and risky as to outcome.

F. APPRAISAL

It is commonly provided in property insurance policies that in case the insurer and insured cannot agree as to the value of the property damaged or lost, each shall select an appraiser, and together, with the assistance of an umpire chosen by the two appraisers if necessary, they shall determine the value. While some of the more extreme policy provisions requiring that any prospective dispute on the policy between insurer and insured be submitted in its entirety to an arbitrator (thereby depriving the insured in advance of any access to the courts) have been stricken, appraisal clauses are generally enforced, since they deal only with the limited issue of amount of proceeds due.

G. SUBSEQUENT DAMAGE

Policies of property insurance commonly preclude coverage for any damage to the property subsequent to the initial damage that occurs as a result of the insured's failure to take reasonable affirmative action to prevent such further loss. Automobile policies even go so far as to provide that reasonable expenses incurred by the insured in affording protection to the damaged automobile shall be deemed to be incurred at the insurer's request. Most courts have interpreted this limitation on coverage as applying only in instances of *negligence* on the part of the insured in protecting the property.

H. NO–ACTION CLAUSES

In order to insure that it will not be named as a party defendant in a direct action by an injured third party prior to judgment being obtained against the insured, a liability insurer will frequently include in the policy a "no-action clause". Typical wording of these clauses is, "no action shall lie against the insurer until the amount of the insured's obligation to pay shall have been finally determined either by judgment against the insured after actual trial or by written agreement of the insured, the claimant, and the company."

The primary purpose of the no-action clause is to prevent the naming of the insurer as a defendant, thereby insulating the insurer from any prejudice that could be occasioned by the jury's knowledge that the tort-feasor is insured. It is thought, not without reason, that the jury would be more inclined to find negligence as well as to be more generous in finding damages if it were certain that an insurance company was paying the judgment. On the other hand, it has been suggested that, given the current prevalence of insurance coverage, most jurors would expect a defendant to be insured to some degree regardless of the name of the case. Some studies have even indicated that the knowledge of the existence of liability insurance has caused jurors, who themselves pay insurance premiums, to decrease the size of the verdicts.

Whichever analysis of the inclinations of jurors is correct, a majority of the jurisdictions that have dealt with the issue have upheld the validity of no-action clauses. In addition, most courts have refused to allow direct actions to lie against liability insurers even in the absence of a no-action clause in the policy.

A minority of courts have held that where a liability policy is issued to satisfy a statutory requirement for liability insurance—as, e.g., in the case of compulsory automobile liability insurance—an injured plaintiff is actually a third-party beneficiary of the insurance agreement, and may therefore maintain an action directly against either insured or insurer or both, whether or not a no-action clause exists in the policy.

I.   DIRECT ACTION STATUTES

A small minority of jurisdictions have attempted to avoid the effect of no-action clauses by enacting "direct action" statutes, which specifically sanction third-party actions against the insurer. A typical statute provides as follows:

"Any bond or policy of insurance covering liability to others for negligence makes the insurer liable, up to the amounts stated in the bond or policy, to the persons entitled to recover against the insured for the death of any person or for injury to persons or property, irrespective of whether the liability is presently established or is contingent and to become fixed or certain by final judgment against the insured." Wis.Ins.Code s. 632.24 (1975).

Under such a statute, the plaintiff is generally permitted to join the insurer and insured as parties defendant in the same action. Furthermore, this type of statute has the effect of invalidating any no-action clause that appears in the policy and eliminates the requirement that the liability of the insured be reduced to a dollar judgment before recovery can be had against the insurer. It does not, however, remove the plaintiff's obligation to prove the insured's liability as a precondition to compensation by the insurer.

The justification for direct action statutes is that they hasten actual recovery by the injured plaintiff and at the same time reduce litigation by accomplishing in one action what previously required two. In addition, they protect whatever third-party beneficiary interest in fact exists. They do this, however, at the expense of whatever prejudicial effect—for or against the insurer—results from disclosure of the existence of insurance to the jury.

CHAPTER SIX

DEFENSES OF THE INSURER

A. GENERALLY

In order to protect the primary interests of the insurer in (1) being able to determine clearly all pertinent aspects of the risk for purposes of deciding whether to issue the policy and at what premium, and (2) being able to contain the risk within the intended bounds once the policy has issued, a series of formalized defensive devices has evolved. These could be categorized as concealment, representations by the insured, conditions, warranties, and limitations or exceptions to coverage.

B. CONCEALMENT

It is universally agreed that there is an affirmative duty on the part of the insured to disclose to the insurer all material facts –i.e., those that would influence the particular insurer in deciding to issue the policy of insurance at all, or to issue it only at a particular level of premium. Although the scope of the duty varies depending on the type of insurance applied for, the rationale is always the same:

"The special facts, upon which the contingent chance is to be computed, lie most commonly in the knowledge of the *insured* only: the under-writer trusts to his representation, and proceeds upon confidence that he does not keep back any circumstance in his knowledge, to mislead the under-writer into a belief that the circumstance does not exist, and to induce him to estimate the risque, as if it did not exist.

The keeping back such circumstance is a *fraud,* and therefore the policy is void." *Carter v. Boehm* (Eng.1766).

Because of the frequent inability of the insurer to inspect the subject matter of the insurance in cases of *marine* insurance, nondisclosure by the insured prior to formation of the contract of any material information renders such a policy void, in spite of any lack of intent to deceive on the part of the insured. While this is the rule in England in regard to all forms of insurance, American courts have applied the rule strictly only to policies of marine insurance. In the case of other forms of policies, such as fire insurance, the subject matter of the insurance is generally available for inspection by the insurer. In the case of life insurance, the insurer can insist on the insured's submitting to an examination by the insurer's physician. This cir-cumstance can lead insureds to believe that all of the information required by the insurer has been obtained, and that they are under no obligation to disclose more. The majority American rule is, therefore, that in cases of life, fire, or casualty insurance, including inland marine insurance, un-less the insured exercises *bad faith* in withholding information that he knows would be necessary to the insurer in evaluating the risk, failure to disclose even material information will not be grounds for voiding the policy.

The burden of proof as to fraud in concealment is on the insurer. In some cases, fraud can be established by inference from the clearly material nature of the information withheld. The insurer is most frequently afforded the benefit of this inference in cases in which the information withheld is extrinsic to the subject matter of the insurance and, therefore, not apparent to the insurer on inspection— e.g., the fact that the insured had made a previous attempt to destroy the insured building.

On occasion, the insured has successfully argued that he was led to believe that the information was not material because it was not made a subject of inquiry in the questions on the application.

In some instances, there is, in the application for insurance, a provision requiring the insured to represent that he has disclosed all material information. Under the cases, such a representation does not seem to enlarge the duty of the insured to disclose *in good faith* all known material information. The same appears to be true of case interpretations of the New York Standard Fire Insurance Policy providing for the voiding of the contract of insurance for failure to disclose any material fact. Only when the insured conceals a fact in bad faith, knowing the fact to be material, will the policy be voided.

Nor is the duty to disclose on the part of the insured increased when the insurer fails to ask any questions of the insured before issuing the policy. The *good faith* assumption of the insured that the insurer has gathered all necessary information elsewhere will prevent voidance of the policy.

Where, on the other hand, the insurer specifically inquires into any matter, it will be presumed to be material to the insurer's decision, despite any lack of objective relevance to the risk.

Since the requirement for voidance is that the concealment by the insured be *misleading* to the insurer, any answer to a question on the application that is obviously missing or incomplete will not be grounds for voiding the policy. Only if an incomplete answer appears to be complete will it result in voidance. For example, if an application for life insurance contains a question as to how many times during the past five years the insured has been hospitalized and for what causes, and the insured describes one hospitalization but fails to mention a second, the incomplete answer will appear to be complete and will, therefore, be grounds for voidance. If the insured had left the answer blank or had merely given a date without specifying the cause, the incompleteness would be obvious, and, therefore, would not be grounds for voidance. The test is whether or not the reasonable insurer would be misled.

Once the contract of insurance becomes binding, the insured ceases to be obligated to disclose any material information that comes to his attention after that point. For example, in the case of life insurance, where there is frequently an appreciable period of time between the submission of the completed application and the issuance of the policy of insurance, the duty on the part of the insured to disclose new material information continues until the insurer becomes bound by the contract. There is a similar duty to *correct* answers on the application which become untrue, but only during that interim period.

The duty to disclose applies only to facts, and not to mere fears or concerns of the insured about his health or the subject matter of the policy. There is also no requirement that the insured disclose facts which the insurer already knows, which relate to a risk excepted from coverage, or as to which the insurer has waived disclosure. Nor is the insured required to communicate publicly known events to the insurer (such as earthquakes, forest fires, etc.) as to which the insurer has equal access to information.

C. MISREPRESENTATIONS

1. Definition

A *representation* is any statement, oral or written, express or implied, made by the insured to the insurer which forms at least part of the basis on which the insurer decides to enter into the contract of insurance. A representation does not become a term of the contract unless it is expressly incorporated into the written document, in which case it becomes a warranty or condition.

2. Avoidance of the Policy

If a representation of the insured is *untrue or misleading,* and is *material* to the risk (as discussed below), and is *relied* upon by the insurer in issuing the policy at the specified premium, the insurer can use this misrepresentation as grounds for avoidance of the policy at any time (unless the policy has become incontestable), or as a defense to payment of proceeds under the policy. The clear majority view is that as long as these elements are present, it is immaterial to the insurer's action or defense that the misrepresentation was made by the insured innocently, with no intent to defraud. A minority of courts, however, takes the position that unless the misrepresentation was made with deliberate intent to deceive the insurer, there will be no grounds for avoidance, even though the representation is materially false.

A universally recognized corollary of the majority position is that a *non-material* misrepresentation— i.e., one that in no way induced the insurer to issue the policy at the specified premium—even if deliberately and fraudulently made, will not be grounds for avoidance or defense by the insurer. See *Employers' Liab. Assur. Corp. v. Vella* (Mass.1975).

3. Materiality

At common law, a representation is considered material if it is such as to induce the reasonable insurer to enter into a contract of insurance that it would otherwise have refused, or to accept a lower premium than it would otherwise have required.

The burden of proving materiality is upon the insurer. While expert witnesses are generally not permitted to testify to the ultimate fact of whether or not a particular representation is material, they are permitted to testify as to the common usage of insurers in declining to insure, or to insure only at a particular level of premium, upon disclosure of the fact concerned. It is generally held that any matter expressly inquired into by the insurer is presumed to be material.

The common law test for materiality has been altered by statute in a number of jurisdictions. One of the most common of such statutes requires for materiality that the misrepresentation must actually have "increased the risk of loss." This type of statute is frequently worded as follows:

"No oral or written misrepresentation made by the assured, or in his behalf, in the negotiation of insurance, shall be deemed material, or defeat or avoid the policy, or prevent its attaching, unless made with the intent to deceive and defraud, *or* unless the matter misrepresented increases the risk of loss." (Emphasis added.)

While this wording would seem to indicate that a fraudulently made but immaterial misrepresentation would be grounds for avoidance by the insurer, the case law interpreting these statutes has consistently retained the common law view that such will not be the case. On the other hand, an innocently made but material misrepresentation is generally held to be grounds for avoidance.

Another type of statute goes so far as to require that the matter misrepresented actually contribute to the loss before it will be grounds for defense. This type of statute, of course, does not apply to an action by the insurer to rescind the policy on the basis of a misrepresentation before a loss occurs.

Where these statutes exist, their requirements cannot be altered or overcome by the terms of the contract of insurance.

4. Reliance

An essential element of a cause of action by the insurer to rescind, or of a defense against payment of proceeds, is *reliance* on the misrepresentation in issuing the policy at the specified premium. If there were sufficient indications in the representations of the insured or otherwise that further investigation by the insurer was called for, and if that investigation would reasonably be expected to have provided the insurer with a true picture, many courts have denied the insurer's defense or petition for avoidance. An obvious case is the situation in which the insured is asked in the application to list the dates and causes of all hospitalizations over the past ten years. If the answer of the insured lists the dates but not the causes, further investigation by the insurer is clearly called for.

If the insurer undertakes to make an investigation of the subject matter of a misrepresentation, and the court determines that if the investigation had been pressed further the truth would have been revealed, a number of courts have held that under those circumstances the insurer cannot claim reliance on the misrepresentation.

5. Obligation of Insured to Correct Representations

Representations are considered to speak to the matter concerned as of the time of effectiveness of the insurance contract—the time at which both parties become bound—unless the representation clearly indicates that it speaks to a different time (as, e.g., a statement that as of the date of filling in the application the applicant is twenty-five years old). For that reason, the insured is under an obligation to correct any representation that becomes untrue at any time before the contract is formed, but is not under an obligation to correct a representation that becomes untrue thereafter. *MacKenzie v. Prudential Ins. Co.* (6th Cir.1969).

This rule can be critical, since a failure to affirmatively *correct* a previous representation which has become false before the contract is formed will be grounds for avoidance or defense in spite of a lack of bad faith on the part of the insured, while a failure to affirmatively *disclose* a material fact which was not the subject of a prior representation will be grounds for avoidance or defense only if bad faith on the part of the insured is established.

6. Interpretation of Representations

Representations are generally interpreted by the courts in such a way as to uphold the contract if logically (and occasionally beyond) possible. For example, if a representation is *substantially* correct, the court will not void the policy or permit a defense upon the grounds of any insubstantial error. For instance, a statement that an applicant has never suffered an injury will be considered to be substantially true (and, therefore, not a misrepresentation) in spite of the fact that he has neglected to mention minor injuries that have left no lasting effect on his health or functioning. Courts have even overlooked the failure to mention major injuries that have left no permanent health impairment. Similarly, a representation that the applicant has not consulted a physician within a specified number of years will not be considered false for failure to mention consultations with a physician for a minor and passing ailment.

7. Belief or Opinion

It is important to distinguish between representations that relate to objective, existing facts, and representations concerning the opinion or belief of the insured. When, for example, a question in an application for life or health insurance asks for statements by the insured concerning the state of his health, courts have interpreted the question as asking for the *opinion* or *belief* of the insured on the subject, rather than a statement of the objective fact. If, therefore, a question asks, "Are you suffering from any disease or infirmity?" and the insured answers as he believes, "No," when, in fact, unknown to the insured, he has a malignancy, the representation of the insured would be considered by the courts to be true.

Also in this category are statements of the insured concerning the value of property that is not susceptible of exact valuation, such as land or a building. Such statements are considered to be statements of the *opinion* of the insured rather than statements of objective facts, and they are not untrue unless they fail to express the actual *state of mind* of the insured at the time.

Similarly, a representation as to the intention of the insured in regard to future conduct or the happening of a future event, unless it is made an express warranty or condition of the contract, is considered to be merely a statement about the present state of mind of the insured rather than a promise that the future conduct or event will actually come about. If, for example, the insured orally states that he will install a fire alarm on the premises, and the insurer relies on this representation in issuing a fire insurance policy at a particular premium, but does not include an express term in the contract regarding the alarm, in the event that the insured does not install the alarm and the building burns, the insurer cannot defend against payment on the grounds of breach of a promise because under the parol evidence rule, any such promise would be merged in the terms of the written contract. The insurer also cannot avoid the policy on the grounds of a misrepresentation unless it can prove that *at the time* the representation was made, the insured did not in good faith intend to fulfill the promise.

In addition, when a representation is made expressly on the basis of a statement of another, the representation expresses only that the statement was made by the other, and does not, without more, go to the truth of the statement.

In each of the above cases, unlike the situation of a statement of objective fact, the representation about the current opinion or belief of the insured can only be false if the opinion or belief of the insured is contrary to his representation. It necessarily follows, therefore, that such a representation could not be false without a deliberate intent to misstate that opinion or belief; and, therefore, with this class of misrepresentation, a fraudulent intent, as well as materiality and reliance, is necessary to provide grounds for avoidance or a defense to payment of proceeds.

8. Return of Premiums

The general rule in the case of voidance of a policy on the grounds of a misrepresentation by the insured is that if the misrepresentation was fraudulent, no recovery of premiums is directed. If, on the other hand, the misrepresentation was innocent, premiums may be recovered by the insured. In the latter case, the premiums go to the insured or his estate, and not to the beneficiary under the policy.

9. Representations by Agents

Just as representations made to an agent of the insurer are considered to be made to the insurer itself (unless the insured has reason to believe that the agent will not pass the information on to the insurer, generally to preclude a refusal of the policy by the insurer and thus loss of the commission by the agent), so representations made by the agent of the insured will be binding upon the insured. On the other hand, the insured is not bound by representations made by third parties, even though materially false and relied upon by the insurer. This rule is applied even as to third parties who are given as references by the insured in the application.

10. Assignee of the Insured

An assignee can acquire no greater rights than those possessed by an assignor. Therefore, any defense available to the insurer against the insured on the grounds of misrepresentation is equally available against an assignee of the insured, unless there is a stipulation to the contrary agreed to by the insurer.

11. Renewal of a Policy

When a fire insurance policy is renewed, it is considered to be on the basis of representations made in originally applying, unless otherwise stated or unless a new application is submitted. The duty is, therefore, on the insured in renewing the contract to advise the insurer of any material changes in the information supplied since the time the original representations were made.

On the other hand, some cases indicate that in the case of accident insurance, if the representation was true when originally made, it is not grounds for avoidance or defense to show that it had become untrue by the time of renewal.

D. WARRANTIES AND CONDITIONS

1. Definition

The terms, "warranty" and "condition", are generally used interchangeably, for all practical purposes, and they refer to representations or promises by the insured, incorporated into the contract itself, on the truthfulness or fulfillment of which it is agreed that the rights of the insured shall depend. The primary differences between a mere representation and a warranty or condition are (1) while the insurer has the burden of proving the materiality of a misrepresentation before it will be grounds for avoidance, the materiality of a warranty or condition is conclusively presumed; and (2) while a representation will not be grounds for avoidance as long as it is *substantially* true, a warranty or condition must be *strictly* complied with in order to preclude avoidance. As with the majority view in representations, good or bad faith on the part of the insured is irrelevant.

The extent of the strictness of the rule that a warranty must be fulfilled to the letter is demonstrated by the fact that warranties dealing with such subjects as the state of the health of the insured are tested by the actual objective fact, rather than, as is the case with representations on such matters, being interpreted as merely stating the *opinion* of the insured.

Before a representation will be considered a warranty or condition, two requirements must be met. First, the representation or promise must be *expressly* included, or incorporated by clear reference, in the contract document. This is frequently done by attaching the application with its questions and answers to the policy and expressly making it a part of the contract. Statements volunteered by the insured on the application, however, that go beyond the information called for by the questions of the insurer will be considered representations rather than warranties, even if the policy generally incorporates the statements on the application as warranties.

The second requirement is that the contract must clearly show that the parties intended that the rights of the insured would depend on the truth or fulfillment of the warranty or condition. Courts have held that merely referring to representations outside of the contract as warranties or conditions is insufficient. There must be a clear statement within the written contract to the effect that the insured warrants the truth of the statements under penalty of loss of rights under the contract (although the actual words, "warranty" or "condition", need not be used). Courts enforce both requirements strictly in order to interpret a statement of the insured as a representation rather than a warranty where there is any doubt or ambiguity for the purpose of preventing possible avoidance of the contract on the grounds of an immaterial misstatement.

2. Affirmative or Promissory Warranty

A warranty can be, in Professor Vance's terminology, either affirmative or promissory. An affirmative warranty is a statement concerning a fact as of the time the contract is entered into and nothing more. If the statement is untrue as of that time, the policy is voidable from its inception. A promissory warranty makes a statement or promise about the future or continuing truth of the matter represented. Courts generally take the position that unless a warranty is clearly shown to be promissory, it will be presumed to be affirmative. For example, a warranty to the effect that a building is used for the storage of concrete blocks will be interpreted, without more, to refer to the time of inception of the policy, and will not be construed as a promise that the building will continue to be used for that purpose.

3. Court Interpretation

In order to take advantage of the favorable rules permitting avoidance of policy obligations for any trivial deviance from the statement of a warranty or condition, insurers at one point began to inundate policies in warranties and conditions that became inequitable traps for unsuspecting insureds. The result was a period of matching wits between the insurers who sought to work forfeitures of insured's rights on the basis of technical violations of warranties and courts that attempted to "interpret" their way around the rigid rule of law in order to work a just result for the insured. The outcome was an array of precedent that is difficult to arrange in any comprehensible order. There are, however, four generalities that can be drawn from the cases. They are as follows.

a.   Where possible, courts will sever a policy so that the breach of a warranty or condition which pertains to one type of risk or one part of the subject matter insured will not avoid the policy as to other risks or other parts of the subject matter.

b.   Where a warranty or condition is only temporarily breached, and the insurer does not take action to have the policy voided before the breach is cured, and the risk is not substantially increased during the period of the breach, many courts now hold that the policy is merely suspended during the breach and is revived when the breach is cured, thereby permitting the insured to collect on losses that occur after that point. Other courts continue to hold that once there is a breach, the policy remains voidable after the breach is cured.

c.   If possible, a court will interpret a clause in a policy as something other than a warranty. For instance, if the statement is not expressly incorporated in the contract, or the rights of the insured are not clearly made to depend on the truth of the statement, it will be interpreted as a representation rather than a warranty or condition. Also, in the case of a clause defining the property insured, such as "furniture located at 112 Main St.," the court will, without more, interpret the clause as merely identifying the property rather than warranting that it will remain at that location.

d.   In the absence of clear language to the contrary, courts will interpret a warranty as affirmative rather than promissory.

4.   Statutes Protective of Insureds

A number of different types of statutes have been enacted for the purpose of protecting insureds against the avoidance of policies on the basis of immaterial technicalities. The following are the most common.

One type of statute provides that no misrepresentation or breach of warranty or condition will constitute a defense against payment of proceeds unless it resulted in a material *increase of the risk*. (Occasionally such statutes use the words, "materially affect the risk.") The purpose of this type of statute is to put warranties and conditions on a par with misrepresentations, permitting a defense for breach only if *materiality* is actually proven.

This type of statute frequently speaks in terms of the misrepresentation or breach of warranty or condition being done with intent to deceive *or* resulting in an increase in the risk. Cases interpreting the statutes have held, however, that while an innocent misrepresentation or breach of warranty or condition that increases the risk will provide a defense for the insurer, a deliberately deceitful misrepresentation or breach which is immaterial to the risk will not provide a defense.

In determining whether or not the breach or misrepresentation has increased the risk, the court will generally not consider the question from the point of view of the belief of the insured, but will rather adopt one of the following three tests: (1) would the breach or misrepresentation, if known, have affected *this* insurer's decision to insure at this premium; (2) would the breach or misrepresentation, if known, affect *a reasonable* insurer's decision to insure at this premium; or (3) as an objective fact, was the risk materially increased? The question of material increase of the risk under any of the three tests is generally held to be one of fact for the jury.

A second type of statute provides that all statements made by the insured will be considered to be representations rather than warranties unless they are fraudulently made. If, therefore, a policy defines a particular statement by the insured as a warranty, it will be permitted to have that effect (rendering the policy voidable in case of any breach, whether it is material or immaterial) only if the statement is made by the insured with deliberate fraudulent intent.

A third type of statute provides that a breach of warranty or condition will constitute a defense for the insurer only if it actually *contributed to causing the loss,* as opposed to simply increasing the risk generally. This is the most severe type of statute for the insurer, since even in cases in which the breach actually has caused the loss, it is frequently impossible to *prove* the causation, as, e.g., in a case in which fire has completely destroyed a section of a building. Some courts have limited the effect of the statute by holding that it does not apply to a *promissory* warranty or any promise to be fulfilled after the contract takes effect.

A fourth type of statute takes a different approach in the case of life insurance by requiring that each policy contain a clause stating that the policy shall be incontestable by the insurer after the policy has been in effect for a period such as one or two years during the life of the insured. This means that if the insured lives for the stated period after the policy goes into effect, the insurer cannot avoid the policy on the grounds of misrepresentation or breach of condition or warranty. The insurer is given that period within which to investigate any such grounds for avoidance, and thereafter, the expectations and financial planning of the insured will not be subject to upset on the grounds of such defenses. If the insured should die prior to the end of the prescribed one or two year period, the incontestability clause does not take effect, and the insurer can use any such defenses in an action brought on the policy at any time thereafter.

In order to raise a defense covered by the incontestability clause, court proceedings in which the grounds for avoidance or defense are raised must be *begun* before the period expires.

Two common exceptions are included within most incontestability statutes. The first provides that the policy will not be incontestable on the grounds of non-payment of premiums, and the second provides that it will not be incontestable on the grounds of breach of conditions relating to military or naval service in time of war.

While the protection for the insured is the most extensive under statutes of this type, they apply in most jurisdictions only to life insurance. There is, however, some movement toward extending their application to health and accident and disability insurance, again for the purpose of precluding a latter day upset in the financial planning of the insured. In a similar vein, a number of states have statutes rendering automobile liability statutes incontestable for the benefit of third party victims, at least to the extent of compulsory coverage.

E. LIMITATIONS ON COVERAGE

1. Types of Limitations

In addition to limiting the risk of liability on a policy by the inclusion of conditions or warranties, insurers frequently include clauses that have the effect of imposing specific exceptions or limitations on the *coverage* otherwise stated in the policy. Such limitations can apply to a number of different aspects of coverage as follows.

1. *Limitation on the subject matter of the policy*—For example, a homeowner's policy may cover the generality of items contained within the house but specifically except from coverage particular items such as a coin collection or cash.

2. *Limitation on the types of peril insured against*—A fire insurance policy may except from coverage any loss caused by a fire resulting from lightning or earthquake.

3. *Limitation as to amount of proceeds payable*—All forms of insurance will specify as the "face amount" of the policy the upper limit of the insurer's exposure to liability under the policy. In the case of property insurance, such as fire insurance, the policy frequently specifies an upper limit of proceeds payable for any loss as well as a formula further limiting payment to the value of the insured's interest in the property damaged. Automobile liability policies generally fix the upper limit of coverage both in terms of the maximum proceeds per person and the maximum proceeds per accident.

4. *Limitation as to period of coverage*—Generally any policy will be specific as to the date of expiration, and in some cases, as with life insurance, will also specify a "grace period" beyond the date of expiration during which the insured may make a premium payment that will renew the policy as of the date of expiration. It is generally held that if death of the insured occurs during the grace period, the insurer is liable for proceeds. A grace

period of one month is commonly required by statute in regard to life insurance.

The date of inception of a policy can be as specified on the policy or can be subject to the happening of some event such as the payment of the first premium or the delivery of the policy to the insured. The question occasionally arises when a policy does not go into effect on the date specified on the face of the policy because of failure to prepay a premium or deliver the policy, as to whether the policy expires one year (plus grace period) from the anniversary date specified on the policy, or one year (plus grace period) from the time the policy actually went into effect. The majority adopt the former position, resulting in a policy period of *less* than one year (plus grace period) for the first year. The minority adopt the latter time period on the grounds that the insured has paid for a full year's insurance (plus grace period).

2. Comparison With Warranties and Conditions

The major difference between a limitation on coverage and a warranty or condition is that if a warranty or condition is breached by some occurrence or circumstance, not only does an insurer have a defense against payment of proceeds, but the policy itself is voidable. On the other hand, an occurrence which falls outside of coverage because of a limitation or exception does not have any affect on the voidability of the contract. The insurer is merely not liable for any loss because of that occurrence.

A second difference is that under certain circumstances, a court will hold that an insurer has waived or is estopped to claim the right to defend or rescind on the basis of a breach of warranty or condition or a misrepresentation, in which case the insurer continues to be liable under the policy. It is generally held, however, that a court will not expand *coverage* beyond that specified in the contract by application of the doctrine of waiver or estoppel.

A third difference is that the statutes which commonly limit the defenses of misrepresentation, warranty, and condition, such as incontestability statutes, "contribute to loss" statutes, and "increase the risk" statutes (discussed above), do not apply to limitations or exceptions to coverage.

3. Distinguishing Between Warranties/Conditions and Limitations on Coverage

Two problems have required the courts to devise tests for determining whether a particular clause in a policy is a warranty or condition or limitation on coverage. The first is the fact that in some instances it is impossible to discern from the wording of the clause which of the three functions it is intended to fulfill. Wording such as "The insurer will not be liable if the loss occurs while the building has remained vacant for a period of thirty days" could be interpreted as either a condition or exception to coverage.

Courts became aware of the second problem when they realized that insurers were side-stepping the effect of statutes aimed at conditions, warranties, and representations by merely rephrasing such clauses as limitations on coverage.

One test for both classifying ambiguous clauses and checking the elusiveness of insurers in shifting their emphasis to limitations on coverage was enunciated in *Simpson v. Phoenix Mut. Life Ins. Co.* (N.Y.1969). If the circumstance which is the subject of the clause is *discoverable* by the insurer through investigation at the time of inception of the policy, the clause is to be classified as a warranty or condition. If the circumstance is not discoverable by the insurer at the time of inception of the policy, it is to be classified as a limitation on coverage. The test, in other words, turns on discoverability. If the insurer *can* discover the circumstance at the time of contracting, it must do so and take whatever action it chooses toward avoidance or be subject to the incontestability and other statutes intended to protect the insured from later claims of breach or fraud. If, for example, the policy conditions the obligations of the insurer on the delivery of the policy to the insured "in good health," the incontestability statute would preclude a defense if the insured were later discovered to have been suffering from a disease that was discoverable at the time of inception of the policy, but would not preclude a defense based on a disease that was not discoverable at that time.

A second test is that developed by Professor Patterson (based on the opinion of Justice Cardozo in *Metropolitan Life Ins. Co. v. Conway* (N.Y.1930)), which was the basis for the New York statute defining the concept of warranty. (N.Y. Insurance Law § 150 (McKinney 1966)). By his definition, a clause is a warranty if it refers to a fact which *potentially* affects the risk, but which need not actually cause the loss in order to provide a defense for the insurer. For example, a provision that a life insurance policy will not cover the death of the insured if it occurs *while* the insured is flying in a private plane would provide a defense to payment of proceeds even if the insured died of a terminal disease, as long as it occurred while the insured was flying in a private plane. The flying merely increased the risk, but need not have been the actual cause of death. Such a clause would be classified as a warranty. On the other hand, a provision that a life insurance policy will not cover death that results from (or is caused by) the insured's flying in a private plane will only provide a defense to payment if the flying directly causes the death. Such a clause would be labeled, under Professor Patterson's terminology, an "efficient" cause, and would be interpreted as a limitation on coverage.

F. INCONTESTABILITY CLAUSE

A standard clause found in most life insurance policies is the "incontestability" clause, which provides that if a certain period of time passes from the inception of the policy to the death of the *cestui que vie,* usually two years, the validity of the policy cannot be contested by the insurer. The effect of this clause is that, in a suit brought by the beneficiary for proceeds, as long as the *cestui que vie* has remained alive for a period of two years from the inception of the policy, the insurer is precluded from defending against the claim on the basis of misrepresentation, breach of condition, or any other claim that the policy is invalid.

The purpose behind the incontestability clause is twofold. First, it protects against stale defenses brought by insurers. Insurers will not be permitted to forestall an adequate investigation into the question of whether the policy should issue and then deny coverage based on the invalidity of the policy several years or more after it was first issued.

The second purpose behind the incontestability clause is to protect the expectations of the insured and the insured's beneficiaries. After the two year period has expired, the insured and his/her beneficiaries should be able to rely on the validity of the policy, especially in light of the fact that life insurance policies are often a critical element of the insured's estate plan.

The use of incontestability clauses in life insurance policies is widespread. In fact, many states have statutes mandating the use of these clauses in life insurance policies. Even in jurisdictions in which incontestability clauses are not mandated, insurers often include them in life insurance policies in order to induce insureds to purchase the policy. In addition, some courts have read into the policy the statutorily mandated terms where a policy fails to incorporate an incontestability clause in contravention of a statute requiring such a clause.

The incontestability clause precludes the insurer's ability to defend against coverage on a variety of defenses such as a breach of condition or misrepresentation. It should be noted, however, that this clause only precludes the insurer's defense as to the validity of the policy. It does not preclude the defense that the coverage sought did not exist under the terms of the policy or was explicitly excluded in the policy. Thus, after the permissible period, the incontestability clause will prevent the insurer from defending a claim by asserting that the policy is invalid based on the insured's misrepresentation in the application. It will not, however, prevent the insurer from asserting the defense that a particular ailment which led to the insured's death was outside the scope of coverage.

Another viable defense an insurer may raise even after the incontestability period has expired relates to the failure of the parties to form a contract. Specifically, the insurer may argue that the policy was void *ab initio* based on, *e.g.,* the insured's lack of insurable interest in the party who is the subject of the life insurance policy. Because a life insurance policy cannot legally be issued to a party who has no insurable interest in the subject of the policy, the policy issued under this pretense is effectively void from the outset, and thus, the incontestability clause in the policy is unenforceable.

Application of the incontestability clause will prevent the insurer from raising a defense of fraud if the insurer attempts to do so after the period permitted under the clause. There is, however, an exception to this rule which holds that if the fraud was so serious as to frustrate public policy if the policy were enforced, the insurer will be permitted to contest the validity of the policy.

Examples of types of fraud which will lead a court to set aside the incontestability clause include cases in which, at the time the policy is secured, the policy holder intends to murder the *cestui que vie* in order to receive the proceeds, as well as cases in which the person applying for the policy impersonates the purported policy holder in order to receive the proceeds of the policy. Essentially, the insurer argues that the policy is void *ab initio,* and therefore, the incontestability clause should not be enforced.

Though the incontestability clause is generally explicit with regard to the length of time during which the policy can be contested, reinstatement of the policy can blur the clearly defined time-frame. For example, if a policy lapses for failure to pay the premium, and the insured provides new information to demonstrate his/her insurability in order to reinstate the policy, but that information is fraudulent, will the insurer be permitted additional time in order to discover the fraud and contest the policy?

Most courts have permitted the incontestability clause period to begin anew in these cases, but only with regard to any new information presented by the insured to cure the lapse. If the contest were based on information relevant to the initial issuance of the policy, the period provided by the original incontestability clause would remain in effect.

Incontestability clauses may also create unique problems in the context of group life insurance policies. For example, the question of whether an individual is eligible for coverage, *i.e.*, whether he/she fits properly within the class covered by the policy, is a question which may or may not fall within the sweep of the incontestability clause. Whether the eligibility issue is controlled by the incontestability clause depends upon whether eligibility is an issue of coverage or of validity.

Some courts have found the question of eligibility under a group insurance policy to be a question of validity of the policy in regard to the person concerned, *i.e.*, whether the individual is eligible to participate in the group policy is a fact that should be discovered within the two year period, and the failure to discover ineligibility cannot be contested after the permissible period. Other courts have found that the question of eligibility relates to whether there will be coverage under the policy, not whether the policy is valid. As a result, the insurer is not barred from contesting coverage after the period provided for in the incontestability clause.

New York's highest court has fashioned a clear test to be used in deciding questions involving the applicability of incontestability clauses. In *Simpson v. Phoenix Mutual Life Insurance Co.*, the Court held that the insurer under a life insurance policy had no defense against a claim by the beneficiary where the insurer could have discovered the misrepresentation at the time the policy was issued. In other words, if the misrepresentation or breach of a clause of the policy was *discoverable* at the time of the inception of the policy, the court will consider the defense by the insurer to fall within the incontestability clause, and the insurer will be deprived of the defense if the contestability period has elapsed during the lifetime of the insure.

On the other hand, if the insured could not have discovered the misrepresentation or breach of a clause of the policy at the time the policy was issued, the court will interpret the risk as a limitation of coverage, and thus, the incontestability clause will be inapplicable, and the insurer will be permitted to deny coverage.

The *Simpson* court applied this test in the context of a case in which the insured's eligibility as a member of the group insured by a group life insurance plan was in question. The court found that the insurer would have been able to discover that the insured was not eligible for the group insurance at the time it issued the policy. Therefore, the pertinent clause of the policy was considered a condition, and the incontestability clause was applicable.

INSURED'S DUTY OF COOPERATION

Though the insurer must fulfill a number of obligations in the context of the insurer-insured relationship, the insured also has several obligations that it must fulfill. Other than the payment of premiums, the primary obligation of the insured is the duty to cooperate with the insurer in the event of a claim. This duty may be defined explicitly in the policy, or it may be implied in the terms of the policy which generally impose an obligation on the insured to cooperate with the insurer.

The duty of cooperation may include, inter alia, attending depositions, hearings, and trial, assisting in settlement negotiations, obtaining evidence, and enforcing subrogation rights. The purpose of this duty of cooperation is twofold. First, it is designed to ensure that the insurer is able to protect its own interests by conducting an adequate investigation and presenting its best case at trial or in settlement negotiations. Second, it is aimed at preventing collusion between the insured and third parties. In order to advance these goals, an insurer may deny coverage in any case in which it can show that the insured breached the duty to cooperate.

Despite the insurer's ability to deny coverage where the insured refuses to cooperate, the insurer's task in proving this breach is not an easy one. Most courts have not only imposed the burden of proving the breach on the insurer, but they have also made that burden a significant one. For example, the insurer must demonstrate that the insured's breach of the duty was substantial and material.

A consistent definition of what constitutes a substantial and material breach is difficult to glean from the available case law. However, it has been held that an insured's concealment of the true identity of the driver of a car who injured a third party is not a material breach where the insured cures the concealment in a timely manner. On the other hand, it has also been held that the insured's refusal to sign a complaint against a third party to enforce the insurer's subrogation rights was a material breach.

Even assuming that the insurer is able to demonstrate a substantial and material breach by the insured, it must also show that it was prejudiced by the breach. Like the requirement of materiality, this requirement is often difficult for the insurer to prove, in part because there is no clear test for what constitutes prejudice. Some courts have defined prejudice as that which causes a jury to rule in favor of the insured and against the insurer on coverage or other defense issues under the policy. Other courts have found prejudice to be that which compromises the insurer's ability to contest the merits of a case brought by a third party (as under liability insurance) or against a third party (as in a subrogated action).

One example of the courts' disparate understanding of "prejudice" is a case in which an insured's misrepresentation as to whether anyone involved in a fatal traffic accident had been drinking was held not to rise to the level of actionable prejudice, despite the insurer's assertions that this misrepresentation impeded its investigation of the claim. On the other hand, another court held that where an insured made an agreement with a third party in which the insured admitted critical facts in return for the third party's promise not to seek from the insured any amount of a judgment that exceeded policy limits, there was a breach of the duty of cooperation.

In addition to the basic elements that the insurer must prove in order to deny coverage based on a breach of the cooperation clause, there are other limitations on the insurer's ability to prevail on the defense. Specifically, if there is evidence that the insured's failure to cooperate was due to mistake, and there was no bad faith involved, the breach may be held excusable.

Furthermore, most courts require the insurer to show that it exercised good faith and diligence in seeking the insured's cooperation. For instance, if the insurer denies coverage on the basis that the insured breached the cooperation clause by not attending the trial, the insurer must demonstrate that it acted diligently and in good faith in trying to secure the insured's attendance. Without such a showing, the insurer will not be permitted to deny coverage on the basis of non-cooperation.

New York has imposed even stronger limitations on the insurer in cases involving non-cooperation by the insured. The courts not only require an insurer to demonstrate that it acted diligently but also that its attempts were reasonably calculated to secure cooperation. Moreover, the insurer must demonstrate that the insured willfully refused to cooperate.

CHAPTER SEVEN

WAIVER AND ESTOPPEL

I. GENERALLY

In order to counterbalance the unconscionable advantages believed by many courts to have been taken by insurance companies through their control over the drafting of complex policy language and their severe use of the device of warranties (particularly under early case law), courts have employed two powerful counter-defense mechanisms for the benefit of the insured—waiver and estoppel. Clear delineation between the two theories has been confused by two phenomena. First, in their eagerness to come to the aid of the insured, a number of courts have mislabeled the theory on which they were finding for the insured either "waiver" or "estoppel", when the elements of neither were present. The true theory in most of these cases was merely the refusal of the court to allow the insurer to reap an unconscionable advantage; but particularly in earlier times, courts felt more comfortable using the more classic terminology of waiver or estoppel. This misuse, which continues to some extent today, has beclouded the definition of the two theories. The distinction between the two has been further confused by courts that follow the language of Mr. Justice Field in *Globe Mut. Life Ins. Co. v. Wolff* (S.Ct.1877): "The doctrine of waiver, as asserted against insurance companies to avoid the strict enforcement of conditions contained in their policies, is only another name for the doctrine of estoppel." Despite such frequent treatment of waiver and estoppel as synonymous, the area can best be understood if the actual distinctions between the two are kept clearly in mind.

II. WAIVER

A. DEFINITION

The doctrine of waiver applies to those situations in which the insurer is aware that it has valid grounds for rescission of the policy or defense to any claim on the policy, and expressly or impliedly, through the acts of its agents (such as acceptance of a premium), conveys to the insured its *voluntary* surrender of such right.

The doctrine will apply only in cases in which the insurer is considered to have actual knowledge of the grounds for rescission or defense, or in which the insurer has knowledge of facts that would put a reasonable person on inquiry and a reasonable inquiry would disclose the pertinent grounds for rescission or defense. It is generally held that knowledge of a general agent of the insurer constitutes knowledge of the insurer, even if the agent fails to pass the information along to the insurer, while knowledge of a mere soliciting agent, with authority merely to solicit and forward applications to the insurer, does not constitute knowledge of the insurer. Since an insurance broker is generally considered to be the agent of the insured knowledge of a broker is not attributed to the insurer.

Waiver can be applied to rights of the insurer arising from the insured's misrepresentation in the application, breach of condition precedent to formation of the contract (such as a requirement of payment of the first premium in cash on delivery of the policy), breach of a condition or warranty during the term of the policy (such as existence of an alarm system in working order), or breach of a condition regarding perfection of a claim after loss (such as a requirement of a specific form of proof of loss within a stated time period).

B. METHODS OF COMMUNICATING WAIVER

1. Express Waiver

The voluntary surrender of a right can be conveyed to the insured by the express statement of an agent of the insurer that a particular circumstance contrary to the terms of the policy (such as the mortgaging of the property, or leaving the property vacant for an extended period of time) will not be relied upon by the insurer to avoid its obligations under the policy. It can also be expressed in the policy itself, as in the case of an incontestability clause, or a written indorsement added to the policy varying the terms or conditions of the policy.

2. Implied Waiver

Courts will frequently find that the voluntary surrender of a known right is implied in any of the following circumstances:

a. Acceptance of a premium for future coverage with knowledge of an existing breach of condition or warranty;

b. Exercise of a right under the policy, such as to demand an appraiser or arbitrator or to take possession of the damaged property;

c. Demand for proof of loss from the insured without a prior non-waiver agreement with the insured (some courts do, however, permit the insurer to demand proof of loss for purposes of informing itself about the claim without subjecting itself to waiver);

d. Acceptance and retention of proof of loss without objection;

e. Exercise of any right or making of any demand under the policy which would be inconsistent with an intent to rescind the policy or deny liability under it; or

f. Failure to specifically plead a defense in an action on the policy by the insured.

It is widely held that mere silence on the part of the insurer upon learning of grounds for rescission or defense prior to the time of a loss is not sufficient to constitute a waiver unless the circumstances would require the insurer to give some affirmative notice in fairness to the insured. For example, if the insured fails to pay a premium, the insurer is not required to notify the insured of its intent to rely on that fact as terminating the policy unless prior waivers of late premium payments would have led the insured to expect that the policy would continue in effect absent notice to the contrary by the insurer.

Some courts have held to the contrary that if the insurer learns of grounds for rescission or defense before a loss, it is required to give reasonable notice of forfeiture to the insured or it will be held to have waived the defense. Similarly, statutes in some jurisdictions specifically require notification by the insurer if it is to rely on the nonpayment of premiums for forfeiture. Even in these jurisdictions, however, no such waiver is implied from the insurer's silence upon learning of grounds for rescission or defense *after* a loss and prior to the entry of a formal defense.

C.   LIMITATIONS ON WAIVER

1.   Public Interest

An insurer or insured can only waive rights under a policy which are for its sole benefit. If there is a public interest in the right, it cannot be waived by either party. For example, neither party can waive the voidability of a policy for lack of an insurable interest. Similarly, where a statute requires that an insurer give a specific form of notice to the insured to effect forfeiture for nonpayment of premiums, the insured cannot waive the right to such notice, and any purported waiver would be considered a nullity.

2. Parol Evidence Rule

The parole evidence rule applies to an insurance policy as well as any other written contract to preclude evidence of any oral or implied agreement between the parties entered into prior to or concurrent with the execution of the agreement evidenced by the written policy which would alter or waive any term of the written contract. There is, however, no rule of evidence which would prohibit proof of an oral or implied agreement of waiver entered into subsequent to the execution of the written policy.

3. Consideration

There is a basic split among the courts in the way in which they conceptualize waiver. Some courts hold that a waiver is an actual agreement between the parties amending their rights and obligations under the original contract (policy). Under this view, consideration flowing from the party benefiting from the waiver is necessary to make the waiver agreement binding. Under this view, a waiver occurring after execution of the policy and before loss would be a substitute agreement to the extent that it conflicted with the original agreement, and it would therefore require consideration. Similarly, waiver of a valid defense after loss had occurred would be a mere voluntary assumption of a duty and would be unenforceable in the absence of consideration.

Other courts take the position that since a misrepresentation in the application or a breach of warranty or condition would not render the policy void, but would merely give rise to a *privilege* on the part of the insurer to rescind the contract or rely on the defense, a waiver in this case is nothing more than the surrender of a privilege. In the view of these courts, consideration is not necessary to make the surrender of a mere privilege binding. (See Vance, Insurance, 3d Ed., p. 504.)

In those jurisdictions in which consideration is deemed necessary, courts have frequently held practically any action or change of position by the insured to his detriment, taken on the basis of a voluntary waiver by the insurer, to be a sufficient substitute. For example, where an agent for an insurer states to the insured that the insurer will not enforce a clause in the policy regarding other insurance or sole ownership, and the insured violates that clause in the belief that it will not affect the enforceability of his policy, it is generally held that the change of position on the part of the insured satisfies the requirement of consideration.

4. Limitation in Regard to Facts

While the parties to an insurance contract have the ability to waive rights and privileges under the contract, a number of courts have taken the position that they cannot by agreement change existing facts. For example, in *Sternaman v. Metropolitan Life Ins. Co.* (N.Y.1902), the application for life insurance contained a clause that purported to be an agreement that the doctor who performed the medical examination on behalf of the insurer should be considered to be solely the agent of the insured. The purpose of the clause was to have the insured, by waiving the actual agency relationship between the doctor and the insurer, assume full responsibility for any misrepresentations made by the doctor in his medical report. The court held the clause void as contrary to public policy, stating that the parties "cannot by agreement change the laws of nature or of logic, or create relations, physical, legal, or moral, which cannot be created." Id.

5. Limitation as to Coverage

The courts have generally agreed that while an insurer may be held to have waived grounds for rescission or defense, the doctrine of waiver will not be used to extend *coverage* under a policy to losses not included, or expressly excluded from coverage.

6. Policy Limitations on Waiver

Policies frequently contain provisions purporting to limit the power of agents to waive conditions, warranties, or rights arising from misrepresentations in the application by requiring that such waivers be effected only by written endorsement by the insurer on the policy. Courts, other than those that impose no obligation on the insured to read and comprehend the policy, generally hold that such provisions are to be given the effect of placing the insured on constructive notice of the requirements for valid waiver contained therein, whether or not the insured has actual knowledge of such a provision. On the other hand, courts have limited the effect of these provisions in various ways. For example, constructive notice of the provision is generally held to apply only to potential waivers that occur after delivery of the policy to the insured. Also, any agent of the insurer who is at a level of authority sufficient to enter into the policy contract on behalf of the insurer (and, therefore, to include the provision in the contract) also has the authority to waive the provision itself. The net result is that such provisions limit only the authority of agents at lower levels. The greatest weakness of these provisions, however, is that while they provide some protection for the insurer against waiver, they do not preclude the insured from claiming estoppel when the insured can show some element of detrimental reliance.

III. ESTOPPEL

A. DEFINITION

Estoppel is generally held to apply to an insurance policy in the circumstance in which an insurer is, or ought to be, aware of its right to defend or rescind on the basis of a misrepresentation or breach of warranty or condition, and expressly or impliedly represents to the insured, who is unaware of the grounds for defense or rescission, that the policy is enforceable, and the insured relies upon the representation of the insurer to his detriment. The insured is considered to have relied to his detriment if, for example, he has paid subsequent premiums or even failed to acquire other insurance. The reason for the requirement that the insured be unaware of the grounds for rescission or defense at the time of his reliance is that estoppel is an equitable doctrine, and the insured must therefore come into equity with clean hands.

The courts are widely split on the question of whether or not an insured is permitted to claim an innocent lack of knowledge of the grounds for rescission or defense if it is a result of his failure to read the policy. Many courts accept the reality that insureds are generally disinclined and frequently incapable of reading and understanding the complex policy language, and therefore impose no such obligation on the insured.

B.   LIMITATION AS TO COVERAGE

As in the case of waiver, the courts are in agreement that while the doctrine of estoppel may be used to render a defense based on misrepresentation or breach of condition or warranty ineffective, it will not be used to extend *coverage* to losses not included or expressly excluded from coverage under the policy.

C.   PAROL EVIDENCE RULE

In view of the fact that estoppel is an equitable doctrine based upon a position knowingly taken by the insurer and detrimentally relied upon by the insured, as opposed to being based upon a separate agreement between the parties (as is the case with waiver), the parol evidence rule has no application. For that reason, estoppel can arise out of actions by the parties occurring prior to or contemporaneous with the execution of the written policy contract, while it is generally held that the parol evidence rule precludes proof of waiver in those instances.

D. LIMITATION TO FACTS

A statement or representation of an insurer will effect an estoppel only if it is a misrepresentation of an *existing fact* (as, for example, that the policy is, as issued, an enforceable contract). Estoppel will not apply if the statement or representation is merely a promise as to future action (as in the case of an oral promise to give notice in the future when each premium will come due), or a statement of intent to surrender a future right. In the latter type of case, estoppel will apply only if the insurer had no intent of honoring the promise at the time the promise was made.

E. COMMON INSTANCES OF ESTOPPEL

Although not an all-inclusive list, the following are the most common circumstances in which estoppel arises.

1. In situations in which the insurer delivers a policy to the insured while the insurer, through its representative, is aware of a misstatement in the

application or an existing breach of a condition or warranty in the policy that would make the policy voidable from its inception, the grounds for voidance being unknown to the insured, courts most frequently hold that the insurer has impliedly misrepresented to the insured that the policy is enforceable. In view of the reliance of the insured in paying the premiums and in not making other arrangements for insurance, the insurer is held estopped to deny that the contract is enforceable.

2. In the case in which an agent of the insurer, aware of the prospective insured's situation, but unaware of a condition or warranty in the policy that he offers to the insured which would be violated from the time of inception of the policy, *negligently* sells the policy to the innocent insured, the insurer is frequently held estopped to defend on the basis of that breach, even though the insured has failed to read the policy on delivery.

3. In cases in which the agent for the insurer deliberately falsifies the answers of the insured on the application *without* the knowledge of the insured, either to assist the insured in getting the insurance or to obtain a commission on the sale of the policy for himself, it is generally held that the knowledge of the agent is attributed to the insurer, and the insurer is estopped to deny that the policy is enforceable.

On the other hand, the insurer will not be estopped to rely on the defense of misrepresentation in the application if the insured had knowledge, or was put on notice by the circumstances, that the agent had falsified the answers. The insured is, in fact, under a continuing obligation to bring the fraudulent answers of the agent to the attention of the insurer if he discovers the falsity at any time between application and delivery of the policy, at the risk of being considered to have participated in the fraud.

There is a split among the courts as to whether the insured should be required to read the application before signing it or when it is returned to him as an attachment to the policy, and should therefore be charged with knowledge of any false answers. A number of courts do not impose this requirement, but rather permit the insured to rely on the professional knowledge and judgment of the agent of the insurer.

4. In the situation in which an insured requests an agent of the insurer to obtain the proper indorsement on the policy to permit him to take action that would otherwise violate a condition or warranty in the policy (as, for example, to enable him to mortgage or sell an interest in his property), and the agent returns the policy to the insured informing him that the indorsement has been obtained, when, in fact, the agent has not obtained the indorsement, or the person whose signature he did obtain did not have the authority to waive the warranty or condition, and the innocent insured relies upon the agent's misrepresentation by violating the condition or warranty, the insurer is estopped to defend against a claim on the basis of that

violation. Notice that in a case of this type, it could *not* be said that the agent *waived* the warranty or condition if he himself lacked authority to enter into such an amending agreement on behalf of the insurer; but it could be held that because of the agent's action, on which the innocent insured relied, the insurer is *estopped* to raise the defense of breach of the warranty or condition.

CHAPTER EIGHT

MEASURE OF RECOVERY

A. GENERALLY

In the case of life insurance, the amount to be paid in the event of loss is specifically fixed by the contract. Similarly, in the case of accident insurance, the proceeds are measured by a specific amount agreed to be paid for loss of a particular limb or faculty, or, as in the case of health insurance, by the medical expenses actually incurred. The more difficult problems of determining the amount of proceeds to be paid in accordance with the principle of indemnity lie in the area of property insurance. Under most forms of property insurance, the contract provides for the payment in the event of loss of an amount up to the "actual cash value" of the property at the time of loss.

1. Articles of Commerce

If the property consists of articles of commerce that are readily replaceable in kind at a determinable market price, as for example copies of a currently available book, or cans of paint, or shipments of cotton or grain, the value universally agreed upon is the market value.

237

2. Unique Property

If the property is of a more unique type, such as a yacht or a building, courts will generally not limit evaluation to a determination of the market value. The measure is rather a conglomerate of several distinct approaches. "Where insured buildings have been destroyed, the trier of fact may, and should, call to its aid, in order to effectuate complete indemnity, every fact and circumstance which would logically tend to the formation of a correct estimate of the loss." *McAnarney v. Newark Fire Ins. Co.* (N.Y.1928).

There are two basic approaches which may be considered in combination with other factors to arrive at a fair figure for indemnification of the insured.

a. *Reproduction Cost Less Depreciation*

Although this measure of proceeds is aimed at determining the cost of replacing the exact depreciated property that was lost, frequently this measure would work a hardship on the insured if it were used as the sole measure of proceeds. For example, the owner and occupier of a fifty-year-old home that is destroyed would have to replace it with a new building, and could have serious difficulty in financing the difference in cost between the new home and its fifty-year-old predecessor. For that reason, modern policies frequently provide "replacement cost insurance," whereby, if the upper limit of liability of insurance was at least, for example, 80% of the full replacement cost of the building at the time of the loss, the insurer agrees to pay the full cost of repair or replacement without deducting for depreciation. Depending on the wording of the contract, the insured may be required to actually repair or replace the building in order to collect full payment. Such a provision is referred to as "replacement insurance," while a provision that permits full recovery without deduction for depreciation whether the insured repairs or replaces or not is referred to as "depreciation insurance."

The purpose in requiring the insured to carry an upper limit of coverage of an amount such as 80% of the full replacement cost of the building before the replacement cost provision becomes effective is to induce insureds to carry high limits of coverage. The premium on the first thousand dollars of coverage is usually the same as the premium on the fiftieth or hundredth thousand dollars of coverage. Yet there are statistically far more small claims made than large claims, and therefore the insurer finds that it makes a much larger profit on the higher limits of coverage than on the lower limits. For this reason, insurers are willing to throw in replacement cost insurance as a reward for the insured's taking out higher limits of coverage.

One danger of which an insured should be aware is that although the policy limit may have equalled or exceeded 80% of the full replacement cost of the building when the policy was initiated, after the passage of years, inflation as well as a rising housing market could cause the limit of coverage to wind up below the 80% figure at the time of a loss, thereby nullifying the replacement cost provision.

b. *Market Value*

i. *Income Producing Property*

In the case of income producing property, such as apartments or office buildings, held primarily as investments, a common method of determining market value is the capitalization of earnings test. Proof of valuation under this method is usually accomplished through testimony of an expert witness, who determines the rate of return on investment that a reasonable investor would require in investing in this type of property. He will also determine, based on the history of previous income and expenses, what amount of profits the property is likely to produce annually. Using these two figures, it is a simple mathematical calculation to determine the amount that a reasonable investor would pay for this property. If, for example, the property will produce $10,000 profit annually, and an investor would want a 10% return on his money if he is to invest in *this* property as opposed to other investments available, the value of the property under the capitalization of earnings method would be $100,000. (The annual $10,000 profit would be a 10% return on the $100,000 investment.)

ii. *Non-income-producing Property*

In the case of *non-income-producing property* (in the sense that it is not held as an investment), such as a home used by its owner, market value would generally be determined by comparing prices paid by willing buyers to willing sellers for similar properties in similar locations. Again the method of proof is generally the testimony of an expert real estate appraiser.

On the other hand, in the leading case of *McAnarney v. Newark Fire Ins. Co.,* supra, the court held that in evaluating non-commercial property, such as a private home, the proper consideration is the value of the particular use of the property *to the owner,* rather than the general market value. This is also the approach used in the case of personal property, such as the family furniture, which may have a substantial use value to the owner and a relatively low value on the market as used furniture. Courts do not, however, carry this to the point of allowing compensation for sentimental value.

c. Obsolescence

A third factor to be considered where relevant is obsolescence, or loss of usefulness of the property being valued. In *McAnarney,* for example, the court took into account the diminution in use value of buildings, designed to be used for the production of malt, after prohibition had eliminated that operation. An appropriate consideration then became the possible other uses to which the buildings could be adapted. In the case of *Doelger & Kirsten, Inc. v. National Union Fire Ins. Co.* (Wis.1969) the court held that in evaluating large wooden patterns costing over $12,000 to reproduce, it was relevant to consider the fact that the product made with the patterns had fallen into total disuse, thereby rendering the patterns obsolete.

In some instances, obsolescence will already have been taken into account in arriving at a valuation through one of the methods discussed above. For example, in determining the price that a willing buyer would pay a willing seller to arrive at market value, obsolescence will of necessity be a subsumed factor.

Courts have occasionally distinguished between obsolescence that has already occurred, as in the case of the patterns, and that which is merely prospective. For example, in *Bailey v. Gulf Ins. Co.* (10th Cir.1969), the court refused to consider as a factor in evaluating a fraternity house that had been damaged, the fact that the city had declared the house to be a nuisance and had ordered it to be demolished. In adopting this view, the court pointed, by way of analogy, to the majority rule that the amount of proceeds is not affected by the fact that the insured is bound by an executory contract to sell the property.

d. Combination of Factors

In combining the various elements discussed, together with such factors as bona fide offers to purchase previously received by the insured and declarations against interest concerning value made by the insured, courts have arrived at an appropriate formula in each case on an ad hoc basis. As stated by the court in *Doelger & Kirsten, Inc., v. National Union Fire Ins. Co.,* supra, in reviewing the trial court's formulation of value based on various factors, "Under the 'broad evidence rule,' we need not find the route travelled by the trier of fact in this case to be the only route that could have been travelled. We need only to find it a proper and acceptable one. This we do. That both parties are outraged by the result reached may be some reassurance that the trial court found and followed a *via media* between two extremes." Id.

e. Election to Replace

An insurer under a policy of property insurance will generally reserve to itself the right to elect to repair or replace the property lost or damaged with materials of like kind and quality within a reasonable time after loss or damage, or to pay the full cost of such repair or replacement to the insured. If the insurer so elects, factors such as depreciation and obsolescence would be irrelevant.

B. COINSURANCE

In many instances, because of separation between buildings or the protection of sprinklers, warning devices or other safeguards, insureds realize that the likelihood of *total* destruction of their insured property by fire is remote. Therefore, by insuring to the extent of, e.g., 30% of the full value of the property, they have, in effect, full coverage. On the other hand, from the point of view of the insurer, since premiums are generally charged on the basis of a certain percentage of each thousand dollars worth of insurance, the cost of the first thousand dollars of insurance is the same as the cost of the fiftieth thousand dollars of insurance. This means that since most claims against the insurer are made in relatively small amounts, the insurer makes less profit on the lower levels of insurance coverage than on the upper levels. In order, therefore, to induce insureds to purchase coverage closer to the full value of the property, insurers of property have borrowed the concept of coinsurance from the practice in marine insurance. Under the coinsurance principle, if the insured does not carry coverage up to a certain specified percentage of the full value of the property insured, as computed at the time of loss, the insured becomes a *coinsurer* on any loss— he must bear a certain percentage of the loss himself—regardless of how small the loss may be.

The standard language expressing this agreement is found in the New York Standard Coinsurance Clause:

"This company shall not be liable for a greater proportion of any loss or damage to the property described herein than the sum hereby insured bears to the percentage specified on the first page of this policy of the actual cash value of said property at the time such loss shall happen. * * *"

The percentage generally chosen is 80%. Under this provision, assume that the value of the property at the time of loss is $100,000, it is insured for $40,000, and there is a loss in the amount of $10,-000. The formula for determining the amount of proceeds would be as follows: amount of proceeds equals the upper limit of coverage ($40,000) divided by 80% of the full value of the property at the time of loss ($100,000), multiplied by the amount of the loss ($10,000).

$$\text{Proceeds} = \frac{\$40,000}{80\% \text{ of } \$100,000} \times \$10,000 = \underline{\$5,000.}$$

Notice that on a loss as relatively small as $10,000, the insured is required to bear one-half of the loss ($5,000) himself.

If, under this example, the insured has obtained coverage in the amount of $60,000, the proceeds on the same $10,000 loss would have been:

$$\frac{\$60,000}{80\% \text{ of } \$100,000} \times \$10,000 = \underline{\$7,500.}$$

In this case, the insured would only have to bear the loss to the extent of $2,500.

If the insured has been induced to insure to the extent of $80,000, the fraction to be multiplied by the amount of the loss would have been $\frac{\$80,000}{80\% \text{ of } \$188,000} = 1$. In other words, *any* loss up

to $80,000 would be paid by the insurer in its entirety, and the coinsurance principle would be effectively inoperative.

It must be borne in mind that in no event will the recovery be allowed to exceed the amount of the actual loss or the upper limit of coverage.

In some few jurisdictions, coinsurance clauses have been rendered illegal by statute. In others, they are permitted only if there is a reduction in premium for accepting coinsurance, and if the insured is given adequate notice of the provision by a conspicuous statement in the policy, or if coinsurance is specifically requested by the insured.

While marine insurance is presumed to be coinsurance under any policy as to which the upper limit of coverage does not equal the full value of the insured property, non-marine insurance is presumed *not* to be coinsurance unless there is a specific provision to that effect in the policy.

One problem of which insureds under a coinsurance policy should be aware is that in insuring property that is rising in value, or under conditions of inflation, the initial coverage may equal or exceed the pertinent percentage of the full value of the property, but subsequently, at the time of the loss, it may have fallen below that figure. In this situation, an insured may believe that the coinsurance provision has been nullified by an adequately high level of coverage, only to find that he is a coinsurer by the time of the loss. The most effective protection against this is to raise the upper limit of insurance to a comfortable level above the specified percentage of the full value of the property to provide a cushion, and to recheck the adequacy of coverage at reasonable intervals.

C. "OTHER INSURANCE" CLAUSES

1. Generally

In order to reduce the moral risk of overinsurance in the case of most types of insurance other than life insurance, the device of "other insurance" clauses is used by insurers to eliminate, or at least reduce, the effective coverage of a policy if the insured obtains other insurance on the same risk. These clauses generally operate either to *void* coverage altogether in the event of other insurance (in some cases, even if the other insurance is found to be unenforceable), or to reduce the policy to one of *excess coverage* over the other insurance, or to limit the insurer's liability to the payment of only the *prorata* proportion of the loss that the face value of the policy bears to the total amount of insurance outstanding on the risk. The last type (prorata) is the most common in use today, and is generally held to be effective in prorating liability among insurers even if the other insurer is insolvent and unable to pay its share of the liability.

In order to trigger an "other insurance" clause, the second insurance policy must both benefit the same party insured and cover the same property, the same interest in the property, and the same risk.

The courts are in disagreement as to whether an "other insurance" clause is to be interpreted to be effectuated only if the other insurance is valid and enforceable. It is the general rule that if the other insurance policy is *void* on its face, it is not within the contemplation of the "other insurance" clause. If, however, the second policy is merely *voidable* because of a misrepresentation or breach of condition or warranty, some courts hold that it is nevertheless sufficient to trigger the "other insurance" clause, particularly if it has not yet been voided, while other courts hold that an "other insurance" clause refers only to other enforceable insurance, and a voidable policy does not qualify. To avoid the uncertainty, insurers will frequently define "other insurance" as "valid or not." Courts will generally apply this definition to include other policies that may be voidable, but not policies that are void on their face.

2. Conflicts Between "Other Insurance" Clauses

As frequently occurs when two separate policies cover the same risk, the "other insurance" clauses can come into conflict, each attempting to defer coverage of the loss to the other. Courts have traditionally tried to reconcile the conflict by determining which of the two policies provides "primary" coverage, and compelling payment of proceeds under that policy first. A number of rules of thumb have been used to classify one policy as primary. For example, courts have variously considered the primary coverage to be under the policy that provides the most specific coverage for the particular loss, the policy first purchased, the policy covering the primary tortfeasor, or the owner's automobile policy as opposed to the driver's policy.

A number of courts have expressed dissatisfaction with all of these arbitrary methods of resolving the conflict, and have adopted the approach set forth by the Oregon Supreme Court in the case of *Lamb–Weston, Inc. v. Oregon Auto. Ins. Co.* (Or.1959). There, the court was confronted with a stand-off between an excess coverage clause and a prorata clause, but its rule is equally applicable whenever there is a conflict between any combination of "other insurance" clauses. The court simply chose to disregard both of the conflicting clauses, and if the loss is less than the combined coverages of both policies, it is to be prorated between the insurers according to the respective limits of their policies. If the loss exceeds the combined policy limits, then each insurer shall pay to the full limit of its policy. The primary benefits of the *Lamb–Weston* rule are that neither insurer receives a windfall by the application of an arbitrary standard, and recovery of proceeds by the insured is not delayed to permit litigation between the insurers.

3. Rights of Contribution Among Insurers

When two or more insurers carry policies which obligate each of them to pay only the proportion of any loss that its coverage bears to the entire coverage on the risk, no right of contribution exists on the part of an insurer that pays more than its prorata share of the loss against the other insurer or insurers. Since the policies are independent contracts, overpayment by one insurer is considered to be voluntary, and it neither gives rise to a cause of action against another insurer, nor does it extinguish the liability of any other insurer to the insured.

D. VALUED POLICIES

A "valued policy" is one in which the full value of the property is agreed to by the insurer and insured at the inception of the policy and is expressly stated in the policy. In the event of total loss, this is the figure to be paid as proceeds rather than the actual value to be determined at the time of loss. A policy in which no specific value is attributed to the property is called an "open" policy. Insurance on property under a marine policy is considered to be valued unless expressly otherwise stated in the policy—i.e., the upper limit of the policy is presumed to be the true value of the property in the event of total loss. Non-marine property insurance, on the other hand, is presumed to be unvalued, unless otherwise stated.

A substantial number of states have adopted statutes related to fire insurance, and occasionally other forms of property insurance, mandating that these forms of insurance be valued, generally by creating a conclusive presumption that the upper limit of coverage is the actual value of the property at the time of total loss. In every instance, either by the specific wording of the statute or as a result of court interpretation, the presumption can be avoided by the insurer by proof that the insured had *fraudulently* overvalued the property. In some states the insurer is permitted to deduct from the specified valuation the amount by which the property has depreciated from the inception of the policy.

The purpose behind these statutes is twofold. First, they protect the insured by preventing the insurer from issuing and collecting premiums on a policy at an excessive value and then in the event of loss reducing the amount of actual proceeds paid by proving that the property was not worth the amount of the upper limit of coverage. Where no total loss occurs, as is the most common instance, the insured can spend years paying premiums on levels of insurance that he does not in fact have. Secondly, by imposing this statutory presumption, it is hoped that the insurer will be induced to investigate more carefully before the policy is written to guard against the kind of overinsuring that leads to the deliberate destruction of the property by the insured, thereby raising the premium rates for all insureds under that type of policy. In actual practice, however, as noted by Keeton (Insurance Law, Basic text P. 142), insurers seem to prefer to run the moral hazard of overinsuring than to incur the added expense of investigation. The net effect of the valued policy statutes seems, therefore, to be counterproductive in terms of enforcing the indemnity principle. They have frequently been criticized as inducements to arson.

In view of the fact that courts consider these valued policy statutes to be for the benefit of the insurance buying public at large, and not just the individual policyholder, they are generally held to apply to *all* policies of the type to which they are pertinent, and their provisions cannot be waived by the insured. Any settlement between the insurer and insured for a figure less than the upper limit of coverage in the case of a total loss is held to be contrary to public policy and void. For the same reason, policy provisions reserving to the insurer the right to repair or rebuild the property have been considered to be violative of the statute and void.

In order to remove the temptations to the insured inherent in overinsuring under these statutes, insurers have attempted to expressly limit coverage to a fraction of the true value of the property—in many cases, three-quarters of the value. Courts have blocked that attempt by declaring such fraction clauses violative of the valued policy statutes.

Total loss is considered to have occurred when the property is rendered completely unfit for the purpose for which it was intended, regardless of the scrap value of the materials remaining. In the case of a building, if any portion left standing must be torn down before new construction begins, the loss is considered total. If a building ordinance prohibits rebuilding of a partially destroyed building, the loss is total.

In the case of less than total loss, in most jurisdictions valued policy statutes are considered not to apply, and the value of the loss is measured by the usual methods. A minority view, however, would permit recovery of a percentage of the face value of the policy determined by the percentage of the property destroyed.

E. APPRAISAL CLAUSES

Two types of clauses that must be differentiated are *appraisal* clauses and *arbitration* clauses. The purpose of each is to facilitate the speedy payment of proceeds without resort to full litigation. Arbitration clauses have generally purported to bind both insurer and insured to submit any dispute regarding either liability of the insurer or amount of proceeds to a board to be composed as specified in the clause. They have met with substantial hostility on the part of the courts, frequently being held void because they oust the court of jurisdiction over the dispute and thereby prevent the insured's access to the judicial system and a jury trial on a matter of contract law. Courts are particularly disdainful of these clauses in view of the "take it or leave it" method of including such clauses in standard form policies. Courts do not evidence the same hostility to agreements to arbitrate arrived at *after* the dispute has arisen between insured and insurer, assumedly on the grounds that in that situation, the agreement is one of informed choice on the part of the insured.

Appraisal clauses, on the other hand, have met with greater success in the courts because they are confined to disputes over the *amount* of proceeds to be paid, leaving the question of liability to the courts. Even appraisal clauses, however, have been declared invalid in cases of total loss in jurisdictions where valued policies are mandated by statute. In these jurisdictions, even in instances in which the insured has consented to submission of the total loss valuation to appraisers, courts have held the *insured* not to be bound by the appraisers' decision (as opposed to the insurer, who *is* held to be bound).

The most common form of appraisal clause is that which originated in the New York standard fire insurance policy. It reads as follows:

"In case the Insured and this Company shall fail to agree as to the actual cash value or the amount of loss, then, on the written demand of either, each shall select a competent and disinterested appraiser and notify the other of the appraiser selected within twenty days of such demand. The appraisers shall first select a competent and disinterested umpire; and failing for fifteen days to agree upon such umpire, then, on request of the insured or this Company, such umpire shall be selected by a judge of a court of record in the state in which the property covered is located. The appraisers shall then appraise the loss, stating separately actual cash value and loss of each item; and, failing to agree, shall submit their differences, only, to the umpire."

If submission of a claim to arbitration is expressly made a condition precedent to bringing an action on the policy, the condition is not held to be void, and the insured fails to comply with the condition prior to suit, the insurer has a full defense to payment. If it is not expressly made a condition precedent, the insured is entitled to proceed directly with a court action on the policy, but he may be subject to a counterclaim for breach of the arbitration clause of the contract.

If the policy does not specify a time period within which a demand for appraisal may be made, the courts will generally fall back on the implied requirement that demand be made within a "reasonable" time. This "reasonable" time, and even a time period specified in the policy, can be enlarged by the court on grounds of unfairness to the insured because of the course of negotiations toward settlement between the parties, or simply on the grounds of not upsetting the reasonable expectations of the insured.

Insurance companies use arbitration and appraisal clauses in a variety of policies, including fire, uninsured motorist, and no-fault insurance. Fire insurance policies, for example, generally include appraisal clauses which are triggered when the value of the property destroyed by fire is in dispute. Uninsured motorist policies often include arbitration clauses requiring the parties to participate in arbitration where liability or damages are in dispute. Likewise, no-fault insurance policies often include arbitration clauses which are aimed at resolving disputes relating either to liability or damages.

CHAPTER NINE

INSURER'S DUTY TO DEFEND

A. GENERALLY

It is customary for an insurer under a liability policy to include a clause in the policy placing on the insurer both a right and obligation to take over the defense of any action brought by a third party against the insured on any cause of action that falls within policy coverage, "even if any of the allegations of the suit are groundless, false or fraudulent." Because of the latter phrase, it is possible that the insurer could be called upon to defend an action as to which there would be no obligation to pay proceeds, because the obligation to defend arises whenever an action is filed against the insured in which the allegations of the third party would bring the claim, if successful, within policy coverage, while the obligation to pay proceeds arises only if the insured ultimately comes under an actual legal obligation to pay.

B. SITUATIONS AFFECTING THE DUTY TO DEFEND

1. Ambiguous Claims

Although as a general rule the duty to defend turns on whether or not the claim stated by the third party falls within or without coverage, in some cases the allegations of the third party either do not address a particular fact that is determinative of coverage or are ambiguous as to that fact. This happens particularly in cases in which the fact which is determinative of coverage is irrelevant to liability of the insured to the third party (as, e.g., when the status of the third party as employee of the insured or the exact date or time of the loss does not affect the insured's liability but does affect coverage under the liability policy). In such cases, courts have generally held that as long as there is *potential* coverage, the insurer is obligated to defend. Some courts in this situation place the burden on the insurer to conduct a reasonable investigation as to coverage, and if such a reasonable investigation would disclose facts dictating coverage, the insurer is held under an obligation to defend. In instances of ambiguity of coverage, some courts have held that if the insurer has refused to defend against the third party action, even though it is later proven in an action on the policy between the insurer and insured that there was in fact no coverage, the insurer is nevertheless liable to the insured for the cost of the defense. On occasion, courts have gone so far as to hold the insurer liable for the tort recovery against the insured in spite of lack of coverage because of the insurer's breach of its obligation to defend.

2. Alternative Claims by a Third Party

While the authorities are not unanimous on this point, when an insured is sued in an action wherein the third party alleges alternatively deliberate and negligent conduct on the part of the insured, some courts have held that the insurer should not be permitted to defend against the action because of the conflict of interest between the insurer and the insured. If the jury's verdict is to go against the defendant-insured, it is to the benefit of the *insurer* that the jury find the insured guilty of deliberate conduct rather than negligent conduct since the judgment will then fall outside of coverage under the liability policy. The *insured's* interests lie on the side of a finding of negligent conduct in terms both of insurance coverage and any possible punitive damage assessment. In view of the conflict of interest, many courts transform the obligation to defend into a liability to pay the costs of the defense as to the claims within coverage. Since the insurer is not permitted to take part in the tort trial, it is also held that the insurer is not collaterally estopped by the judgment in that action to claim in any action on the policy that the conduct of the insured was in fact deliberate and outside the scope of coverage.

3. Multiple Causes of Action

The fact that a third party claimant joins other causes of action that do not fall within policy coverage with a cause of action which is within coverage does not remove the obligation of the insurer to provide a defense as to the cause of action within coverage.

4. Untrue Statement of Facts in the Complaint

While the general rule is that the duty to defend in any particular case turns on whether or not the allegations of the tort claimant's complaint bring the cause of action within coverage under the liability policy, a different situation may be presented where the allegations of the complaint do not comport with the true facts. For example, if the complaint states a cause of action that falls without coverage (as, e.g., a cause of action for the deliberate tort of assault and battery), but the actual facts indicate a cause of action within coverage (as, e.g., a case of mere negligence), a number of courts take the position that to permit the insured to lose the benefit of the insurer's defense simply because of the manner in which the tort claimant chose to state the cause of action would be to defeat the reasonable expectations of the insured under the policy. These courts have created an exception to the general rule in finding a duty to defend in spite of the allegations of the tort complaint. On occasion this result has been based on a duty on the part of the insurer to reasonably investigate the situation. More conservative courts have imposed the duty to defend only in the instance in which the insurer knows or has reason to know that the true facts fall within coverage, despite the wording of the tort complaint.

In the reverse situation, wherein the alleged facts fall within coverage while the true facts fall without coverage, courts generally apply the normal rule of requiring the insurer to defend in accordance with the cause of action alleged in the tort complaint.

5. Unnecessary Allegations

Courts are split on the question of whether or not allegations in the tort complaint which are unnecessary to the cause of action stated should be credited in determining the insurer's obligation to defend. Consider, for example, the situation in which the tort claimant alleges gratuitously that he is an employee of the insured, although his status as employee is irrelevant to his cause of action. If there is an employee exclusion in the liability policy of the defendant such that this unnecessary allegation could eliminate the obligation of the insurer to defend, should the allegation be considered or disregarded? Needless to say, the issue only arises when the unnecessary allegation is challenged for truthfulness by either the insurer or insured. Some courts take the position that an unnecessary allegation that would defeat the duty to defend and which is challenged by the insured should be disregarded in determining the insurer's duty to defend in order to prevent upsetting the reasonable expectations of the insured under the policy. Similarly, some courts take the position favored by Keeton that an unnecessary allegation that would dictate an affirmative duty to defend and which is challenged by the insurer should be disregarded because of the high possibility that the tort claimant introduced the false allegation fraudulently or in collusion with the insured purely for the purpose of creating insurance coverage. Other courts take the opposite point of view, crediting even unnecessary allegations of the tort claimant in determining whether or not there is a duty to defend, particularly in the latter instance favoring a duty to defend.

C. DISCHARGE OF DUTY TO DEFEND BY PAYMENT OF PROCEEDS

There are three basic viewpoints on the question of whether or not payment of proceeds in the amount of the policy limit discharges any obligation to defend an action against the insured as well. Some courts take the position that once the insurer has paid over to the insured the full amount for which it can be held liable under the policy, it has rendered full performance, and the subordinate duty of providing a defense does not survive independently. Some courts feel that once the insurer is stripped of any financial interest in the outcome of the tort action against its insured it would be inappropriate to require or permit it to undertake the defense.

The second viewpoint enunciated by a number of courts is that the insurer can extinguish its obligation to defend by payment of the full policy limit to a third party tort claimant or claimants in partial or full settlement or satisfaction of judgment (though not by tender or payment of the policy limit to its own insured), thereby leaving the insured on his own as to disposition of the claims against him. This resolution is pertinent to the situation in which there are multiple claimants as a result of the same incident, and the insurer settles with or pays the judgments to the early claimants, thereby exhausting the policy limit per incident. Under this approach, the insurer would not have to defend against the subsequent actions of other claimants.

Under either of these two viewpoints, however, there is authority for the proposition that an insurer who undertakes initially to provide a defense for the insured cannot thereafter prejudice the position of the insured by withdrawing from the litigation prior to its conclusion.

The third viewpoint espoused by some courts is that the obligation to provide a defense is independent of the obligation to indemnify the insured for liability, and, therefore, survives the payment of the policy limit to anyone.

D. REMEDIES AVAILABLE TO INSURED FOR FAILURE TO DEFEND

In the event that the insurer breaches its duty to provide a defense for the insured against a third party's tort claim, courts have held the insurer liable to the insured for the following damages:

1. All costs and attorney's fees incurred by the insured in providing his own defense, including witness fees, court costs, investigation costs, appellate bonds and other appellate costs, as long as they are reasonable;

2. The amount of any judgment against the insured or settlement between the insured and claim-

ant as long as such settlement is reasonable in
amount and entered into in good faith (some courts
limit the amount of recovery under this category to
the policy limit, while others allow recovery of the
full settlement or judgment amount irrespective of
policy limit); and/or

3. Damages to compensate the insured for additional harm suffered because of the insurer's unjustified breach of its duty to provide a defense,
such as mental suffering.

If the insurer refuses to defend when the insured
is sued for claims both within and without coverage,
the insurer is generally held liable for all expenses
of suit plus the amount of any settlement or judgment attributable to the claims that fall within
coverage.

By way of other consequences, if the insurer
improperly refuses to defend, the insured has the
right to take control of the defense contrary to the
usual contract terms, and the insurer cannot avoid
payment under the policy on the grounds that the
defense was not conducted as it would have conducted it, or that an appeal was or was not taken.
The insurer can also lose the right to intervene in
the action, and the insured is free to enter into any
reasonable, good faith settlement with the tort
claimant and still collect under the policy in spite of
a clause in the policy forbidding settlement by the
insured or precluding reimbursement except for loss
sustained and paid by the insured in satisfaction of
a judgment after trial of the issues.

The insurer's unjustified refusal to defend also relieves the insured of its obligations under the policy to forward to the insurer proof of loss, notice of the incident, or any other papers connected with the suit. The insured is also held relieved of its obligation to cooperate and assist the insurer with the defense.

Some courts have gone so far as to hold that an unjustified refusal to defend amounts to a waiver of any other possible defense in regard to lack of policy coverage or non-compliance of the insured with policy conditions.

E. REMEDIES FOR BREACH OF DUTY OF CARE

Courts have imposed on insurers the duty of acting with reasonable care in performing their obligation to defend. If, therefore, an insurer assumes its duty of defense but performs it negligently, such as by failing to discover or press a particular defense, failing to turn up evidence, or failing to meet deadlines in filing an answer or notice of appeal, the insurer can be held liable to the insured for the full amount of any judgment against the insured even though it exceeds policy limits.

F. REMEDIES FOR UNTIMELY WITHDRAWAL OF INSURER

If, out of an abundance of caution, the insurer enters upon the defense of the insured in spite of the fact that it was not actually obligated to defend because of non-coverage or forfeiture by the insured, but then subsequently withdraws from the defense in an untimely way with the result that the insured is prejudiced in conducting its own defense, the insurer can be held liable for the full amount of any judgment or reasonable settlement. The theory generally relied upon is estoppel.

G.   METHODS OF SELF–PROTECTION FOR THE INSURER

1.   Declaratory Judgment Action

In view of the dangers involved in being held to have unjustifiably refused to defend an insured, including exposure to the payment of any judgment or settlement without policy limit, insurers frequently take the precautionary step of bringing a declaratory judgment action against the insured for a safe determination of any issues that could be determinative of coverage or of its obligation to defend.   In this way, the insurer can be sure in advance of the justification of its refusal to defend.

2.   Nonwaiver Agreement

At times, the insurer will wish to assume the defense of the third party tort action as a precaution against later being held to have unjustifiably refused to defend.   On the other hand, if it does so assume the defense, the majority of courts hold that it thereby waives any claim of forfeiture of coverage by the insured or lack of coverage under the policy of which it had knowledge. Courts have applied this rule of waiver even in cases in which the facts concerning the forfeiture or noncoverage were equally well known by the insured. (Note: this rule of waiver does not apply to a case in which the insurer is itself a defendant under a direct action statute.)

One device for enabling the insurer to enter upon the defense of the tort action as a precaution, while at the same time preserving its ability to claim noncoverage or forfeiture in the event of a settlement or judgment against the insured, is a *nonwaiver agreement* entered into between the insurer and insured. The insurer agrees to continue with the defense, while the insured agrees that the insurer shall retain the right to contest any issues relating to coverage in the event of liability of the insured. One danger of which the insurer must be aware is that if it is found by the court to have been too reticent about extending or accepting offers of settlement because it is relying on an undisclosed hope for a second chance to escape payment of proceeds by raising the issue of noncoverage in any subsequent action by the insured on the policy, the court is liable to void the nonwaiver agreement altogether. Also, by way of a *caveat,* the attorney for the insurer can face personal problems of conflict of interest in advising the insured to enter into a nonwaiver agreement with the insurer, particularly if the attorney has not fully explained to the insured the nature of any conflict of interest created by the nonwaiver agreement for the insurer when it attempts to defend against the tort action for the insured with one eye on the interests of the insured and the other on its own interests in fostering findings of fact that will lead to a conclusion of noncoverage.

3. Reservation of Rights Notice

A weak alternative to the nonwaiver agreement is the "reservation of rights notice," which is a unilateral statement by the insurer in writing notifying the insured of the insurer's intention to continue with the defense while retaining the right to press all issues that could lead to a finding of noncoverage. The primary purpose of the notice is to make the insured aware of the insurer's full intentions so that the insured cannot later claim that the insurer waived its rights to claim noncoverage or is estopped to make such a claim because the insured was misled into believing that the insurer had accepted liability on the policy. Such notice is also intended to make the insured aware of the fact that the insurer may decide to withdraw from the defense of the tort action at any time, and, therefore, the insured would be well advised to hire his own attorney and conduct his own investigation.

Some courts give full effect to the nonwaiver notice as a protection against the claim of estoppel by the insured. Some of these courts hold as a corollary that after receipt of a nonwaiver notice, the insured has the right to take over the defense of the third party's tort action without breaching the defense clause of the policy.

Other courts will not give effect to the insurer's unilateral claim of right both to retain control of the litigation and preserve the claims of noncoverage that put the insurer into a conflict of interest position with the insured. These courts insist that for a reservation of rights notice to be effective, it must be assented to by the insured, thereby rendering it tantamount to a nonwaiver agreement.

H. INSURER'S CONTROL OF THE DEFENSE

1. Generally

In cases in which the only claims pressed against the insured are claims of the type that would be within coverage of the liability policy, even if the total possible exposure of the insured exceeds the policy limit, the insurer has both the responsibility for the defense and the right to control the defense. An insurer will, however, generally permit private counsel of the insured to participate in an advisory capacity where the insured's exposure exceeds the policy limit.

In the event that claims within coverage are joined with claims that are not within coverage in the third party's complaint, the obligation to defend remains on the insurer as to the claims within coverage, but it no longer has the exclusive right to control the litigation. There is an obligation to share control with counsel representing the insured's interests in defending against claims not covered by the policy.

2. Conflicts of Interest Affecting Insurer's Right to Control

The most common situations giving rise to a conflict of interest between the insurer and insured in cases in which the attorney for the insurer is defending the insured are as follows:

a. Cases in which the insurer contends that the insured and the third party claimant are in collusion, and that the third party claim is an attempt to defraud the insurer;

b. Cases in which the conduct of the insured could be found to be either negligent or intentional, and it is in the best interests of the insured to argue negligence so that policy coverage will apply and such defenses as contributory negligence and assumption of the risk will be available, and in the best interests of the insurer to have the jury find intentional conduct so that any liability will be outside of policy coverage; and

c. Cases in which the *tactical* choice of defense by the insurer conflicts with the personal interests of the insured, as, for example, when the insurer's attorney chooses to admit professional negligence on the part of an insured doctor or other professional and try the case solely on damages.

In cases of this type, a number of courts have taken the position that once the insurer has met its obligation of fully informing the insured of the conflict of interest, the insured has the right to refuse to allow the insurer's attorney to represent him, and to charge the insurer for the reasonable costs and attorney's fees incurred in defending the action. Similarly, the insurer is permitted to opt to withdraw from the defense and merely pay the reasonable costs and attorney's fees involved in the defense of the insured. In either case, most courts hold that the insurer is not precluded by the findings of the court in the tort action from raising any issue of collusion or noncoverage. Some courts disagree in holding the insurer bound by the trial court's findings in the action between the insured and the third party. Needless to say, if the insurer decides to continue with the defense of the tort action for fear that it will not be as well defended by the insured's counsel or that the insured will settle for a higher figure than would be the case if the insurer's counsel were handling the negotiations, the insurer generally does so at the expense of being bound by the jury's determinations in the tort action of any facts that will determine coverage or noncoverage.

I. MULTIPLE COVERAGE

In cases in which the insured carries two or more liability policies, each of which covers a part of the claim of the third party, some courts have held that if one insurer carries the entire burden of the defense while the others refuse to take part, the laboring insurer does not have a cause of action against the other insurers for contribution, since the duty to defend was contractually owed only to the insured and not to other insurers. Other courts disagree in permitting the defending insurer to bring an action against the other insurers for pro rata contribution according to the ratio of their liability for payment of any judgment.

J. DUTY IN REGARD TO APPEAL

As a general rule, the duty to defend does not *automatically* carry with it the obligation to prosecute an appeal in the event of a verdict against the insured. The majority impose the obligation on the insurer to take into account the interests of the insured as well as its own interests in deciding whether or not to appeal, and will impose liability on the insurer for acting in *bad faith* toward the insured in refusing to appeal. A minority of courts impose the stricter standard of reasonable care in making the decision. There is, however, authority to the effect that the insurer will not be held liable for negligent failure to appeal unless the insured can show error in the judgment of the trial court and that the third party tort claimant would be unable to win on a re-trial.

Under either the standard of good faith or due care, the courts seem far more willing to impose the duty to recompense the insured for his expenses in prosecuting his own appeal than to impose liability for the judgment in excess of policy limits.

Courts have split on the question of whether the insurer is required to post an appeal bond to cover the entire amount of a judgment or only that portion of the judgment within policy limits.

In the event that the insurer fails to provide for an appeal bond and obtain a stay of execution, with the result that the insured is compelled to satisfy the judgment or settle with the tort claimant to prevent execution against his property, the insurer cannot avoid payment of the judgment to the extent of policy limits on the grounds that the insured has breached the policy provision precluding settlement or payment by the insured without the consent of the insurer.

K. DUTY IN REGARD TO SETTLEMENT

1. Court–Created Duty

It is usual for insurers to use policy language that reserves to themselves the right to negotiate and settle any action as they may deem expedient. In spite of the strictly pro-insurer language of the clause, courts have implied the duty to consider the interests of the insured when the insurer is negotiating a settlement. This duty is created out of consideration, among other factors, of the fact that the interests of the insured in the tort action against him or her are surrendered exclusively into the hands of the insurer.

For a full discussion of this duty, see Chapter Eleven, dealing with bad faith causes of action, infra.

L. ASSIGNMENT OF CLAIMS AGAINST INSURER

A majority of courts have ruled that assignment of the claim of the insured against the insurer for breach of its duty to defend is valid. A frequent result, therefore, is that the insured assigns his claim against the insurer for the excess of the judgment or settlement above policy limits to the third party tort claimant. The third party claimant then simply collects the *entire* amount of the judgment from the insurer. In cases, therefore, in which the insured's cause of action against the insurer is not defeated by the fact that the insured is insolvent and would never pay the excess liability himself, the only real beneficiary of the insured's cause of action is the tort claimant who would otherwise receive less than the full amount of his judgment. This consideration favors the disallowance of claims for excess liability against the insurer in cases in which the insured is insolvent.

A minority of jurisdictions hold that the action of the insured against the insurer for breach of its duty to defend or settle is a tort action and is, therefore, unassignable. In such jurisdictions, the action would also not survive the insured.

M. CONFLICT OF INTEREST IN COUNSEL

As discussed above in this chapter, the insurer has a duty to defend a claim against the insured any time there is a possibility of coverage under the policy. Where there is a dispute over the issue of whether the insurer is actually obligated to extend coverage, the insurer will often undertake the defense in order to avoid the potential for a subsequent bad faith claim. The insurer will generally undertake representation, however, only after reserving the right to deny coverage under the policy. In these cases, the insurer selects the attorney who will represent the insured, and that attorney controls the litigation.

There has been a considerable amount of litigation on the issue of whether this triangular arrangement among insured, insurer, and attorney is appropriate, or for that matter, ethical. The seminal case addressing this issue is *San Diego Navy Federal Credit Union v. Cumis Insurance Society Inc.*

In *Cumis,* the California Court of Appeals faced a situation in which an insurer agreed to defend its insured against a claim for wrongful discharge but reserved its right to deny coverage on the punitive damages claim. The insured subsequently retained independent counsel to defend the wrongful discharge claim, because it believed that an attorney hired by the insurer would face a conflict of interest in representing the insured's interests while being retained and paid by the insurer.

This conflict of interest resulted from the fact that it was in the insured's interest to prove that if it was liable at all, its conduct had not been deliberate, that punitive damages were inappropriate, and thus, that coverage was required. It was in the insurer's best interests, in the event of a plaintiff's verdict, to have a finding that the insured acted deliberately; and, thus, the insurer would not be obliged to provide coverage, since damages for deliberate acts and punitive damages were excluded from coverage. Thus, the attorney who had been hired by the insurer, but who was theoretically supposed to represent the interests of the insured, was enmeshed in a conflict of interest.

Though the insurer in *Cumis* actually paid two invoices for the independent counsel's services, it later took the position that there was, in fact, no conflict of interest that would require independent counsel and, therefore, denied further payment for independent counsel's services.

The insured sued the insurer claiming that 1) it was entitled to independent counsel and 2) that the insurer was responsible for paying the fees of independent counsel. The trial court agreed with the insured, and on appeal, that decision was affirmed. The appellate court held that where the insured and the insurer have conflicting interests—*i.e.,* where it is in the interests of the insurer to demonstrate non-coverage of the act under the policy, while it is in the interests of the insured to demonstrate that its acts are covered under the policy—and where the conflict in these interests has been created by the insurer's reservation of rights to contest coverage, "the insurer must pay the reasonable cost for hiring independent counsel by the insured."

The backlash from the *Cumis* case has been widespread. For example, several cases brought immediately following *Cumis* indicated that *Cumis* was interpreted by the courts to require the insurer to provide "*Cumis* counsel" in any situation in which the insurer defended under a reservation of rights. The California courts were quick to clarify and restrict the holding, stating that there is no conflict of interest requiring *Cumis* counsel unless the counsel retained by the insurer can affect coverage by the manner in which he/she controls the case. For example, in a case in which the policy excludes coverage for deliberate acts, *Cumis* counsel would have the ability to affect coverage by the manner in which he/she presents the defense. If the defense attorney presents evidence tending to show that the insured's acts were deliberate, the outcome is more likely to be favorable to the insurer. Alternatively, if the defense attorney presents evidence that the insured did not act deliberately, the outcome may be more favorable to the insured. Thus, in that case, the defense attorney in the underlying tort action has the ability to affect coverage, and, consequently, an impermissible conflict exists. No such impermissible conflict would exist if the basis for the reservation of rights were, for example, a breach of condition by the insured, that was not relevant to any issue that would arise in the underlying action against the insured.

One of the most significant results of the *Cumis* decision was the enactment of California Civil Code section 2860. Enacted in part to contain the potential expansive reach of the *Cumis* holding, this statute codified the holding of the case and attempted to clarify the rights and duties of *Cumis* counsel.

As noted above, following the *Cumis* decision, some courts interpreted the decision to mean that a conflict arose *whenever* the insurer reserved rights to disclaim coverage. The statute follows the more restrictive holdings in stating that an impermissible conflict arises only in cases in which the outcome of an issue which is both relevant to the underlying lawsuit and the issue of coverage could be controlled by the defense counsel provided for the insured by the insurer. Furthermore, no conflict shall be considered to arise "as to allegations of punitive damages" or "solely because an insured is sued for an amount in excess of the insurance policy limits." As noted in the subsequent case of *Golden Eagle Ins. Co. v. Foremost Ins. Co.,* the duty to provide independent counsel is based not on insurance law, but rather on the ethical requirement that an attorney avoid representing conflicting interests.

The statute also provides specific language by means of which the insured can make a knowing and intelligent written waiver of the right to have independent counsel provided.

Among the complexities introduced by the requirement of *"Cumis"* counsel is the extent and type of cooperation mandated between the independent counsel and the insurer's counsel. Under the statute, a duty is imposed on both the independent counsel and the insured to disclose all information relevant to the underlying action except "privileged materials relevant to coverage disputes." Furthermore, both independent counsel and the insurer's counsel "shall be allowed to participate in all aspects of the litigation. Counsel shall cooperate fully in the exchange of information that is consistent with each counsel's ethical and legal obligation to the insured." Added to that, it is provided that "[n]othing in this section shall relieve the insured of his or her duty to cooperate with the insurer under the terms of the insurance contract."

As stated in the case of *Employers Insurance of Wausau v. Albert D. Seeno Construction Company,* independent counsel is required not only to disclose to the insurer any information relevant to the action, except for matters relating to coverage and therefore privileged, but also to *consult* with the insurer on all issues relating to the action. The court noted that these duties do not place the independent counsel and the insurer in an attorney-client relationship, which means that the insurer cannot move to disqualify the independent counsel for breach of that duty. The court suggests, however, that the insurer could bring a claim for breach of the covenant of good faith and fair dealing.

It should be noted that these terms requiring joint participation and consultation between counsel, and cooperation with the insurer by the insured, might turn out to be more easily stated than accomplished. For example, in cases of differences of opinion on tactics or even the acceptance of or the making of an offer of settlement, what exactly is the relative role and control of each counsel? This is not clarified under the statute.

Also under the statute, if the insurer is required to provide for independent counsel, the insurer can require that independent counsel chosen by the insured have certain qualifications, such as a minimum of five years of litigation experience and substantial experience in defending the type of litigation underlying the claim. The insurer can also insist that the independent counsel have errors and omissions coverage.

In the event of uncertainty as to whether a conflict requiring independent counsel has arisen, case law suggests that a declaratory judgment action by the insurer would be an appropriate procedure. Whether or not the plaintiff in the underlying action should be allowed to intervene in the declaratory judgment action would be an issue within the discretion of the court.

One final note is that a review of case law in jurisdictions other than California also reveals a trend toward recognizing the need for independent counsel in cases which present conflicts of interest. The insurer will be obligated to compensate independent counsel if the conflict can be shown.

Notwithstanding the confusion surrounding *Cumis* and the subsequent codification of its holding, it has had a widespread impact on the insurance industry. Insurers are now often forced to expend substantial sums in order to finance the services of outside counsel, while also retaining their own counsel to represent the interests of the insurer, thereby adding to the costs of liability insurance. In addition, what was formerly a simplified system involving one counsel appointed by the insurer to control the litigation has been made considerably more complex. Under the new sensitization to the conflict of interest, while it is to be presumed that independent counsel will manage the defense, the relative roles of the insurer's counsel and independent counsel in that litigation in terms of reaching the ultimate decisions on tactics, witnesses, settlement, etc., remain unclear.

CHAPTER TEN

SUBROGATION

A. DEFINITION

Under the equitable doctrine of subrogation, if A owes a debt to B, and C pays that debt under some form of legal compulsion—i.e., not as a volunteer—C becomes entitled to bring B's cause of action against A to recover the amount paid. C is said to be subrogated to B's claim against A. Courts of equity have applied the doctrine in the context of insurance in the following way. If A negligently causes damage to B's property, and the C insurance company indemnified B under its contract of insurance with B, C insurance company is subrogated to B's claim in tort against A to the extent of C's payments to B. Subrogated rights arise in the insurer by action of law, regardless of whether or not they are provided for in the insurance contract or in any transactions between the insured and third party. They apply to all causes of action the insured may have against the third party in regard to the loss concerned, whether founded in tort or contract law. If at the time the insurance policy is taken out there is a contract whereby a third party has assumed the risk that is insured against—i.e., the third party is obligated to pay the insured a sum that will offset the loss insured against—the insurer is subrogated to the contractual cause of action of its insured. This occurs, for example, when an insurance policy covers a mortgagee's interest. If the insurer pays proceeds because of damage to the mortgaged property, it is subrogated to that extent to the mortgagee's rights in contract against the mortgagor.

On the other hand, the insurer can be subrogated only to those causes of action that the insured possesses, subject to most defenses good against the insured (such as contributory negligence). If an insured has released a prospective tort-feasor prior to entering into the insurance contract, as, for example, in a lease or bill of lading, the insurer has no greater right against the tort-feasor than the insured would have. If, however, the insured releases a tort-feasor *after* the contract of insurance is entered into (at which time the right of subrogation automatically attaches) he will be held to have breached his contract with the insurer, thus presenting the insurer with a defense against payment of any claims under the policy. If, after a loss and payment by the insurer, the third party, with knowledge of the insurer's rights, obtains a release from the insured as part of a settlement, that release will be ineffective as a defense against the insurer's subrogated claim. If, however, the tort-feasor settles with the insured without knowledge of the insurer's rights, any release obtained will be effective against the insurer.

B. RATIONALE

The doctrine of subrogation in the insurance context has been closely interwoven with the doctrine of indemnity. The most frequently cited reason for its application is to prevent an insured from profiting from his loss—i.e., obtaining a double recovery, once from his insurer and once from the tort-feasor. The interrelationship between the subrogation and indemnity doctrines explains as rationally as possible the delineation between the types of insurance to which subrogation applies and those to which it does not apply (as will be discussed below).

A second reason cited for this application of subrogation is that it comports with public policy to allow the ultimate economic burden to be borne by the party causing the loss in the first place. This both prevents a tort-feasor from profiting from insurance paid for by the insured in the event that the insured would forego suit once made whole by his insurance, and imposes a burden that might act to deter the commission of torts.

A possible third reason, that of ultimately reducing insurance rates by virtue of subrogated recoveries by insurers, has simply not come to pass. Insurers consistently fail to introduce the factor of such recoveries into rate-determining formulae, but rather apply such recoveries to increasing dividends to shareholders.

C. APPLICATION OF SUBROGATION TO LINES OF INSURANCE

Primarily because of the close association of subrogation with the indemnity principle, it has not been universally applied to all lines of insurance. The following is a delineation of its application or non-application in each individual line.

1. Property Insurance

Because property insurance is the most clear form of indemnity—payment measured and limited by the value of the thing lost—subrogation applies most universally to this line of insurance. A subrogation clause is commonly included in property insurance policies, but it seldom does more than state rights that would arise under the law in any event.

2. Liability Insurance

Here again, the basis of payments by the insurer is indemnification of the insured for sums that the insured is obligated by law to pay to a third person. The insurer is, therefore, generally subrogated to the insured's claims over against a primary tortfeasor, or claims for indemnity or contribution against a third person.

3. Life and Accident Insurance

a. Life Insurance

Because of the overall classification of life insurance as a form of investment rather than indemnity, subrogation rights do not arise by action of law in this line of insurance. The obligation of the insurer is to pay a sum of money that is fixed solely by the contract between the parties and is in no way measured or limited by any actual dollar value of the life that is lost. In fact, by its nature, the loss is not susceptible of economic measurement, and, therefore, there is no concern for the prevention of a double recovery by the beneficiary.

In denying subrogation rights, courts have also raised the technical rationale that at common law, any personal cause of action dies with the deceased, and any statutory cause of action for wrongful death belongs to the personal representative of the deceased rather than the owner or beneficiary. There is, therefore, no cause of action in the owner or beneficiary of the policy to which the insurer could be subrogated.

A distinction can be drawn between the various forms of life insurance in that, while limited payment and endowment policies are clearly investments, short term life insurance is equally clearly a form of indemnity. Similarly, in the case of property insurance, many individual policies, such as marine policies, more closely resemble life insurance than property insurance in that, in the event of loss, they call for the payment of a sum fixed by contract rather than a sum measured by the value of the property at the time of the loss. In dealing with such individual policies, courts have taken a broad approach, simply applying subrogation rights to property insurance and denying it in the case of life insurance, regardless of differences within each classification.

b. *Accident Insurance*

Because the amount payable for any specific injury is fixed by contract without assessment of the economic value of the loss, accident insurance more closely resembles life insurance than property insurance, and, therefore, subrogation rights do not attach to accident insurance.   As stated in the landmark decision of *Gatzweiler v. Milwaukee Elec. Ry. & Light Co.* (Wis.1908), "The insured buys and pays for the right to have from another a specified sum upon the happening of a specified event.   Payment for the insurance is in the nature of an investment.   The money value of the thing covered by the insurance does not enter into the transaction at all."

One additional current that runs through decisions on both life and accident insurance is the feeling that all available compensation from insurance and recovery from the tortfeasor is seldom sufficient to meet the needs of the injured person or the survivors.   There is, therefore, little interest in applying the subrogation device to prevent excessive recovery by the insured.

4.   Medical, Surgical, and Hospitalization Insurance

Authoritative case law is scant to indicate whether or not subrogation rights arise at law without stipulation in the insurance contract in the area of medical, surgical, and hospitalization coverage, but such case law as is available indicates that subrogation is generally denied.   In one case, *Michigan*

Hosp. Serv. v. Sharpe (Mich.1954), the court disallowed a claim in subrogation by the Michigan Hospital Service (Blue Cross), on the unsatisfactory ground that when the Service paid the subscriber's hospital expenses, it was merely fulfilling its contractual obligation to supply such services to the subscriber and was, therefore, paying a debt for which it was *primarily* liable, rather than indemnifying the subscriber for a debt primarily owed by the subscriber. Cast in this posture, the Service is not entitled to subrogation, because subrogation by its nature does not arise in one who merely pays a debt for which he is primarily liable. The reason that such an approach is unsatisfactory is that the story can be told equally plausibly in either of two ways: either the Service can be cast as an insurer indemnifying the subscriber for the hospital costs he incurs, or it can be cast as a conveyor of the hospital services which it must purchase directly from the hospital in order to deliver them to the subscriber. Either view is equally rational. It would seem, therefore, that the court has concluded that subrogation is inappropriate in the case of hospital or medical coverage, and has chosen the version that leads inevitably to its denial.

One further indication in this area has been the persistent failure of insurance companies to seek subrogation absent some specific stipulation in the policy. This implies a tacit assumption by insurers that it is not available at law.

The state of subrogation *at law* in this area is currently somewhat confused by the dramatic decrease in instances in which it would be an issue because of the proliferation of express stipulations for subrogation in this type of policy. This is particularly true in relation to medical payments coverages in automobile policies.

5. Casualty Insurance

The pattern of subrogation rights that arises at law in the case of casualty insurance is more complex than in the case of either property or life insurance. The existence of subrogation rights tends to depend upon the nature of the insured and the nature of the third party concerned, as well as the specific type of insurance. For example, as noted by Keeton in Insurance Law, Basic Text, pp. 148–9, in the case of insurance against loss through forgery, if the insured is the drawee-bank under a forgery bond, the insurer is subrogated to the bank's cause of action against the innocent third party who cashed the check for the forger. If, on the other hand, the insured is an employer under a general fidelity bond on his employee, the insurer is not subrogated to the employer's claim against an innocent third party such as the drawee-bank. In both cases, however, the insurer would be subrogated to the claim against the forger. The lines of this patchwork quilt seem to be drawn on the basis of a balance of equities between all parties concerned.

6. Workmen's Compensation

Usually, subrogation rights, whether of the employer or of the employer's insurer, are specified in the workmen's compensation act of the particular jurisdiction. Absent statutory provision, there is a split among the states as to whether the insurer is entitled by law to subrogation. Those that deny the legal right of subrogation do so by analogizing workmen's compensation to life or accident insurance.

According to Vance (Insurance, 3d ed., pp. 798–9), subrogation rights under workmen's compensation statutes follow three basic patterns:

a. The insurer can recover from the tort-feasor only the amount it was compelled to pay the employee, and the employee can then sue to recover any excess value of the damage suffered;

b. If the employee elects to accept compensation payment, the insurer is subrogated to the entire claim of the employee against the tort-feasor; or

c. Once the insurer has paid compensation benefits, it is subrogated to the entire claim of the employee against the tort-feasor, but it holds that portion of the recovery in excess of its compensation payment in trust for the employee or his dependents.

D. REMEDIES

1. Against a Third Party

The insurer steps into the shoes of the insured in being subrogated to any cause of action against a third party who has caused the loss for which the insurer has become obligated to indemnify the insured, as well as any third party who is contractually bound to the insured to assume primary liability for the loss. The third party cannot escape liability to the insurer by direct payment to the insured or by obtaining a release from the insured as long as the third party was at the time of payment or release aware of the subrogated rights of the insurer. The third party could potentially, therefore, wind up paying twice for the same loss—once to the insured in derogation of the insurer's rights, and secondly to the insurer.

2. Against the Insured

a. *Prior to Payment of Proceeds*

In the event that the insured compromises the subrogated claim of the insurer by settlement with the third party or by giving a release to the third party, the insured is held to have breached its contract of insurance, and the insurer has a partial or complete defense against an action by the insured on the policy. This defense is not available to the insurer if, at the time of the settlement or release, the third party was aware of the insurer's subrogated rights because such a release or settlement would not prejudice the rights of the insurer against the third party.

b. *After Payment of Proceeds*

In the event that the insurer has paid proceeds to the insured under the policy and the insured has settled with or released the third party, the insurer has a cause of action against the insured for breach of contract. To establish harm caused by the breach, the insurer must "show that in fact it might have recovered against [the third party] as a wrong-doer." *Hamilton Fire Ins. Co. v. Greger* (N.Y.1927). It has been suggested that this rule should be interpreted as meaning that the insurer must only show that the prospects were such that it would have effected *some recovery* by way of settlement with the third party, rather than requiring proof that the insurer would have recovered judgment against the third party were it not for the insured's settlement or release. See Keeton, Insurance Law, Basic Text, p. 165.

In the event that the third party was aware of the insurer's rights at the time of release or settlement with the insured, the insurer's claim against the third party is still intact, and therefore no damages flow from the breach by the insured.

As an alternative, the insurer can petition the equity court to impose a constructive trust for its benefit on the funds in the hands of the insured, received from the third party in derogation of its subrogation rights. The net result is that the insured is compelled to account to the insurer for the portion of those funds that represent the proceeds of the claim against the third party as to which the insurer was subrogated.

Notice that the amount of recovery by the insurer can vary depending on whether it chooses to use the insured's breach of subrogation rights as the basis for a defense against payment of proceeds or the basis of a cause of action in breach of contract or constructive trust.

E. DIVISION OF FUND RECOVERED FROM THIRD PARTY

Courts have taken differing approaches to the distribution between the insured and insurer of any fund recovered from a third party. In the absence of stipulations to the contrary in the insurance policy, the majority of courts direct that the insured is to be compensated first out of the fund to the extent to which his loss exceeds insurance proceeds. The insurer is then to be compensated up to the amount of proceeds paid to the insured, and the remainder of the fund, if any, goes to the insured. An alternative approach is to compensate the insurer first for proceeds paid, with any remainder going to the insured. One final approach is to split the fund pro rata between the insured and insurer according to the percentage of the loss borne by each. Needless to say, the only instances in which the particular approach adopted by the court will be of concern to the insured or insurer are those cases in which the fund recovered from the third party is less than the total value of the loss.

F. DEFENSE TO SUBROGATION

1. "Volunteer" Defense

Under the traditional doctrine of subrogation, an insurer who pays a claim on a policy "voluntarily", as opposed to being legally obligated to pay, is not entitled to subrogation. For example, if an insurer pays a claim in excess of policy limits, or one that is not within policy coverage, or one that falls within an exclusion, to the extent that the insurer was not legally obligated to pay, it is considered a volunteer. Similarly, where an insurer is only obligated to pay its *pro rata* share of a loss under an "other insurance" clause, it is considered a volunteer to the extent of any payment in excess of that share.

This defense to subrogation has met with sparse success in terms of fact situations under which courts will label the insurer a "volunteer" because it discourages insurers from settling claims with insureds promptly. Courts tend to allow the defense only in cases in which circumstances indicate that the insurer paid the claim in the face of a clear, valid defense, and disallow it consistently when liability under the policy is in dispute. It is generally disallowed in cases in which the insurer pays a claim in spite of a defense based on a breach of condition that an insurer would ordinarily be willing to overlook. As Keeton suggests, even in situations in which the defense would be available, the insurer can obviate it by simply taking an assignment of the claim against the third party from the insured (if assignment is permitted in the jurisdiction), or by use of the "loan receipt" (See section on REAL PARTY IN INTEREST, infra, for an explanation of the function of the loan receipt.)

2. Defense of Insured

It is a general rule of limitation on insurer subrogation that an insurer cannot be subrogated to a claim against a named insured under the same policy. For example, if, under a single policy, the interests of both bailee and bailor in a piece of property are covered, and the property is destroyed through the negligence of the bailee, when the insurer pays the proceeds to the bailor, it cannot be subrogated to any claim against its other insured, the negligent bailee. To allow subrogation in this instance would make the insurance policy illusory as to the bailee. The issue frequently arises as to whether the interests of both bailee and bailor, or lessee and lessor, were intended to be covered by the policy in order to determine whether the insurer can be subrogated to a claim for negligence against the bailee or lessee.

G. REAL PARTY IN INTEREST

1. Procedural Rule

It is in the practical interest of the insurer to be able to prosecute its subrogated claim against the third party in the name of the insured in order to prevent the inevitable bias of the jury against an insurer. Such an interest would seem as rational and legitimate as its interest, generally protected by the courts, in keeping the fact of liability insurance coverage of a defendant from the jury. In fact, some jurisdictions have permitted insurers to bring subrogated claims in the names of their insureds in spite of the fact that the relevant procedure statute of the jurisdiction required that all actions be prosecuted in the name of the real party in interest. The New York civil practice act specifically provides that "Except where otherwise prescribed by order of the court, an * * * insured person who has executed to his insurer either a loan or subrogation receipt, trust agreement, or other similar agreement * * * may sue or be sued without joining with him the person for or against whose interest the action is brought." N.Y.Civ.Prac.L.R. § 1004 (McKinney 1963). Other courts have required that the insurer be named as party plaintiff, particularly when it has paid the loss in full, and have dismissed actions brought in the name of the insured alone.

2. Loan Receipts

In order to avoid being in the position of the real party in interest (and, therefore, named party plaintiff) in a claim against a third party, and yet retain the right to the proceeds of the action, insurers have employed with some success the device of the loan receipt. Rather than *pay* the insurance proceeds to the insured, the insurer "loans" the amount of the proceeds to the insured with the stipulation that the insured is to repay the insurer out of any recovery or settlement against the third party. Some courts have upheld the loan receipt device, while others have disallowed it as a method of obviating the real party in interest rule.

H. CONVENTIONAL SUBROGATION

The term of art for a right of subrogation provided by contract between the insurer and insured (whether in the policy itself or in a separate agreement entered into at the time of payment of proceeds) is "conventional subrogation". While in most instances the contract provision merely restates rights that already exist at law as a creation of equity, as noted by Keeton (Insurance Law, Basic Text, p. 153), courts have permitted the parties far more freedom of contract in terms of enlarging subrogation rights than they have in the area of insurable interest—another area dominated by the indemnity principle. For example, legal subrogation is generally denied in the area of health insurance, while conventional subrogation (for example, in regard to medical payments coverage in automobile insurance policies) is fairly consistently sustained. In the case of *Michigan Hosp. Serv. v. Sharpe,* referred to above, legal subrogation under a Blue Cross policy that contained no stipulation for subrogation was denied to the Hospital Service. In the companion case of *Michigan Medical Serv. v. Sharpe* (Mich.1954), a cause of action against the subscriber for failure to comply with the contractual subrogation clause was permitted. Similarly, in the leading case of *Gatzweiler v. Milwaukee Elec. Ry. & Light Co.* (Wis.1908), involving a policy of accident insurance, the court assumed that "in the absence of some stipulation to the contrary a contract of casualty insurance is not * * * one of indemnity giving rise in the circumstances of this case to the right of subrogation as against the party wrongfully causing the injury, and yet the parties might give it that character by a stipulation to that effect * * *"

The minority of courts that have denied the validity of conventional subrogation in the area of health or accident insurance have done so on the grounds that it is tantamount to assignment of a cause of action for personal injury which is prohibited in the jurisdiction. The majority of courts seem to have recognized that the fears of champerty and maintenance which lie behind the common law and statutory rules making personal injury claims non-assignable are not relevant to subrogation claims because the latter are not available to volunteers, nor does the amount of the subrogated claim exceed the amount paid out by the insurer. It is, therefore, not a field for profiteering by buying up law suits on the part of insurers.

In spite of this liberality, courts have drawn the line at life insurance. Attempts to introduce conventional subrogation into this area have met with virtually no success in that such subrogation clauses have been declared void.

Another limitation on the wide-ranging effectiveness of conventional subrogation is the fact that where the defense of voluntariness has been held good against legal subrogation, it has also been held good against conventional subrogation.

CHAPTER ELEVEN

BAD FAITH CAUSES OF ACTION

A. GENERALLY

In a further effort to protect the interests of insureds in their dealings with insurance companies, the majority of state courts have fashioned a cause of action out of an amalgam of tort and contract principles that is generally known as the "bad faith cause of action". The well-spring of the theory is the ancient doctrine of contract law that there is implied on both sides of every contract a covenant of "good faith and fair dealing" to see that the other party to the contract is not hindered in reaping the benefits of the contract. The cause of action itself, however, is, in many jurisdictions, considered to be one sounding in tort.

Although the implied covenant runs to both parties to any contract, in the context of insurance policies, the courts have chosen to apply it solely as the foundation for a cause of action by insureds against insurers.

The cause of action arises in two contexts—1) that of third-party claims, in which the insured is seeking defense and indemnification from liability to a third party, and 2) that of first-party claims, in which the insured is seeking indemnification from the insurer for a loss suffered by the insured personally. The bases for the causes of action in bad faith in the two contexts, as well as the remedies available, are sufficiently distinct to require treating each separately.

B. THIRD–PARTY CLAIMS

1. Context

The conflicting interests between insured and insurer in the area of third-party claims that led courts to fashion the bad faith cause of action for the protection of insureds can best be appreciated by considering the following situation. An insured has a liability policy with an upper limit of $50,000. An action is brought against the insured for $100,-000 by a third-party under a theory that falls within the coverage of the policy. The insurer assumes control of the defense of the action, and, in the course of litigation, the third-party offers to settle the action for $50,000. Assuming that the third-party has a reasonably sound case on liability and damages, and that the offer of settlement is therefore an attractive one from the point of view of the defendant/insured, the insurer is now under the pressure of divided loyalties. Looking solely to the interests of the insurer, it would be preferable to decline the offer, since the insurer stands to lose no more if the jury comes in with a plaintiff's verdict for the full $100,000 than if the case is settled for $50,000. In either situation, the insurer's liability would be no more than $50,000 under the policy limits. If the case is allowed to go to the jury, there is always the chance of a defendant's verdict, or a finding of damages in an amount less than $50,000. From the point of view of the insured, however, to decline the offer of settlement within policy limits in order to gamble on a defendant's verdict is to gamble with the insured's money, since any verdict over $50,000 would have to be paid out of the pocket of the insured. Since control of the defense of the action, including the right to decide to accept or reject a settlement offer, is rightfully assumed by the insurer under the terms of the policy, the issue arises as to what duty is owed by the insurer to give consideration to the interests of the insured in making its decision on settlement.

2. Development of the Cause of Action

a. *Early Case Law*

Early case law on this subject was consistent in supporting the insurer's absolute right to make an unfettered decision on settlement. In 1923, for example, the New York court looked solely to the wording of the policy to define the rights of the parties and found that "there is nothing in the policy by which the insurance company obligated itself to settle, if an opportunity presented itself." *Auerbach v. Maryland Cas. Co.* (N.Y.1923). The Massachusetts Supreme Judicial Court went even further in holding in 1931 that "an insurance company, * * * has an absolute right to dispose of an action brought against its assured * * * in such way as may appear to it for its best interest." *Long* *v. Union Indemnity Co.* (Mass.1931). It concluded that the insurer need not even consider the interests of the insured if the two are in conflict.

b. California Origin of the Cause of Action

While other courts subsequently imported the implied covenant of good faith and fair dealing into the insurance context generally, it was the California District Court of Appeals, in the seminal case of *Brown v. Guarantee Insurance Company* (Cal.App. 1957), that gained the attention of courts across the country by employing that doctrine to create a specific cause of action against an insurer for failure to consider the interests of the insured in refusing to settle an action by a third party. The insured had been sued in tort for $15,000. The insurer under an automobile liability policy assumed the defense and rejected an offer of settlement at the policy limit of $5000 without even informing the insured of the offer. The insurer expressly took the position that "unless [the insurer] could save some money on the settlement, [it] had no reason to settle" the case.

i. Balancing the Interests of Insured and Insurer

The court in *Brown* began by recognizing the conflict of interest between the insured and insurer and placed great weight on the fact that the insurer alone had control of the decision to accept or reject settlement.

In working its way to a solution, the court was sensitive to the necessity for treading a careful path between the interests of the two parties rather than adopting an approach that would strongly favor either. If a serious and enforceable burden were not imposed on the insurer to give due consideration to the interest of the insured in having the action settled within policy limits, the insurer would be free to go on gambling, however recklessly, with the insured's funds in terms of any recovery over policy limits. On the other hand, if the duty imposed on the insurer to give weight to the insured's interest were too one-sided, the insured would be in a position to demand that the insurer accede to unreasonable, or even possibly fraudulent settlement offers on the part of the third-party plaintiff to avoid even larger penalties when sued by the insured.

ii. Selection of a Standard

The court in *Brown* opted for the creation of a cause of action in tort, and in defining the underlying duty, the court adopted the concept of the universal implied covenant in every contract, the duty to exercise "good faith and fair dealing." This phrase, however, gives little concrete guidance in actual fact situations. The court, therefore, went on to place a practical limit on the extent of that duty. "The insurer is under no duty to compromise a claim for the sole benefit of its insured if to continue the fight offers a fair and reasonable prospect of escaping liability under its policy or of getting off for less than the policy limit."

In this early case, the California court also feared dropping the level of culpability that would result in a breach of the insurer's duty to its insured from an act of actual bad faith to an act of mere negligence. The concern of the court was that since experienced trial attorneys frequently differ on the highly subjective decision to accept or reject a settlement offer, the negligence standard would leave too much room for speculation by inexperienced jurors. The negligence standard might force an insurer to accept an ill-advised settlement out of fear that a jury—never known for its proclivity to favor insurance companies against insureds—might use the reasonable person standard as a means of shifting the amount of the third-party judgment in excess of the policy limit from the insured to the insurer.

The California court was also concerned about the possible extent of the remedy. Insurers base their acceptance of a particular risk for a particular premium on the fact that the risk is capped by the policy limit. If an insurer is to be deprived of the protection of the policy limit and be held liable to the full extent of the judgment against its insured, it should be done only as a result of the kind of substantially culpable conduct connoted by the term, "bad faith". According to this court, the negligence standard should only be applied in determining whether or not the insurer employed reasonable diligence in investigating the factual basis for the third party's claim in order to make a good faith decision on settlement.

iii. Criteria for Determining Bad Faith

To this point, the court in *Brown* had specified what the practical definition of bad faith should not be. In pinning down exactly what bad faith is, the court listed eight factors for consideration which have been widely cited by other courts in adopting the bad faith cause of action. The factors are:

"1) the strength of the injured claimant's case on the issues of liability and damages;

2) attempts by the insurer to induce the insured to contribute to a settlement;

3) failure of the insurer to properly investigate the circumstances so as to ascertain the evidence against the insured;

4) the insurer's rejection of advice of its own attorney or agent;

5) failure of the insurer to inform the insured of a compromise offer;

6) the amount of financial risk to which each party is exposed in the event of a refusal to settle;

7) the fault of the insured in inducing the insurer's rejection of the compromise offer by misleading it as to the facts; and

8) any other factors tending to establish or negate bad faith on the part of the insurer."

No single factor is intended to lead to an automatic conclusion of bad faith, but rather the intent is that the pluses and minuses of all of the factors be weighed in reaching a decision.

In the years following the *Brown* decision, nearly every court that faced the issue followed the lead of the California court in instituting a substantially identical cause of action for bad faith.

c. *The Negligence Standard*

By 1965, however, the California court again took the lead by doing exactly what the *Brown* court feared in lowering the standard for insurer liability from bad faith to mere negligence. By the time the California court affirmed the negligence standard in the case of *Crisci v. Security Insurance Company* (Cal.1967), the test in California had become whether or not a reasonable insurer would have accepted or rejected a particular offer of settlement if there had been no policy limit.

Only a minority of the courts of other states have followed the California court in *expressly* reducing the standard from bad faith to negligence. As noted by a number of commentators, however, the net effect of at least two developments over the years has been the blurring of any practical distinction in the outcome of actual cases between the two tests. The first development was the fact that in many approved charges to the jury, the bad faith standard is set forth, but then the jury is instructed that it may consider negligence on the part of the insurer as an indication of bad faith. The second development is that some courts will staunchly adhere to the bad faith standard but then define that standard in terms of what the reasonable insurer would do if there were no policy limit. In each case, the distinction between the standards is hopelessly blurred, and the resulting practical test is one of negligence.

d. *Strict Liability Standard*

In 1967, the California court was again in the lead in tentatively exploring the wisdom of dropping the standard to the rock-bottom level of strict liability. The court was presented with a particularly blatant example of bad faith on the part of the insurer in *Crisci v. Security Insurance Company* (Cal.1967). The plaintiff had fallen through a stairway negligently maintained by the insured and was left for a period of time hanging fifteen feet above the ground. There were not only serious physical injuries, but also a strong indication that the experience brought on a severe psychosis in the plaintiff. It was apparent to the insurer's counsel and claims manager that a verdict of at least $100,000 was likely. On the gamble that the jury would believe the defendant's psychiatrists and totally reject the testimony of the plaintiff's psychiatrists, the insurer rejected a settlement offer in the amount of the policy limit, $10,000. In fact, the insurer took the position that it would not pay one cent toward settlement. The jury returned a verdict for the plaintiff in the amount of $100,000. and the insured sued the insurer for the excess of the verdict over the policy limit.

The California court had no difficulty in determining that the insured had met the burden of proving violation of the "prudent insurer" standard. It went on, nevertheless, to press strongly for a revision downward of the standard of conduct that would result in insurer liability. The court took the position that "whenever the insurer receives an offer to settle within policy limits and rejects it, the insurer should be liable in every case for the amount of any final judgment whether or not within policy limits." In other words, the insurer would be held strictly liable for failure to accept *any* offer of settlement, no matter how strong the defense. The court reasoned that the implied obligation of good faith and fair dealing is one arising under the contract of insurance, and contractual obligations are strictly enforced. The court exhibited further rigidity in reasoning that it is always in the interests of the insured to have the action settled within policy limits, and, therefore, rejection of an offer of settlement within those limits would always be conclusive evidence that the insurer had placed its own interests above those of the insured.

In constructing this doctrine of strict liability, the California court left no flexibility for the possibility of a baseless or even fraudulent action brought by the third party against the insured. Rejection of any offer of settlement within policy limits would apparently lead directly to the abandonment of policy limits.

It is perhaps because of recognition of the fact that the strict liability theory proposed in *Crisci* would make insurers the defenseless targets of fraudulent plaintiffs, and that the public—the ultimate judgment debtors in actions against insurers—would finally bear the cost in the form of increased premiums, that no jurisdiction to date has clearly adopted the strict liability standard. Even in California, the proposed rule discussed in *Crisci* was merely dicta.

3. Contract v. Tort

While a number of courts have failed to classify the cause of action for bad faith as sounding either in tort or contract, those that have chosen to classify are split. Some jurisdictions have shown consistency in determining that a cause of action that is based on an implied covenant in a contract must itself be an action in contract. Others have used the "good faith and fair dealing" covenant merely as a basis for defining the duty owed by the insurer to the insured, and have concluded that the action is one in tort.

While the specific categorization of the cause of action has not appeared to affect the remedies available against the insurer, it does determine which of the two statutes of limitations is to be applied.

4. Assignment of Cause of Action

The majority of courts have followed the lead of the California Supreme Court in the early case of *Comunale v. Traders & General Ins. Co.* (Cal.1958), in upholding the assignability of the insured's cause of action against the insurer for bad faith failure to settle the underlying tort action. Assignment has been upheld even where the policy itself conditions assignment of any interest under the policy on consent of the insurer. This provides protection for third-party plaintiffs who successfully prosecute tort actions against judgment-proof insureds, and also prevents an insurer from exercising bad faith in negotiating settlement of the tort action with impunity. The minority of courts that do not permit assignment appear to fear collusion between the third-party plaintiff and the insured in opening the pocket of the insurer beyond policy limits.

In assigning the cause of action for bad faith, however, the courts have imposed the limitation that only the claim for the excess judgment over policy limits is assignable, as opposed to any claim for emotional distress or punitive damages. For the same reasons, courts have generally allowed suits by third-party plaintiffs under direct action statutes only to the extent of the policy limits.

Absent an actual assignment by the insured, however, it is generally held that the third-party plaintiff does not have a cause of action against the insurer for a bad faith refusal to settle the underlying tort action, since the duty to act in good faith runs solely to the insured. The courts have also rejected the notion that the third-party plaintiff is a third-party beneficiary of the implied promise to exercise good faith in negotiating a settlement, since the only interests to be protected by this good faith negotiation are those of the insured and insurer. The third-party plaintiff is in the position of an adversary to both. A minority of courts have, however, permitted a third-party plaintiff to bring an action against the insurer by attachment of the "debt" owed to the insured because of the tortious, bad faith conduct, after the third-party plaintiff has obtained a judgment against the insured.

5. Excess Insurer

If the insured has taken out a policy of excess liability insurance, any excess of the tort judgment against the insured over the limits of the primary policy will fall on the excess insurer. This means that the actual victim of the primary insurer's bad faith refusal to settle within primary policy limits is the excess insurer. In order to prevent primary insurers from acting in bad faith with impunity, and to encourage primary insurers to settle tort claims, the courts have generally permitted an excess liability insurer that has been economically harmed by the primary insurer's bad faith refusal to settle to bring the bad faith cause of action against the primary insurer.

The theory under which the excess insurer is generally permitted to proceed against the primary insurer is that of subrogation to the bad faith claim of the insured against the primary insurer. Courts generally deny the existence of a direct claim for bad faith in the excess insurer against the primary insurer because of lack of privity of contract between the two. A minority of jurisdictions have even denied the existence of a subrogated cause of action in the excess insurer. The majority of courts, however, reason that the bad faith claim is one sounding in tort and is therefore a proper subject for subrogation.

The beneficial effects of permitting subrogation in the excess carrier that have swayed the majority are the following. First, since the amount of the underlying tort recovery over the primary insurer's limits is borne by the excess insurer, the insured is not economically hurt by the primary insurer's bad faith refusal to accept a reasonable offer of settlement within policy limits, and is therefore not likely to prosecute a bad faith claim. This would leave the primary insurer free to unreasonably refuse to settle the tort action and, in effect, gamble on a defendant's verdict at trial with the excess insurer's money. Allowing the excess insurer to bring the subrogated bad faith claim puts pressure on the primary insurer to settle the tort suit for a reasonable figure, which is in the public interest.

The second benefit of subrogation is that it makes the excess insurer's exposure more truly co-extensive with the insured's potential liability over the primary insurer's policy limit because it factors out the risk of unreasonable refusal to settle by the primary insurer. Since this is the risk upon which the excess insurer bases its premiums, a fair result is reached for the excess insurer.

In *Fireman's Fund Insurance Company v. Maryland Casualty Company,* the court dealt with the situation in which the insured effectively released the primary insurer (Maryland) from any bad faith claim. The issue was whether or not this release affected any rights of subrogation in the excess insurer (Fireman's Fund). The court noted that there are six elements essential to the subrogated rights of any insurer: 1) the insured has suffered a loss for which a wrongdoer causing the loss (in this context, the primary insurer guilty of bad faith refusal to settle) should be held accountable, 2) the insurer (here excess) has, in whole or in part, compensated the insured for that loss under a legal (excess policy) obligation to do so, 3) the insured has an assignable cause of action against the wrongdoer (primary insurer guilty of bad faith) which he/she might bring but for being compensated by the insurer (excess), 4) the insurer (excess) has suffered damages because of the wrongdoing (bad faith of the primary insurer), 5) justice requires that the loss fall on the wrongdoer responsible (primary insurer guilty of bad faith), and 6) the amount of the loss to the insurer (excess) is in a definite sum—i.e., the amount of the excess policy proceeds.

The court found that neither the third nor fourth element was present in the *Fireman's Fund* case, because the insured had released the primary insurer of any liability for bad faith. The insured, therefore, had no cause of action to which the excess insurer could be subrogated. Since a subrogee stands in the shoes of the subrogor (insured), the subrogee acquires no greater rights than the subrogor has in the action. Furthermore, the subrogee would be subject to all of the defenses that the wrongdoer (primary insurer) could raise against the subrogor, such as release.

It might be suggested that when a primary insurer chooses to reject an offer of settlement from the plaintiff in the underlying tort suit, the obtaining of the signed consent on the insured to the rejection of settlement would protect the primary insurer against a subsequent subrogated cause of action for bad faith by the excess insurer.

6. Remedies

The remedy most typically applied in the event of an insurer's violation of its duty toward the insured in rejecting settlement within policy limits is that the insurer is held liable for the excess of any resulting judgment for the third-party against the insured over the policy limit. Generally added to this amount are the costs of bringing the bad faith cause of action against the insurer. In some cases, courts have allowed damages for mental suffering caused to the insured by the insurer's bad faith refusal to settle, and if the violation is particularly egregious, punitive damages have been permitted.

A final note on the issue of punitive damages in bad faith cases concerns the affect of an insured/defendant's assignment of a bad faith claim to a plaintiff where punitive damages have already been awarded to the plaintiff against the insured/defendant. It has been held that where an insured assigns his or her bad faith claim to a plaintiff after a jury trial in which compensatory and punitive damages were awarded to the plaintiff, the assignment of such a claim is not effective as a basis for the plaintiff's suing the insurer in bad faith for the punitive damage portion of the award. Although the insurer's refusal to settle the case may have been an act of bad faith, the punitive damages are based upon the *insured's* blameworthy behavior, not the subsequent actions of the insurer; thus, the imposition on the insurer of an excess judgment based on the punitive damages have been held to violate public policy.

7. Insolvency of the Insured

A number of courts have addressed the issue of the effect of the insolvency or bankruptcy of the insured on the insured's cause of action against the insurer for its bad faith refusal to settle a tort claim. The majority of courts have held that once an excess judgment against the insured has become final, the insured's cause of action for bad faith against the insurer is unaffected by the inability of the insured to pay the excess. Frequently in this situation, the action is brought against the insurer by the third-party plaintiff after assignment of the cause of action by the insured. The net result of this assignability is that when an insurer is deciding whether or not to accept an offer of settlement from the third-party plaintiff, the insurer is required to make its decision as if the insured were capable of paying the excess.

While the minority of courts agree with the majority that an insured need not *actually* pay the excess judgment to the third-party plaintiff in order to have standing to bring the bad faith action against the insurer, if the insured is incapable of making such payment, these courts consider the insured to have suffered no damage from the refusal of the insurer to settle with the third-party plaintiff, and therefore the insured cannot collect the amount of the excess judgment from the insurer.

8. Release

When an insured releases a third-party tortfeasor from liability, that release is generally binding on a first-party insurer so that the insurer cannot then proceed in subrogation of the claim. The same idea applies in the context of bad faith actions against third-party insurers. For example, in *Romstadt v. Allstate Ins. Co.* (N.D.Ohio 1994), the District Court for the Northern District of Ohio held that the plaintiff's release of the insured/defendant in a tort action extinguished any bad faith claim against the defendant's insurer by the plaintiff as assignee of the insured/defendant's bad faith claim against its insurer for failure to settle. On the eve of trial, the insured accepted a settlement offer which provided that the plaintiff would receive a certain sum. In exchange, the plaintiff would release the insured from all claims and would agree not to seek satisfaction from the insured personally with regard to any amount of the settlement which exceeded policy limits. The insured agreed to assign her bad faith claim against her liability insurer to the plaintiff, who would then seek satisfaction of the excess amount from the insurer.

When the plaintiff filed a bad faith action against the defendant's insurer seeking the amount of the settlement which exceeded the defendant/insured's policy limits, the court found that the assignment was ineffectual. The insured had never been exposed to excess liability because of the nature of the release, and thus the insured had no basis for a bad faith claim. No bad faith claim, therefore, could be brought by the plaintiff as assignee.

C. FIRST–PARTY INSURANCE

1. Generally

The second context in which the cause of action for bad faith has arisen is that of first-party insurance. This involves insurance covering losses suffered directly by the insured as opposed to losses to third-parties for which the insured may be held legally liable. The primary examples of first-party insurance that have been the subjects of bad faith actions are accident, life, health, disability, hospitalization, medical payments, fire, theft, and uninsured motorist insurance.

2. History

It was again the California court that established the leading precedent for a cause of action in bad faith for failure to pay the claim of an insured. In *Gruenberg v. Aetna Ins. Co.* (Cal.1973), the insured brought action against his insurer for failing to pay the proceeds of a fire insurance policy on his restaurant. The restaurant had burned under suspicious circumstances, and allegedly, the insurer implied to the authorities that the insured had deliberately set the fire. The insured was charged with arson, and pending criminal proceedings, the insured refused to be interviewed by the company regarding the fire. The charges were ultimately dropped, but the insurer refused to pay the proceeds, claiming that the insured had breached the policy requirement that he be examined under oath regarding the loss at the insurer's request. The insured then brought suit alleging that the insurer had acted in bad faith by implying to the authorities that the insured had set the fire in order to establish grounds upon which to deny liability on the policy. In upholding the viability of the insured's cause of action, the California Supreme Court extended its holding in the area of third-party bad faith actions to first-party actions as well. The court held that the duty of good faith and fair dealing required not only that the insurer accept reasonable settlements in third-party insurance cases, but also that the insurer not unreasonably withhold payments due its insured under a policy of first-party insurance. The court further held that this duty is implied by law, and that therefore the breach of this non-consensual duty constituted a tort separate and distinct from any action in contract under the policy. The duty of good faith is absolute and continues as long as the policy is in effect, even if the insured breaches any of his duties under the contract.

3. Majority View

A slight majority of jurisdictions have followed the California approach in holding that an independent tort arises for a bad faith failure to pay the insured on a first-party insurance claim. These decisions follow the *Gruenberg* line of reasoning that the failure to exercise good faith in deciding whether or not to pay a claim is a breach of the implied duty of good faith and fair dealing, and therefore actionable as a tort.

4. Minority View

A substantial minority of courts have denied the bad faith cause of action for first-party claims. Some courts do so because of statutory remedies which penalize insurers for failure to settle claims with insureds, holding that such statutory remedies are exclusive. Other courts hold that no separate tort arises in the first-party context because of the distinction between the third-party and first-party situations. In the third-party context, the insurer owes a fiduciary duty to the insured whose interests the insurer represents in controlling the defense of the underlying action, whereas, in the first-party context, the insurer and insured are actual adversaries.

5. Standard of Proof

Courts adopting the first-party cause of action for bad faith have used caution in preserving a meaningful right in insurers to contest a claim where there is a reasonable basis for denying liability for proceeds under a policy. The courts have regularly refused to reduce the level of breach on the part of the insurer that will constitute bad faith to mere negligence in failing to pay proceeds. Some deliberate conduct is generally required, although that conduct need not be unlawful or malicious.

The applicable standard has been defined as the existence of "no lawful basis for the refusal coupled with actual knowledge of that fact" or "intentional fail(ure) to determine whether or not there was any lawful basis for such refusal." *Chavers v. National Security Fire & Casualty Ins. Co.* (Ala.1981).

One court further defined the lack of a lawful basis for refusal to pay in terms of specific elements:

"a) an insurance contract between the parties and a breach thereof by the defendant; b) an intentional refusal to pay the insured's claim; c) the absence of any reasonably legitimate or arguable reason for that refusal (the absence of a debatable reason); d) the insurer's actual knowledge of the absence of any legitimate or arguable reason; e) if the intentional failure to determine the existence of a lawful basis is relied upon, the plaintiff must prove the insurer's intentional failure to determine whether there is a legitimate or arguable reason to refuse to pay the claim." *National Security Fire & Casualty Ins. Co. v. Bowen* (Ala.1982).

Yet another, perhaps more stringent, definition of the required standard of proof that has been accepted in principle by several courts is that the insured must be entitled to a directed verdict on his claim on the policy at the time that his claim on the policy is denied by the insurer—i.e., he must be entitled to recover the insurance proceeds claimed as a matter of law—in order to establish a bad faith claim against the insurer for failure to pay proceeds.

One apparent anomaly created by the fact that the entitlement to a directed verdict on the policy claim is judged as of the time of the refusal of the claim by the insurer for purposes of the bad faith claim is that the insured could wind up collecting on the bad faith claim and ultimately losing on the contract claim for proceeds under the policy. If the insurer unreasonably delays in investigating the claim, its initial refusal could come at a time when it has as yet turned up no lawful basis for denying the claim. This could result in a verdict for the insured on a tort claim of bad faith. Yet the insurer might subsequently conduct an investigation that would produce evidence on the basis of which it could successfully defend against the contract action on the policy itself. The defendant's verdict on the contract action could, in fact, strengthen the bad faith tort action, since the later discovery of evidence by the insurer would be an indication of inadequate investigation before its initial refusal of the insured's claim. Courts are inclined to take unreasonable delay in investigating a claim on a policy as a serious matter since such delay frequently places inordinate economic stress on the insured at the time of a serious financial loss, and squeezes the insured into acceptance of an unfair compromise of its claim against the insurer.

6. Defenses

In their concern for the preservation of the ability of an insurer to legitimately contest an insured's claim to proceeds, the courts have denied a cause of action for bad faith in cases where there has been an arguable question of non-coverage under the policy, a reasonable dispute over interpretation of policy or statutory language, misrepresentation by the insured in the application for insurance, failure of the insured to supply information regarding the claim, evidence of suicide or deliberate destruction of insured property by the insured, inflation of the claim, or questions of lapse of the policy or running of the statute of limitations. This list is illustrative, and not exhaustive.

7. Statute of Limitations

Jurisdictions permitting the cause of action for bad faith as a tort separate from any contract action under the policy have generally been consistent in applying the statute of limitations pertinent to tort (rather than contract) actions. A more difficult question arises in determining when the statutory period begins to run—i.e., when the bad faith cause of action has accrued. Clearly, an actual bad faith refusal to pay by the insurer will begin the period. It has also been held in some instances that the period commences when the insured has the knowledge of facts which would lead a reasonable insured to the discovery of a bad faith refusal by the insurer.

8. Remedies

In bad faith causes of action under first-party insurance policies, awards fall into the following four categories.

a. Policy Proceeds

The most basic element of recovery by the insured is the amount of proceeds of the policy that have been withheld by the insurer. While this recovery could be had in a standard breach of contract action under the policy, there are two advantages to bringing the action in tort for bad faith. The first is that serial payments that have not yet come due could not be recovered in a breach of contract action, while a number of courts, such as the California Supreme Court in *Egan v. Mutual of Omaha Ins. Co.* (Cal.1979), for example, permit recovery of the present value of the future proceed installments if there has been bad faith on the part of the insurer in refusing to pay any of the earlier installments. The theory of those courts refusing such recovery even under a bad faith claim is that if the serial payments are not yet due, there can be no bad faith in the insured's failure to pay them.

b. Emotional Distress

The second major category of recovery is compensation for the emotional distress of the insured that results from the insurer's bad faith failure to pay proceeds. The ordinary rule regarding emotional distress in other contexts is that recovery can only be had if the plaintiff proves that the distress was severe and accompanied by other provable harm. The first case in which the court suggested the possibility of such recovery absent proof of these additional items was *Gruenberg v. Aetna Ins. Co.* (Cal.1973). This case has generally been followed in regard to emotional distress damages by those courts that choose to adopt the bad faith tort theory in first-party insurance cases. Still other courts that limit the plaintiff-insured to a breach of contract suit have allowed recovery of damages for emotional distress on the theory that peace of mind is part of what an insured purchases with an insurance policy.

c. Economic Harm

The second category of compensation is for economic harm that is the direct and foreseeable result of the refusal of the insurer to pay the proceeds of the policy. Such resulting losses have included loss of rents, loss of credit, loss of profits, and loss of business good will.

d. Punitive Damages

In view of the fact that punitive damages are created and regulated by statute, the requirements of proof are also specified in local state statutes. If the plaintiff meets the statutory burden of proof, punitive damages can be allowed in either first or third-party insurance cases.

One issue that occasionally arises is whether or not the insurer's employee responsible for the action that amounts to bad faith is at a sufficient managerial level to impute the employee's conduct to the corporate insurer. The California Supreme Court in *Egan v. Mutual of Omaha Ins. Co.,* supra, took the position that if the insurer's employee is given the authority to handle the insured's claim with little or no supervision, that employee's actions will be imputed to the insurer for punitive damages purposes.

In the case of *Neal v. Farmer's Ins. Exchange* (Cal.1978), the California Supreme Court specified three criteria to be considered in fixing the amount of punitive damages. They are: 1) the degree of reprehensibility of the insurer's act; 2) the amount of actual harm as measured by the amount of compensatory damages; and 3) the over-all wealth of the insurer for purposes of judging the deterrent effect to be achieved by a particular amount of punitive damages.

It should be noted that the Supreme Court of the United States has taken a restrained approach in reviewing the appropriateness of punitive damage awards. In *TXO Productions Corp. v. Alliance Resources Corp.* (S.Ct.1993), a case involving an action for slander of title, the Court generally rejected the defendant's plea to intervene in cases where punitive damage awards exceed compensatory damage awards by a significant margin (e.g. punitive damages are more than four times the amount of compensatory damages), or where the punitive damage award exceeds any other punitive damage award given in that jurisdiction. Moreover, the Court upheld the jury's ability to consider allegedly unfair actions of the defendant toward the plaintiff other than those that were the direct subject of the cause of action, as well as the level of wealth of the defendant, in determining punitive damages.

It is clear that this ruling offers highly favorable precedent for plaintiffs who are awarded significant punitive damages in bad faith causes of action, even though the court was not dealing directly with a bad faith cause of action. The use, however, of bifurcated proceedings, where evidence of the company's financial condition is prohibited in the proceedings until punitive damages have been found to be appropriate might lessen the effects of the Court's non-intrusive approach.

e. *Attorney's Fees*

Prior to the creation of the cause of action for bad faith, an insured could recover attorney's fees only if the insurer wrongfully refused to defend an action against the insured by a third-party plaintiff—and then only those attorney's fees expended by the insured in defending against the action of the third-party plaintiff could be recovered. This follows the general rule that attorney's fees incurred in bringing a tort action are not recoverable as compensation. Some courts carry that rule over to bad faith actions, disallowing recovery of any attorney's fees by the insured.

In the case of *Brandt v. Superior Court* (Cal. 1985), however, the California Supreme Court resolved a disagreement among the California district courts by holding that when an insured is reasonably compelled to obtain the services of an attorney in order to compel the insurer to pay the proceeds that are due under a policy and are being withheld by the insurer in bad faith, the insured should be able to recover certain reasonable attorney's fees as an element of the *damages* proximately caused by the tortious conduct of the insurer. The court is careful to distinguish the portion of attorney's fees attributable to the recovery of the proceeds due under the policy from the portion of attorney's fees attributable to obtaining any recovery beyond those proceeds for the tortious aspect of the refusal to pay, such as, e.g. damages for emotional distress. The distinguishing feature is that the former attorney's fees are actual damages proximately caused by the insurer's withholding funds that are owed to the insured, while the latter attorney's fees are similar to those incurred in bringing any tort action. Therefore, only the former attorney's fees are recoverable by the insured. The court compares these fees to medical expenses incurred in treating injuries caused by the tortfeasor.

The court in *Brandt* suggested the following jury instruction:

"If you find (1) that the plaintiff is entitled to recover on his cause of action for breach of the implied covenant of good faith and fair dealing, and (2) that because of such breach it was reasonably necessary for the plaintiff to employ the services of an attorney to collect the benefits due under the policy, then and only then is the plaintiff entitled to an award for attorney's fees incurred to obtain the policy benefits, which award must not include attorney's fees incurred to recover any other portion of the verdict."

The court also notes that this recovery of attorney's fees is only permitted if the insured establishes that the withholding of proceeds was a matter of bad faith, as opposed to mere error, as in interpreting the policy or a statute.

Included in the insured's recovery should be any attorney's fees reasonably incurred in *negotiating a settlement* of the dispute over the proceeds due.

The reasoning that the court applied to attorney's fees would seem to apply equally to such other proximately caused damages as witness fees and other expenses of a legal action to recover proceeds under the policy.

9. Subrogation

An insurer's subrogation rights may also be affected by bad faith. For example, it has been held that an insurer that wrongfully denies coverage to an insured—*i.e.,* one that acts in bad faith—waives its contractual rights to subrogation. In the case of *Burnaby v. Standard Fire Ins. Co.,* the court examined, *inter alia,* the effect of an insurer's bad faith denial of the insured's claim under a homeowner's insurance policy. The insurer denied coverage based on its belief that the insured had misrepresented his loss history and also that the loss had occurred before the inception of the policy. The court held that there was substantial evidence to support a finding for the insured on both issues. As a result, the court affirmed the jury's conclusion that the insurer had unjustifiably denied coverage of the insured's claim. The court went on to reject the insurer's claim that it should be subrogated to the insured's claims against the parties responsible for the damage to the insured's home. The court based its rejection of the insurer's subrogation claim on its finding that the insurer had acted in bad faith in denying coverage from the outset.

The *Burnaby* holding is also significant because it recognizes that insurers cannot be permitted to deny coverage wrongfully and then defend subsequent suits by the insured against it for failure to honor the policy on the ground that the insured interfered with the insurer's subrogation rights by settlement with the third-party tortfeasor or any other form of release or waiver.

D. RECIPROCAL CAUSES OF ACTION

To date, the cause of action based on the implied duty of good faith and fair dealing has been a one-way street. Although theoretically the implied duty applies with equal force to both parties to the insurance contract, the courts have never held that there is a reciprocal cause of action in the insurer for breach of the duty by the insured. The reasons generally given for this one-sided approach are 1) the inequality of bargaining position and control of the claims process between the two parties, 2) the fact that the insured is buying financial and emotional protection from a possibly disastrous loss, while the insurer is merely performing the administrative task of distributing losses among the class of those who choose to insure, and therefore the insured stands to lose more from the bad faith of the insurer than the insurer would lose from the bad faith of the insured, and 3) the disparity in sophistication in regard to the insurance contract between the parties. The net result has been the clear imposition of a higher level of duty of good faith on the insurer than on the insured.

1. Comparative Bad Faith

The closest the courts have come to the recognition of a bad faith cause of action in the insurer was the creation of the doctrine of "comparative bad faith" by the California court in *California Casualty General Insurance Company v. Superior Court* (Cal. App.1985). In that case, the plaintiff-insured made a claim under the uninsured motorist coverage of her policy. The insurer refused payment, and the matter went to arbitration. The plaintiff subsequently brought action against the insurer for violation of the duty of good faith and fair dealing in failing to promptly investigate and process the plaintiff's claim. The defendant-insurer filed a motion for leave to amend its answer to include the affirmative defense of violation of the duty of good faith and fair dealing on the part of the insured in failing to provide timely information to the insurer necessary to process the claim. The court held that "an insured's breach of the implied duty of good faith and fair dealing which contributes to the insurer's failure to pursue or delay in pursuing the investigation and payment of a claim may constitute at least a partial defense to the plaintiff's damage action for the breach of its duty of good faith and fair dealing based on such delay or failure. * * *" Id. The California court has thereby instituted a doctrine of comparative fault in the area of bad faith causes of action.

CHAPTER TWELVE

REINSURANCE

A.   GENERALLY

There are various situations in which an insurer desires to reduce the amount of its exposure to liability on outstanding policies. This can occur, for example, when business reversals or excessive losses make its current potential liability for losses under existing policies a threat to its solvency. In such situations, an insurer can reduce or eliminate the threat by taking out liability insurance with another insurance company (called a "reinsurer") to indemnify itself against liability on its own policies. Such insurance is referred to as a contract or "treaty" of reinsurance. This is not to be confused with the situation in which the original insured simply takes out two or more policies insuring the same risk with two or more insurers. Nor does it cover the situation in which an agent cancels a policy with one insurer and substitutes a policy with another insurer. Reinsurance occurs only when the original insurer becomes an insured (or reinsured) by a contract with another insurer (reinsurer).

With the exception of mutual insurance companies (which are frequently not given the authority to reinsure), any insurer authorized to issue original insurance may also engage in reinsuring risks of the same nature. There are, however, companies that specialize in the business of reinsurance.

The reinsurance contract can provide that the reinsurer will indemnify the insurer for the full amount of any liability incurred on a policy, no matter how large or small, up to the limits of the reinsurance contract, or it can provide that the reinsurer will indemnify the insurer for only a specific proportion of any such liability, similar to the sharing of a loss between an insured and insurer under a policy of co-insurance. In fact, some statutes prohibit the insurer from reinsuring the total risk on any policy, requiring the insurer to retain some portion of the risk without indemnification.

B.   INSURABLE INTEREST

Since the doctrine of insurable interest applies to contracts of reinsurance, the original insurer is not permitted to contract for reinsurance in excess of the policy limits of the policies it is reinsuring. Nor can its contract of reinsurance cover a greater time period than that of its exposure under its policies. Similarly, if the insurer settles a claim with its insured for less than the liability stated in its policy, many courts hold that the insurer can collect from its reinsurer no more than the settlement sum plus any expenses incurred in reaching settlement. There are, however, courts that have held that the reinsurer is liable for the full amount of the insurer's original liability and does not get the benefit of the settlement.

C. STATUTE OF FRAUDS

Since under the usual contract of reinsurance the obligation of the reinsurer is to indemnify the original insurer, and no obligation is owed by the reinsurer directly to the original insured, the reinsurer is not considered to be the guarantor of any debt of the insurer, and therefore the contract is not within the statute of frauds and need not be in writing to be enforceable.

D. INDEMNITY v. LIABILITY INSURANCE

There are two possible interpretations of the reinsurer's obligation under a contract of reinsurance. Either the contract is considered to be indemnity insurance, whereby the reinsurer is liable for the payment of proceeds only to the extent that the insurer has actually suffered out-of-pocket loss by the *payment* of a claim; or the contract is considered to be liability insurance, whereby the liability of the reinsurer arises as soon as the insurer becomes *liable* for the payment of proceeds on its original policy. In the latter case, the insurer need not actually *pay* the claim of the insured in order to be entitled to proceeds on its contract of reinsurance. In fact, in cases of insolvency of the insurer, where it is impossible for the insurer to pay the claim of the insured, the obligation of the reinsurer to pay the full amount of the insurer's *liability* on its policy remains intact. In such a case, the original insured has no priority claim to proceeds paid by the reinsurer to the insurer because of the insured's claim of loss. Instead, those proceeds from the reinsurer go into a general fund available to all creditors.

As between these two interpretations of a contract of reinsurance, courts lean heavily toward interpreting the contract as one of liability rather than indemnity insurance in the absence of very explicit language in the contract to the contrary. Otherwise, the use of reinsurance to protect the insurer against insolvency would be meaningless, since in the event of insolvency of the insurer and consequent inability of the insurer to pay the claim of the insured, the reinsurer would in turn be under no obligation to pay proceeds. Needless to say, interpreting the contract as one of liability insurance affords consequent benefits to the original insured in providing a more effective backstop for the insurer's solvency.

E. DEFENSES OF THE REINSURER

The defenses of fraud, misrepresentation, and concealment on the part of the reinsured are applicable to void contracts of reinsurance in the same way that they affect policies of original insurance. There is generally a duty on the part of the reinsured to inform the reinsurer of facts within its knowledge that would reasonably affect the decision to reinsure, particularly if the reinsured is aware that a loss has already taken place under the original policy.

If the reinsured does anything to increase the risk of its potential liability under the original policy after the contract of reinsurance is executed, such as the granting of permission to the insured to do something with relation to the subject of the insurance that will increase the risk of loss, the reinsurer is generally relieved of liability.

In an action by the reinsured against the reinsurer on the contract, the reinsurer can raise any defense that the reinsured might have raised under the original policy in an action by the original insured, such as breach of warranty or condition or misrepresentation, since these protections for the insurer, built into the original policy, form part of the basis for the decision of the reinsurer to accept the contract of reinsurance.

When a claim arises against the original insurer on a policy which has been reinsured, as to which claim there is a question about the liability of the insurer, the insurer is obligated to give notice to the reinsurer, which will, in turn, decide whether the claim is to be paid or defended. If the reinsurer gives no instructions, the insurer is entitled to decide for itself whether or not to attempt a defense.

As long as the reinsurer has had notice of the action by the insured against the original insurer, any judgment against the insurer is also binding on the reinsurer.

F.   RIGHTS OF THE ORIGINAL INSURED AGAINST THE REINSURER

The rights of the original insured against the reinsurer depend on the terms of the contract of reinsurance. If the contract provides for payment of proceeds solely to the reinsured, the original insured has no standing whatever to claim directly against the reinsurer. Even in the event of insolvency of the original insurer, the insured has no claim to any proceeds from the reinsurer superior to that of any other creditor of the original insurer. There are, however, cases in which the original insured has been permitted to bring an action by levying on the debt owed by the reinsurer to the original insurer.

If the reinsurance contract binds the reinsurer to pay any claim for which the original insurer becomes liable on its policy directly to the original insured, however, such a contract is generally construed to create third party beneficiary rights in the original insured, such that the original insured can bring action on the reinsurance contract directly against the reinsurer. An action of this type does not automatically cancel all liability owed to the insured by the original insurer. In fact, the insured can bring an action against either or both insurer and reinsurer and is not compelled to elect between remedies, but the insured can collect a total of no more than the amount of his loss.

CHAPTER THIRTEEN

BONDS

A. PRINCIPAL/SURETY RELATIONSHIP

1. In General

Suretyship is the relationship occupied by the person liable for the payment of money or the performance of an act by another. The suretyship relationship, therefore, requires three parties. First, the "principal" is the party whose performance or debt is the subject of the transaction. Second, the "surety" is the party who must undertake to pay or perform in the event that the principal does not. The surety binds itself along with the principal who is already bound. Third, the "obligee" is the party to whom the debt or performance is owed.

As a result of the suretyship relationship, the surety will suffer a loss in the event that the principal fails to pay or perform. Since the surety indemnifies against losses resulting from acts of the principal, the surety, not the obligee, is responsible for seeing that the principal performs. Similarly, if the principal does pay or perform, liability of the surety will completely terminate.

2. Non-commercial Suretyship Distinguished

The suretyship relationship may arise in numerous non-commercial or non-insurance situations. For instance, it is possible that one may become a surety by operation of law even where the principal object of the contract is other than to create a suretyship relationship. In this case the surety is said to be involuntary. Alternatively, one may deliberately undertake a suretyship, but do so only as a matter of accommodating the principal. Insurance companies, however, often undertake to act as a compensated surety in their regular course of business. As voluntary sureties, they typically use an instrument known as a bond (see, "Bonds Generally", supra) where the chief object of the contract is to become a surety.

3. Rights of the Obligee

Since the main purpose of requiring a surety is to protect the obligee in the event that the principal does not pay or perform, the obligee is generally given wide latitude in its ability to seek payment or performance from the surety. The obligee is, thus, able to enforce payment or performance by either the principal or the surety.

One of the most important aspects of the rights of the obligee is that actions or non-actions of the principal generally will generally not be held to release the surety. In order for release of the surety to be premised on actions of the principal, the action must be one which would release the principal as well. In other words, it must be action sufficient to extinguish the principal's obligation to the obligee. For example, even the failure of the principal to pay the premium required by the surety bond will not release the surety from his obligation to the obligee. Failure to file the bond, even if required by statute, has also been held not to release the surety.

The obligee is also entitled to a certain type or quality of performance by the principal before the surety is released. In the case of a construction contract, for example, defective work by the principal will not release the surety unless the obligee has acquiesced or there has been unreasonable delay in discovering the defect. In addition, performance by a stranger generally will not release the surety from its obligation to the obligee. In the case of a suretyship to secure a debt, however, payment of the underlying debt by a stranger will be sufficient to release the surety.

The obligee's rights as against the principal and the surety are legally distinct from each other and may be pursued independently. Thus, the existence of a suretyship does not prohibit the obligee from proceeding *in equity* against the principal even though it may have an action *at law* on the bond against the surety. In addition, the obligee is entitled to engage in conduct toward the principal which is consistent with its rights at law or in equity without fear of releasing the surety by virtue of this conduct. This leaves the door open for forbearance, indulgence, or even passiveness toward the principal on the part of the obligee. This common law rule may be altered either by contract or, in some cases, by statute. However, traditionally the obligee does not owe the surety a specific duty of diligence to proceed against the principal.

4. Rights of the Surety

Like the obligee, the surety also has several rights which define its role in the suretyship relationship. One of the most important rights of the surety and one that distinguishes suretyship from other types of insurance is that if the surety is required to pay or perform, the surety may proceed against its principal. If the surety pays a judgment, it stands in the shoes of the creditor and may, in turn, sue on the judgment. Similarly, a judgment in favor of the principal will be sufficient to release the surety. A partial judgment in favor of the principal will release the surety to the same extent that the claim against the principal is reduced.

Whereas ordinary insurance requires the insurance company to establish a likelihood of loss and base premiums on an expected amount of loss, the surety has the ability to recover money paid to the obligee from its principal. There is no benefit to the public or need for the surety to spread the risk of loss as is the case with other types of insurance. In theory, therefore, the surety could collect premiums and recover all proceeds paid on behalf of its principal. In reality, however, there is an element of risk because often times the reason the surety has had to pay or perform is that the principal is simply unable to pay or perform for the obligee or surety.

Another right of the surety is that the obligee owes the surety a duty of good faith and fair dealing. The obligee must also honor and observe the express terms of the surety bond. For example, provisions with regard to notice must be followed. The obligee must refrain from action which would increase the risk to the surety or alter the position of the surety. Lastly, as with many other types of insurance, a surety may obtain re-insurance. Absent language to the contrary, the re-insurance is for the benefit of the surety and the re-insurer is only obligated to the surety. The obligee may not maintain an action directly against the re-insurer.

5. Defenses of the Surety

Although the obligee is generally given broad protection under the law of suretyship, there are several defenses which may be used by the surety to protect its rights and interests.

Perhaps the broadest defense available is that the surety will not be liable if the agreement between the obligee and principal is held invalid or unenforceable. Similarly, if called upon to pay or perform, the surety may also defend by showing that the underlying agreement has been satisfied. Alleging, however, merely that the agreement was incapable of performance at the time that it was entered into will not release the surety.

Release of the principal by the obligee will also release the surety, even if the obligee only intended to release the principal. Release of one or more co-principals, has also been held to release the surety. A covenant by the obligee not to sue the principal has been held to release the surety. If the agreement called for more than one alternative act or obligation, a showing that any one of the alternative acts or obligations has been satisfied will discharge the surety. Absent the obligee's knowledge or acquiescence, however, performance in an unlawful manner will not be a defense for the surety.

The surety also has several defenses available which set the outer limits of the rights of the obligee discussed infra. As stated, for example, the obligee may indulge the principal or forebear enforcement with regard to the obligation of the principal. Where, however, the obligation of the surety is agreed to expire a specified time after completion of a project, the surety's obligation cannot be enlarged by an extension of time for completion that is unauthorized by the surety. Similarly, the surety will ordinarily be discharged where material changes to the status of the parties of the contract are made without the surety's consent. Deceit or fraud on the part of the obligee which operates to the prejudice of the surety will also result in the discharge of the surety. Lastly, the obligee is also held to a special standard when it possesses collateral securing the principal's obligation. The obligee is required to hold the collateral for the benefit of the surety, and any voluntary or negligent act or omission of the obligee which diminishes the value of the security may result in the release of the surety.

As a *caveat,* however, it is also possible for the surety, by its own conduct, not only to waive particular defenses, but also to waive its status as surety and become obligated as a principal. Additionally, express waiver, taking security at the time it becomes surety, undertaking to settle liability with the obligee via a new contract, or statute may all prevent discharge of the surety.

6. Co-sureties

One particular aspect of suretyship which may lead to dispute is the status and creation of co-sureties. This is particularly a problem where sureties may, in dealing with the principal or obligee, become co-sureties without knowledge that they have become co-sureties. Absent agreement otherwise, co-sureties, as between themselves, will only be liable for a proportionate share of the obligation. It varies by jurisdiction whether release by the obligee of one co-surety will result in the release of all co-sureties. Generally, security or indemnity obtained by one surety will inure to the benefit of all co-sureties.

B. BONDS GENERALLY

1. Generally

The principal/surety relationship is the foundation for a discussion of the insurance-like instrument that memorializes the relationship when the surety engages in that relationship commercially. In most cases, the instrument is known as a bond. It is a written obligation that binds the surety to pay a certain sum upon the happening of some specified event.

The bond is comprised of two parts—the obligation and the conditions. The obligation sets forth the duties of the parties to the bond while the conditions set forth the occurrences that will trigger the obligations.

2. Requirements for a Valid Bond

There are several elements that are required to create a valid bond. One of these mandates that the obligor/surety on the bond sign the bond instrument. The obligee may be required to sign the document as well.

Related to the requirement of execution is the requirement that the bond be properly delivered by the obligor. The obligor is not required, however, to physically deliver the bond instrument to the obligee, but may, instead, simply manifest, in words or action, an intention to deliver the instrument to the obligee.

Just as with any other contract, the bond is not valid unless it is founded upon sufficient consideration. What constitutes sufficient consideration is to be determined under normal contract law and generally amounts to the payment of an agreed premium.

Fraud and duress may be obstacles to finding a valid bond. If the bond was secured by the obligee on the basis of fraud, it is void unless the obligor knew of the fraud when the bond was signed or unless the fraud was, in part, perpetrated by one with authority to bind the obligor. A bond secured by duress is voidable upon a showing that the duress actually induced the execution of the bond.

A final requirement for a valid bond is that it not be used for an unlawful purpose. For example, a bond with a condition that requires delivery of overseas goods in violation of import laws is void.

3. Categories of Bonds

Though there are a number of types of bonds (e.g., performance bonds, payment bonds, and fidelity bonds), there are three main categories into which these types fall. The first of these categories is the statutory bond, which, as the name implies, is both required and governed by statute. It is the statute that dictates the obligations and conditions under the bond, and the bond must be entered into in accordance with the statute in order to be valid. Any bond which is issued to satisfy a statutory requirement and which differs in its terms or coverage from the statutory requirement will generally be held to bind the obligor to the requirements of the statute.

A second category of bonds is known as the common law bond. If a bond does not satisfy the statutory requirements of a bond, it may, nonetheless, be valid as a common law bond. So long as the bond is based on sufficient consideration, was voluntarily executed, and does not contravene public policy, it will be treated as a valid bond. Thus, a bond that satisfies all of the statutory requirements except, *e.g.*, the statutorily specified form of execution, may nonetheless be valid as a common law bond.

The third category of bonds is the bond exacted *colore officii*. This category of bonds is used when a public officer or judge requires an individual over whom he/she has authority to execute a bond. For example, a judge may require a bail bond to issue before releasing a criminal defendant, guarantying the appearance of the defendant at subsequent hearings. It is important to note, however, that if a public official orders a bond without authority of a statute, that bond will be invalid because it is considered to be involuntarily executed.

4. Construing Bonds

Bonds are generally construed under basic contract principles. Thus, a court reviewing a bond should look to the plain language of the bond instrument in an effort to effectuate the intent of the parties. Since, however, commercial bonds are generally drafted by the obligor and issued without negotiation of most of the terms, the doctrine of *contra proferentem* will be applied to any term that is ambiguous, and the meaning favoring the obligee will be adopted. In addition, a court will attempt to give full effect to the intention of the parties to the bond, construing all of the terms of the bond in accordance with their fair or plain meaning.

5. Liability Under the Bond

Liability under a bond will be determined in accordance with the provisions of the bond instrument. For example, the bond instrument will generally provide for the time at which the obligor's potential liability begins and the duration of that potential liability under the bond, as well as the circumstances that will trigger liability. Courts will not expand the obligor's liability beyond the fair or plain meaning of the terms of the bond.

6. Termination of Obligations Under the Bond

There are several ways to terminate the obligations set forth in a bond. The most basic method of terminating the bond is by agreement between the parties. Alternatively, the bond may be annulled if the contract upon which the bond is based (as, *e.g.,* under a performance bond) is canceled.

Another method of terminating the obligations under a bond is by a showing of fraud. However, in order to bring about termination, the party alleging fraud must prove: 1) that there was a false representation; 2) that the representation pertains to a material matter; and 3) that the false representation caused the loss or damage.

Mistake on the part of the obligor as to the obligations under the bond is not a defense to enforcement of the bond, *i.e.,* it is not grounds for terminating the bond.

C. TYPES OF BONDS

1. Construction–Related Bonds

One of the most common uses for bonds is in the construction industry. In this setting, the typical relationship between the parties is that the project owner is the obligee, a general contractor or subcontractor is the principal, and a commercial surety guarantees the performance or payment of the contractor. Although closely related and often used together, three basic types of bonds are often used or even required in construction.

a. *Bid Bonds*

Bid bonds are often required to protect the project owner from the vagaries of the competitive bidding process for large construction projects. They protect the project owner in the event that the successful low bidder for a construction contract is either unwilling or unable to enter into the construction contract or is unable to obtain the necessary performance or payment bonds. The obligees damages are routinely set out in the bond instrument and fit one of three general categories. First, the damages may be the difference between the principal's bid and the next highest bid. Second, damages may be set as a percentage of the principal's bid. Third, damages may be the difference between the principal's bid and the next highest bid, but limited to a fixed percentage of the principal's bid. Of course, it should be remembered that bid bonds are a specific type of suretyship, and, therefore, the surety is only required to pay if the principal, who is primarily liable, does not.

Since the primary purpose of a bid bond is to protect the project owner/obligee, the surety has very few defenses which are distinct from defenses of the principal. For example, it has been held that even where the bid bond was issued as a result of mistake on the part of the surety's agent and in contravention of the company policy, the surety was still held liable under the bond. Therefore, the vast majority of defenses by the surety will be tied to successfully defending on the underlying obligation of the principal/contractor. These defenses generally fall into two categories.

The first group of defenses available to the surety are those relating to changed circumstances surrounding the bid or a failure by the obligee to comply with the conditions of the bid invitation. One clear situation in which this will serve as a defense is where the obligee changes the requirements for the bid. In this case, both the principal and surety will be released from liability. In addition, it has been held that the surety is released from liability where the principal clearly indicates that his bid deviates from the bid specifications. In this instance, the principal's deviating bid is viewed as a counter offer. The principal and surety have also been held to be released where the obligee does not comply with the bid invitation requirements, as where the obligee either delays in accepting a bid, delays in preparing the construction contract, or delays in awarding the construction contract.

The second group of defenses potentially available to the principal and surety relate to mistake on the part of the principal. Simple failure by the principal to sign the construction contract on time will not release the principal or the surety, and they will be held liable on the bond. The trend, however, is in favor of releasing the principal and surety when there has been a mistake in the preparation of the bid. Courts will generally consider five factors in determining whether to release the principal and surety from liability. The first consideration is whether the mistake was made in good faith. Second, the court will consider the degree of the principal's negligence. Gross negligence or worse is not likely to constitute a forgivable mistake. The third consideration is whether the bid as it stands would result in the contract being unconscionable. This will generally relate to the severity of financial loss the principal and surety would suffer. Fourth, the court will consider whether release of the principal and surety would be prejudicial to the obligee. The fifth consideration is whether the principal and surety provided timely notice of the mistake to the obligee.

b. *Performance Bonds*

Performance bonds are often required on construction projects in order to insure that the project is completed according to the construction contract. Specifically, the bond protects the obligee in the event that the contractor/principal defaults. It is not the case, however, that when the contractor/principal defaults, the surety will automatically step in and complete construction. Rather, the bond protects the obligee for costs of completion in excess of the contract price up to the face amount of the policy. In certain instances, the surety may waive this dollar limit if the surety undertakes to complete the construction itself and the cost of construction exceeds the amount covered by the bond.

One aspect of performance bonds which often proves difficult for the surety is the problem of determining when to become involved in the project. Ordinarily, the surety has no right to interfere in the relationship between the owner and contractor until called upon to do so. This will happen when either the obligee declares the principal in default of the contract or the principal declares that it is defaulting on the contract. In some situations, however, waiting for a default to be declared is an inefficient solution from the perspective of the surety. For example, it is possible that the surety's total loss may be minimized by providing financing or guaranteeing additional financing to the principal where to do so would allow the principal to avoid defaulting on the contract. Also, since the principal's default is often the result of severe financial difficulty, the surety must be aware of the impact that bankruptcy laws will have on the surety's ability to access funds already paid by the obligee to the principal. Lastly, since most performance bonds are underwritten by compensated sureties, the surety will be held to the standards of an insurance company and may be subject to punitive damages in the event that it is found to have acted in bad faith.

Like other sureties, the liability of a surety on a performance bond is limited to the liability of its principal. Therefore, a finding that the underlying agreement between obligee and principal is invalid will also release the surety.

There are other disputes which may arise between the obligee and surety which could release the surety either partially or entirely. The surety may, for example, successfully argue that the obligee defaulted on the contract. This defense typically relates to a failure by the obligee to make progress payments to the principal as called for by the construction agreement. Among the defenses which may be offered by the surety which will result in a partial release, perhaps the most significant arises when the obligee has overpaid the principal. For example, in an extreme case, the obligee may have disbursed seventy percent of all payments to the principal, while only thirty percent of the work has been completed. The surety can then claim to be released to the extent of the overpayment on the theory that the money for payment is actually held by the obligee for the benefit of the surety in the event that the surety is required to complete the project.

Similarly, a dispute may also arise that will result in a partial release in the event that some of the losses are attributable to the obligee's failure to timely approve change orders or costs attributable to design problems.

Once the surety has been called in to satisfy its obligations under the performance bond, there are three basic options, aside from disputing its liability, available to the surety. First, it may decide to offer the obligee a cash settlement. This is referred to as "buying back the bond". Second, the surety may decide to finance the principal to the extent necessary to complete performance. Third, the surety may "relet" the contract. This is usually done by either getting another contractor to take over the existing contract or by entering into a separate agreement with another contractor to complete performance.

c. *Payment Bonds (Miller Act Requirements)*

Payment bonds guarantee that sub-contractors and materialmen will be paid for services and materials provided for the completion of the construction contract. In the past, a special materialmen's lien was used to accomplish the same purpose. The development of payment bond requirements arose out of a disfavor of encumbering public lands due to the failure of a contractor to pay sub-contractors or materialmen. Today, payment bonds are almost universally required by statute on public projects and have also become prevalent in private construction.

Although the exact terms of a payment bond will vary, the Miller Act, codified at 40 U.S.C. section 270, establishes the requirements for payment bonds used in federally funded projects and is typical of statutes requiring contractors to guarantee payment of sub-contractors and materialmen with payment bonds. Generally, the Miller Act requires that before awarding a contract valued over $25,000 for the construction, alteration, or repair of a federal government facility, the contractor must provide a payment bond. The Act does not require that the federal government be a party to the contract, but covers projects sponsored by the federal government and projects paid for primarily with federal funds. Determining whether the Miller Act applies essentially involves inquiring whether the project uses federal funds and is intended to benefit the general public. The Miller Act does not, however, require the penal sum of the payment bond to exceed $2.5 million, regardless of the size of the project.

The parties entitled to recover under a Miller Act payment bond are generally divided into two categories, and the rights and duties of an obligee will vary depending on how they are treated under the Act. First-tier claimants are defined as sub-contractors and materialmen in a direct contractual relationship with the contractor. Second-tier claimants are defined as sub-sub-contractors and materialmen who have contracted with a sub-contractor who is in a direct contractual relationship with the contractor. Parties more remote than second-tier claimants have no claim under the bond. For example, the sub-sub-contractor would be able to recover under the bond for money owed to it by a subcontractor, but an employee of the sub-sub-contractor does not meet the requirement and could not recover under the bond. A court may, however, apply these privity requirements less stringently where sham relationships have been created to avoid the bond requirements.

Since the ability to recover on a Miller Act bond is tied to one's contractual relationship with the contractor, the definition of "sub-contractor" under the Miller Act has a great impact on a party's ability to recover. In *Clifford F. MacEvoy Co. v. United States ex rel. Calvin Tomkins Co.* (S.Ct. 1944), the Supreme Court defined a sub-contractor under the Miller Act as "one who performs for and takes from the prime contractor a specific part of the labor or material requirements of the original contract, thus excluding ordinary laborers and materialmen." Id. at 109. This limited definition of sub-contractor is particularly relevant to a sub-sub-contractor who is trying to recover as a second-tier claimant based on the relationship to a sub-contractor. For example, where X agreed to supply all of the concrete for a site and Y provided to X the sand and gravel used in mixing the concrete, X was held to be merely a materialman and not to meet the definition of sub-contractor. When X failed to pay for the sand and gravel, Y was unable to recover on the Miller Act bond provided by the general contractor because Y had no relationship with a "sub-contractor".

First-tier and second-tier claimants are also held to different requirements with respect to notice under the Miller Act. First-tier claimants are not subject to any notice requirement and must only wait 90 days from the date the last service or material was supplied to bring suit. Second-tier claimants are required to give written notice, stating with substantial accuracy the amount claimed and identifying the sub-contractor dealt with, within 90 days from the date the last material or labor was supplied. In the case of unpaid labor, the 90 days will generally begin to run from the last date that work called for in the contract was performed. Additional labor or labor provided to repair or correct defects will not be allowed to extend the 90 days. Similarly, where there has been a failure to pay for materials, a subsequent delivery more than 90 days from the first will not be held to prevent the expiration of the notice period for the first shipment. Courts are split as to whether the notice must be sent or received within the 90 days. A showing of actual notice, however, will often suffice. Furthermore, mere notice to the contractor's surety will not be sufficient to preserve a Miller Act claim.

Once notice has been given, the party seeking payment has one year within which to file suit for unpaid claims. The one year limitation is ordinarily construed strictly, but the surety may be estopped from asserting the one year bar where the surety's conduct induced the claimant to wait more than one year.

Once a claimant has overcome the privity and notice requirements, the Miller Act allows for a fairly wide array of claims to be recovered under the payment bond. Labor is recoverable at the then prevailing rate or at the contract rate. Materials for which recovery may be had include materials incorporated into the structure, materials consumed in erecting the structure, the cost of repairs necessitated by the use of equipment on the project, rental costs for equipment used in construction, and other materials used in performance of the contract. A Miller Act bond is not, however, designed to insure that a sub-contractor will profit or to reimburse for costs which are not directly related to the particular project. As a result, the cost of equipment which is available for use on other jobs and the cost of repairs which increase the value of equipment or make it available for use on other jobs are not recoverable.

The surety for a Miller Act payment bond is entitled to set-off for previous payments made to the claimant or the cost of corrective work necessitated by the claimants improper construction. This defense is in addition to those related to the claimant's improper notice, etc.

2. Fidelity Bonds

a. *Generally*

Insurance designed to cover losses emanating from the lack of honesty or "fidelity" of an employee is known as a fidelity bond. The parties associated with the bond are: 1) the insured employer, 2) the surety or insurer, and 3) the bonded employee.

The fidelity bond is construed under general principles of insurance law. Thus, ambiguities in the bond will be construed against the surety, *i.e., contra proferentem*. Further, clauses in the bond are to be given a reasonable meaning so as to further the intentions of the parties.

b. Coverage Under the Fidelity Bond

Issues of coverage arise on several levels. For example, the question may arise as to *who* is covered under the bond. A question may also arise as to *what risks* are covered. Finally, *when* the event occurred may be critical to determining whether there will be coverage.

i. Parties Covered Under the Fidelity Bond

Under a fidelity bond, only employees of the insured employer are covered. Employees are loosely defined as those who pursue some form of duty for the employer in the office or on the premises of the employer. To further refine this definition, many courts focus on the element of control that normally exists between an employer and an employee.

Where an employer has no control over the actions of the individual, there will be no "employee", and thus, no coverage under the bond for acts committed by that person. Where, however, an employer exercises complete control over the actions of the individual, the individual is an employee for purposes of coverage under the bond. Cases that fall in between these extremes are litigated and judged according to the particular circumstances involved.

ii. Risks Covered Under the Fidelity Bond

The typical fidelity bond will provide coverage for the dishonest or unfaithful acts of an employee committed while the employee is acting within the course and scope of his/her employment. If the acts were either committed outside the course and scope of employment or were not dishonest within the meaning of the bond, no coverage will be provided.

The test for determining whether a particular act was "dishonest" is as follows: Was the act committed with manifest intent: 1) to cause the insured to sustain a loss, *and* 2) to obtain financial benefit for the bonded employee or another person or entity? If the answer to both aspects of this question is in the affirmative, the insured will be permitted to collect under the bond.

It should be noted that some bonds have provisions that deviate from this model. For example, some bonds require 1) collusion between the bonded employee and another, and 2) a loss that inures only to the benefit of the bonded employee in an amount equal to or greater than, *e.g.,* $2,500, if there is to be coverage under the bond.

iii. Timing of Loss

The timing of the dishonest act is also important to the determination of coverage. The bond, itself, will generally set forth the time period within which risks are covered. It is safe to say that acts committed *and* discovered during the life of the bond are covered (assuming the other conditions for coverage are satisfied), while acts committed prior to or after the life of the bond will not be covered. It is important to note that some courts will also permit coverage where the act occurred during the policy period and the insured discovered the culpable act within a reasonable time (*e.g.,* one year) after the termination of the bond.

iv. *Notice of Loss*

Related to the timing and discovery issues is the issue of notice of loss to the surety. Many fidelity bonds require that the insured notify the surety of a loss at the "earliest practicable moment", while other bonds provide that notice of loss must be provided within a certain time period, *e.g.,* within 90 days of the date of the loss. Some states have statutes governing the minimum time allowed for notice of loss, and any provision providing for a shorter period will be void. Generally, the notice period begins to run from the point of discovery of the loss, rather than from the time of the dishonest act.

What constitutes "knowledge" of the insured as to the acts committed by the bonded employee is subject to two different interpretations. Most courts interpret the insured's knowledge objectively, asking whether a reasonable insured would have known of the employees acts. Other courts, however, consider the insured's knowledge on a subjective basis, looking to when the insured actually knew of the loss.

c. *Litigation on the Bond*

If the surety denies coverage under the bond, the insured bears the burden of proving, in an action for breach of contract, that there was a loss, that this loss was caused by the acts of the bonded employee, and that this loss was covered under the bond. Litigation on the bond is not likely to result in cases where the dishonesty is clear and subject to easy documentation. Litigation is likely, however, in situations 1) where the conduct is not clearly dishonest under the terms of the bond (*e.g.*, where it is questionable whether the employee acted with manifest intent to cause a loss or to obtain a financial benefit); 2) where there is an issue of compliance with all of the conditions of the policy, such as timing or sufficiency of notification of the insurer; and 3) where the amount of the loss is disputed.

As is the case with other insurance policies, claims on a fidelity bond can be subject to the defenses of misrepresentation and breach of condition by the insured. In addition, the surety may assert a variety of defenses including acquiescence of, or participation by, the insured in the acts of the bonded employee, unauthorized release by the insured of the bonded employee which would defeat rights of subrogation in the surety, or change in duties or employment of the bonded employee.

d. Subrogation

The most valuable remedy for a surety found to be liable on a bond is generally that of subrogation. This is generally provided for in the bond. Under the subrogation agreement, the surety is subrogated to any action that could be brought by the employer against the culpable employee or a third party who acted in concert with, or with knowledge of, the employee's unlawful acts.

e. Third Party Claims Against the Surety

As a general principle, third party claims against the surety are not favored by courts. The mere fact that the insured is liable to a third party does not create the same liability in the surety. Thus, where a bonded bank employee makes unauthorized withdrawals from a customer's account, the insured bank may be liable to the customer, but the surety may not be liable to the customer. In cases, however, where the language of the bond relating to parties who can sue under the bond is ambiguous, some courts have permitted a third party to sue the surety directly for losses the third party sustains as a result of the actions of the bonded employee.

Claims brought by the insured against the surety as a result of third party claims against the insured are more problematic for the courts. The question in these cases is whether the insured is covered under the bond for a loss suffered as a result of a suit against the insured by a third party who was harmed by an employee of the insured. The majority of courts have permitted such a cause of action against the insurer under limited circumstances, including, *inter alia,* proof of actual loss by the insured as a result of a judgment against the insured in favor of the third party, settlement with the third party, or, in some instances, voluntary payment to the third party.

The minority view, on the other hand, is that such actions by the insured against the insurer for losses caused by damage to a third party who was injured by the bonded employee may not lie because of lack of coverage.

f. Termination of the Bond

Termination of the insurance provided under the fidelity bond may occur in a variety of ways. For example, the bond may explicitly provide for termination at the end of a specified period. The bond may also provide for termination upon the discovery by the insured of a dishonest or fraudulent act of a bonded employee. Finally, the bond may provide for termination in the event that either the insured or the surety provide sufficient notice to the other party of its desire to terminate the bond.

3. Public Official Bonds

Public official bonds are similar to fidelity bonds in that they may be used to indemnify against the dishonesty of public officers. Under a public official bond, the principal is the state or municipal officer whose conduct is the subject of the bond. The obligee under the bond is either the governmental entity or the public officer's supervisor. The surety may be held liable up to the face amount of the bond.

There are some rules and coverages, however, which are particular to public official bonds. Most importantly, the coverage of a public official bond is generally governed by the statute or ordinance which requires it. Thus, where the bond does not encompass all of the requirements of the statute or ordinance, the statutory requirements will be read into the bond. If, however, the bond instrument provides coverage which is broader than that required by the statute or ordinance, courts will generally hold the surety bound by the more expansive language in the bond.

In conformity with most statutes requiring them, public official bonds generally guarantee that the public official will faithfully perform his/her duties, in addition to guaranteeing the public official's fidelity. Examples of actions which a public official bond might be required to cover as a failure of the official to faithfully perform his/her duties include the situation in which the official improperly disburses public funds, or in which a sheriff fails to properly serve process on behalf of a plaintiff. The public official bond will only cover failures which are a part of a public officer's official duties. Thus, it has been held that where a significant alteration was made to the officer's duties to include functions not directly related to the office, the surety was not liable for malfeasance of the latter. Where, however, only minor additions were made which were similar to the officer's existing duties, the surety was held liable for the officer's failure to faithfully perform the additional duties.

4. License and Permit Bonds

License and permit bonds are bonds which are required to be acquired in order to qualify for a license or permit to participate in one of many publicly regulated activities. These bonds are generally required for one of two purposes. First, they may be required in order to exact compliance with the rules and regulations governing the activity. In this case, it is likely that a violation will result in a forfeiture of the face amount of the bond as a penalty. Second, they may be required in order to indemnify the public for any damages which result from the regulated activity. In this case, the surety is only required to pay for the amount of damage actually caused. As with other bonds, the surety under a license or permit bond is only required to pay claims in the event that the principal is not able to make payment. In addition, it is necessary to examine the bond instrument as well as the statute or ordinance requiring the bond in order to determine the extent of coverage. In the event that bond coverage falls short of the statutory requirement, the statutorily required coverage will prevail.

CHAPTER FOURTEEN

REGULATION OF INSURANCE
I. GENERAL

Regulation of the business of insurance emanates from three primary sources—the courts, the various state legislatures, and the regulatory agencies created by statute in each of the states. Perhaps the front line of regulation is that manned by the courts in devising and applying such doctrines as waiver and estoppel in individual cases for the protection of insureds, and in occasionally taking the blunt stand that an insurance policy shall be deemed to provide exactly what a reasonable insured would expect it to provide. This form of regulation by the courts is the subject of a number of other chapters of this book. This chapter will, therefore, focus on the history and current state of regulation at the hands of the various legislatures and the agencies they have created.

II. HISTORY

Prior to 1944, the insurance industry had been enjoying relative freedom from interference by the federal government. The consistent, if somewhat fictional, party line of the courts was capsulized by the United States Supreme Court in the leading case of *Paul v. Virginia* (S.Ct.1869) with the statement that the "issuing [of] a policy of insurance is not a transaction of commerce." The purpose in creating and fostering this fiction seems to have been to preserve the only existing body of regulatory and tax law imposed on the insurance industry—that of the states. The primary advantage of this ruling to insurance companies was that it left them free to cooperate with each other in gathering and processing experience data on the basis of which to predict the probability of losses for the various risks assumed, and to use rating bureaus to help in the actual determination of appropriate premium rates. They were also able to cooperate in the fixing of specific categories of coverage and the development of standard policy forms. The early "no commerce" decisions were the only thin veil of protection that stood between these practices, considered essential to the insurer's ability to function, and the federal anti-trust provisions of the Sherman and Clayton Acts.

The axe finally fell in 1944 when the Supreme Court handed down the decision of *United States v. South–Eastern Underwriters Ass'n* (S.Ct.1944). An association of two hundred fire insurance companies and twenty-seven individuals were indicted under section one of the Sherman Anti–Trust Act for fixing non-competitive rates and section two for monopolization. This case presented a different context for the question of whether or not the issuance of insurance was interstate commerce. The cases in which that question had arisen earlier involved the issue of whether the states were to be denied the power to regulate the insurance business by virtue of the Commerce Clause. In *South–Eastern Underwriters,* the issue was whether the *federal* Congress should be deprived of the power to regulate the industry under the Sherman Act, and the Court held that consistency with other decisions classifying various forms of business as interstate commerce compelled the holding that the insurance business fell within that category.

Mr. Justice Jackson dissented because of the historic context of the case. He feared that the Court's decision would cause disruption of the "tax liabilities, refunds, liabilities under state law to states or to individuals, and even criminal liabilities [of insurers]." He felt that Congress should be permitted to orchestrate the orderly transfer of regulation from the states to the federal government without having that unexpected burden suddenly thrust upon it by the Court's decision.

In the uncertain void following the *South–Eastern Underwriters* case, the insurance industry found that as between the two, it would much prefer the state form of regulation, with which it was familiar and under which it had learned to operate successfully, to the unknown federal legislation that might force radical changes in the industry, particularly in its manner of cooperatively determining rates. The industry therefore assembled all of its political clout behind a draft proposal of an organization formed in 1871, following the *Paul v. Virginia* decision, the National Association of Insurance Commissioners

(NAIC), which proposal was eventually enacted by Congress in the form of the McCarran–Ferguson Act (15 U.S.C.A. §§ 1012–1014).

The major thrust of the McCarran–Ferguson Act is contained in Section 1:

"Congress declares that the continued regulation and taxation by the several States of the business of insurance is in the public interest, and that silence on the part of the Congress shall not be construed to impose any barrier to the regulation or taxation of such business by the several States."

This general principle is clarified in Section 2:

"(a) The business of insurance, and every person engaged therein, shall be subject to the laws of the several States which relate to the regulation or taxation of such business.

"(b) No Act of Congress shall be construed to invalidate, impair, or supersede any law enacted by any State for the purpose of regulating the business of insurance, or which imposes a fee or tax upon such business, unless such Act specifically relates to the business of insurance. * * *"

With the enactment of the McCarran–Ferguson Act, placing the power of legislation clearly in the hands of the "several States," the insurance industry became acutely aware of the need for uniform, rather than fragmented, legislation to facilitate the ability of insurers to do business across state lines. At this point, the National Association of Insurance

Commissioners (NAIC), and an organization created at the behest of NAIC by representatives of all parts of the insurance field, called the All–Industry Committee, formulated model statutes in each of the appropriate areas of insurance regulation. These statutes have been widely adopted by the states, particularly in the area of rate regulation, and will be discussed below.

III. LEGISLATIVE REGULATION
A. GENERALLY

While the pattern of current state statutes governing insurance seems somewhat spotty and fragmented, there are three distinct areas of protection that are sought to be covered:

1. The control of rates for the purpose of seeing that they are not inadequate, excessive, or discriminatory;

2. The prevention of unfair practices, both toward the insureds and the competition, by insurers; and

3. The prevention of insolvency of insurers for the protection of insureds.

B. RATING LEGISLATION

1. Generally

It is the purpose of legislation in the area of rate-making to insure that rates are sufficiently high to cover the payment of proceeds, appropriate profits for the insurer, and the costs of administration, while at the same time insuring that they are neither discriminatory among individuals presenting the same risks nor generally excessive.

Shortly after the passage of the McCarran–Ferguson Act, the All–Industry Committee prepared model acts for the regulation of rate-making, particularly in the areas of fire, marine, inland marine, and casualty insurance, that have been adopted by nearly all of the states. While there have been isolated instances of states assuming full control of the promulgation of rates to be charged by insurers (most frequently in the area of automobile insurance), the most common approach is as follows. Insurers are permitted to work cooperatively, frequently as members of rating bureaus, in devising rate schedules. These schedules are then submitted to the state administrative agency in charge of regulating insurance (frequently headed by a Commissioner of Insurance) for its approval. In some cases, affirmative approval is necessary, while in others, the schedules are considered approved if the Commissioner does not respond negatively within a specified period after filing. In the event of disapproval by the Commissioner, the insurer is generally afforded a process for appealing the decision of the Commissioner through the court system. Various powers of enforcement are granted to the Commissioner to see that the approved rate schedule is adhered to by the insurer, frequently through referral of the matter to the Attorney General of the state.

2. Discrimination

One of the most difficult areas to regulate is that of discrimination in rates charged for various policies. If, for example, insureds presenting high risks are grouped with insureds presenting low risks, and all are charged an equal premium, those at the high end will pay too little, while those at the low end will pay too much and wind up subsidizing those at the high end. There is, however, great difficulty in striking the optimum balance between the benefits to the insureds in breaking down the rate schedules into as many categories of policyholders as possible, so that each pays only for the degree of risk his situation presents, and the benefits of avoiding, as far as possible, the increased costs of administration (and consequent increased premiums) that accompany a more finely classified system of rates. An error on the side of creating too many categories can easily result in increased administrative costs (and, therefore, increased premiums) that will more than offset any reduction of premiums for the lower risk insured. This is a form of discrimination that is far more difficult to deal with than the more obvious and clear-cut forms such as discrimination on the basis of race or religion.

It is also a major concern of regulatory agencies that insurers be prevented from charging different premiums, whether to benefit a favored client or for any reason whatsoever, to insureds who present the same relative risk of loss.

C. REGULATION OF UNFAIR COMPETITION

Under the pressure of threatened competition from the Federal Trade Commission, the states were quick to adopt legislation to prevent unfair trade practices. Section 1(b) of the McCarran–Ferguson Act provided that after a three year grace period, the Sherman Act, the Clayton Act, and the Federal Trade Commission Act would "be applicable to the business of insurance *to the extent that such business is not regulated by State law.*" (Emphasis added.) The All–Industry Committee provided the means by which the states could rapidly occupy the field of regulating unfair competition to the exclusion of the Federal Trade Commission under the McCarran–Ferguson Act by drafting model acts prohibiting such practices as false advertising, misrepresenting a competitor's product, and dealing on the basis of misleading comparisons between the insurer's product and that of a competitor (so-called "twisting" statutes).

Currently, the most tentative division between state and federal regulation lies along the line laid down by section 2(b) of the McCarran–Ferguson Act. The question of whether or not a particular area of unfair competition is sufficiently "regulated by State law" to foreclose federal intervention (particularly by a watchful Federal Trade Commission) depends frequently on whether the court will be satisfied with the *mere existence* of a state statute on the subject, or whether the court will look behind the statute to examine the extent of actual enforcement of the statute by state officials. In the case of *Federal Trade Comm'n v. National Cas. Co.* (S.Ct.1958), the Supreme Court was satisfied that the area of deceptive advertising was sufficiently regulated by the states concerned simply because they had enacted appropriate statutes. The Court did, however, leave room for the drawing of the distinction between "legislation" and "regulation" in the future, which distinction could be based on an examination of the effectiveness of state regulation.

D. CURRENT LEGISLATION

Legislation is currently pending to repeal the McCarran–Ferguson Act for the purpose of bringing the insurance industry under more pervasive federal regulation. It should be noted that even under the McCarran–Ferguson Act, there is extensive regulation of the insurance industry by such bodies as the Interstate Commerce Commission, the Securities Exchange Commission, the Internal Revenue Service, and the Federal Emergency Management Agency. The primary goal of the proponents of repeal appears to be subjecting the insurance industry to the antitrust constraints of the Sherman, Clayton, and Federal Trade Commission Acts.

Among those proposing repeal, three options seem to be suggested: 1) total repeal of McCarran–Ferguson, 2) repeal only of the anti-trust exemption, or 3) total repeal with certain safe harbors, such as the ability to engage in concerted activity to collect data on loss experience and to develop and use standard policy forms.

The opposing sides on the issue of repeal have formed along the lines of the following arguments.

1. Pro Repeal of the McCarran–Ferguson Act

a. Immunity from federal antitrust enforcement has left the insurance industry free to restrict competition by such practices as artificially inflating prices, limiting the types of products available (e.g., restricting the availability of occurrence, as opposed to claims made liability insurance), using tying agreements (refusing to sell the line of insurance desired by the buyer without requiring the purchase of a package of other lines as well), allocating sectors of the market among insurers, and disallowing agents to compete with each other by discounting their commissions. These abuses could most effectively be rectified by opening the field of enforcement to the federal authorities under the antitrust acts.

b. More effective and uniform civil remedies and punitive awards could be made available to combat bad faith dealings by insurers in handling claims.

c. Uniform nationwide regulation of marketing practices and policy language would provide greater protection for the public in buying an essential product that is generally not well understood.

d. Uniformity of regulation would provide a consistency in the law that would benefit insurers as well in dealing in interstate commerce.

e.   Duplication of effort in devising and updating regulations for fifty different jurisdictions would be eliminated.

f.   A federal insurance commissioner or regulator would be less susceptible to local political pressures applied by the insurance industry.

g.   The federal Congress is better funded, equipped, and staffed to study the problems of the insurance industry on an industry-wide basis.

h.   Local state regulation can result in the protection of in-state insurers to the disadvantage of out-of-state insurers.   All insurers would receive more even-handed regulation from enforcement of a federal body of law.

i.   Life insurance, in particular, has come to compete with other forms of wealth management such as stocks and mutual funds.   The latter do come under federal regulation, and in order to promote a fair competitive atmosphere, the former should as well.

2.   Against Repeal of the McCarran–Ferguson Act

a.   State regulation is established, understood by the industry and practitioners in the field, and tested by a substantial body of case law.   Federal regulation is an unknown, and the uncertainty of how to proceed under a new system of regulation could have a detrimental effect on an industry essential to the financial planning of a major proportion of the population.

b. Limitation of the ability of insurers to share such information as actuarial data could force smaller insurers to merge with larger insurers in order to have a data base from which to operate safely. This would be counter-productive in fostering competition.

c. Limitation of the ability to use standard forms would be dangerous to insurers, given the proclivity of courts to "interpret" any new policy language contrary to the interests of the insurer, and confusing to insureds in comparing the products of different insurers.

d. Unless federal regulation were intended to totally preempt existing state regulation (probably an impossible burden on any federal agency), introduction of federal authorities into the field would invite power and jurisdictional struggles between federal and state authorities.

e. The uniformity of federal regulation could actually be counter-productive, since it would eliminate the advantage of the state authorities in tailoring their regulations to the particular needs of their diverse communities. The needs of a mid-west farming community, for example, differ from those of New York or San Francisco.

f. Local authorities currently are able to experiment with new approaches (such as no-fault auto insurance) on a local basis without affecting the entire industry.

g. Where duplication of effort in devising regulations is a problem, model acts produced by the

National Association of Insurance Commissioners (NAIC) have proven effective.

Whatever measures come to be enacted into law by the Congress will undoubtedly be only a first step in gerrymandering the lines of most effective regulation by the federal and state authorities. Experimentation and revision will undoubtedly be the course of legislation for the next decade in accommodating the concerns expressed above.

E.   REGULATION OF UNAUTHORIZED INSURERS

Another serious concern of the regulators is that of protecting in-state insureds against the inability to bring suit on their policies against out-of-state insurers, particularly those dealing in a mail-order business, because they have not subjected themselves to service of process within the state. The All–Industry Committee provided the states with a model act entitled the Uniform Unauthorized Insurers Service of Process Act. It provides for the acquisition of jurisdiction over an out-of-state insurer by an in-state insured through service of process on the state Commissioner of Insurance.

IV.   METHODS OF STATUTORY REGULATION

A.   LICENSING

The primary form of state control over the insurance industry is through statutes requiring that every insurer, local or out-of-state, that intends to write insurance in the state, as well as every agent and broker who will take part in the sale or servicing of policies within the state, shall be licensed by the state. In this way, the state regulatory agency can pass on the economic stability and methods of operation of every insurer, as well as the levels of competence and ethics of every agent and broker. It can also require the appointment of an agent for service of process within the state by each insurer. Under the licensing power, states generally even regulate by statute the types of investments permitted to be made by insurers in order to insure conservative handling of the funds that ultimately stand behind the policies of insureds.

B. STANDARD FORM REQUIREMENTS

One of the most direct forms of control exerted on insurers by the states is the statutory prescription of the language to be contained in an insurer's policies. For example, in 1943, the New York Standard Fire Insurance Policy was developed and has since come to be the statutorily required form for fire insurance policies in most jurisdictions. Variations to suit individual needs can only be accomplished through written indorsements added to the policy. Other forms of insurance lend themselves less to this extensive type of standardization and are, therefore, made subject only to the inclusion of specific standard clauses, such as incontestability clauses in life insurance policies and clauses relating to the requirements of proof of loss.

C. ANNUAL STATEMENTS

State statutes uniformly require that each insurer doing business in the state, whether domestic or out-of-state, file an annual statement of its financial condition with the state regulatory agency. This is the primary means of alerting the agency to any danger of threatened insolvency (with the resulting inability to honor obligations to insureds) on the part of any insurer.

D. BANKRUPTCY PROVISIONS

Since the federal bankruptcy act excludes insurers from eligibility under the liquidation provisions of Chapter 7, most states have enacted statutes which provide for the managing and distribution of the assets of an insolvent insurer. The general pattern is that in the event of insolvency, all policies are terminated, and the insureds become unsecured creditors to the extent of the reserve value of their policies. In some cases, the insolvent insurer's assets are transferred to another insurer (or group of insurers), which in turn assumes all liability under existing policies and continues the insolvent insurer's business.

E. PENALTY STATUTES

In order to insure good faith by an insurer in making prompt payment of proceeds on its policies, some states have adopted penalty statutes. For example, section 767 of the Illinois Insurance Code provides that in any action by or against an insurer in which the issue is the liability of the insurer, or the amount of the loss, or the unreasonableness of the insurer's delay in settling a claim, if the court finds that the action or delay is "vexatious or unreasonable" on the part of the insurer, the court may impose as taxable costs against the insurer reasonable costs and attorney fees, *plus* 25% of the insured's recovery, or the excess of the insured's recovery over any offer of settlement by the insurer, or $5,000 whichever is less.

While most such penalty statutes are aimed at insurers who refuse to pay a claim out of bad faith, some statutes make the awarding of a penalty turn on the mere winning or losing of the lawsuit by the insurer.

While the Supreme Court has upheld the constitutionality of these statutes, it has held that they can only be applied to policies issued in the forum state.

*

INDEX

ESTOPPEL
Agent of insurer, 233ff
Circumstances, 233ff
Defined, 231
Limitations,
    Coverage, 232
    Facts, 233
Negligence of insurer, 234
Parole evidence rule, 228
Reliance, 231f
Waiver distinguished, 223

FIRE
Friendly fire, 126ff
Hostile fire, 126ff
Implied exception, 126ff
Smoke, soot, and heat damage, 127

FIRE INSURANCE
Defined, 29ff
Friendly fires, 29f, 126ff
Hostile fires, 89ff, 29f, 126ff
Other coverages included, 30

GROUP INSURANCE
Adverse selection, see Adverse Selection
Agency of representative, 16ff
Assignment, 19
Authority to terminate, 18
Certificates of participation, 13
Change of beneficiary, 19
Conflict of laws, 20
Contributory, 15, 17f
Defined, 13
Group representative, 13f, 16f
Master policy, 13
Non-contributory, 15, 17f
Notice to members, 18f
Standing to sue, 19f
Types of insurance, 13f

HEALTH INSURANCE
    Generally, 35f
Construction, 41f
Indemnity plans, 37f
Limitations on coverage, 39ff

†